School Violence

Recent Titles in the
CONTEMPORARY WORLD ISSUES
Series

Women and Crime: A Reference Handbook
Judith A. Warner

World Sports: A Reference Handbook
Maylon Hanold

Entertainment Industry: A Reference Handbook
Michael J. Haupert

World Energy Crisis: A Reference Handbook
David E. Newton

Military Robots and Drones: A Reference Handbook
Paul J. Springer

Marijuana: A Reference Handbook
David E. Newton

Religious Nationalism: A Reference Handbook
Atalia Omer and Jason A. Springs

The Rising Costs of Higher Education: A Reference Handbook
John R. Thelin

Vaccination Controversies: A Reference Handbook
David E. Newton

The Animal Experimentation Debate: A Reference Handbook
David E. Newton

Steroids and Doping in Sports: A Reference Handbook
David E. Newton

Internet Censorship: A Reference Handbook
Bernadette H. Schell

Books in the **Contemporary World Issues** series address vital issues in today's society such as genetic engineering, pollution, and biodiversity. Written by professional writers, scholars, and nonacademic experts, these books are authoritative, clearly written, up-to-date, and objective. They provide a good starting point for research by high school and college students, scholars, and general readers as well as by legislators, business-people, activists, and others.

Each book, carefully organized and easy to use, contains an overview of the subject, a detailed chronology, biographical sketches, facts and data and/or documents and other primary source material, a forum of authoritative perspective essays, annotated lists of print and nonprint resources, and an index.

Readers of books in the Contemporary World Issues series will find the information they need in order to have a better understanding of the social, political, environmental, and economic issues facing the world today.

School Violence

A REFERENCE HANDBOOK

SECOND EDITION

Laura L. Finley

 ABC-CLIO

Santa Barbara, California • Denver, Colorado • Oxford, England

Copyright 2014 by ABC-CLIO, LLC

All rights reserved. No part of this publication may be reproduced, stored in a retrieval system, or transmitted, in any form or by any means, electronic, mechanical, photocopying, recording, or otherwise, except for the inclusion of brief quotations in a review, without prior permission in writing from the publisher.

Library of Congress Cataloging-in-Publication Data

Finley, Laura L.
　School violence : a reference handbook / Laura L. Finley. — Second edition.
　　pages cm. — (Contemporary world issues)
　Includes bibliographical references and index.
　ISBN 978–1–61069–623–4 (hardback) — ISBN 978–1–61069–624–1 (ebook) 1. School violence—United States. 2. School shootings—United States. 3. School violence—Law and legislation—United States. I. Title.
　LB3013.32.F563　2014
　371.7'82—dc23　　　　　　　2014021906

ISBN: 978–1–61069–623–4
EISBN: 978–1–61069–624–1

18 17 16 15 14　　1 2 3 4 5

This book is also available on the World Wide Web as an eBook. Visit www.abc-clio.com for details.

ABC-CLIO, LLC
130 Cremona Drive, P.O. Box 1911
Santa Barbara, California 93116-1911

This book is printed on acid-free paper ∞

Manufactured in the United States of America

Preface, xv
Acknowledgments, xix

1   BACKGROUND AND HISTORY, 3

Types of School Violence, 4

Measuring School Violence, 12

Brief History of School Violence Incidents, 18

Legislation and Court Decisions, 37

Supreme Court Cases, 40

Conclusion, 47

Further Reading, 48

2   PROBLEMS, CONTROVERSIES, AND SOLUTIONS, 63

Effects of School Violence, 63

Biological Theories, 66

Psychological Theories, 70
    Rational Choice Theory, 72
    Social Strain Theories, 74
    Social Learning Theories, 79
    Social Control Theories, 81
    Labeling Theories, 82

Conflict Theories, 83

Integrated Theories, 85

Feminist Theories, 86

Risk Factors, 87

Individual, 87

Family, 94

School, 97

Community, 99

Protective Factors, 100

Individual, 100

Family, 100

School, 101

Community, 105

Interventions, 105

Anonymous Tip Lines, 105

Profiling, 106

Dress Codes and Uniforms, 107

Metal Detectors, 108

Video Cameras, 110

Conflict Resolution and Peer Mediation, 110

Peaceable Schools, 111

Restorative Justice, 112

School Police Officers, 112

Canine Searches, 114

Zero Tolerance Laws, 115

Other Laws, 116

Conclusion, 121

Further Reading, 121

3   PERSPECTIVES, 133

A Student's Perspective on the Dangers of Bullying:
Lashanti Jupp, 133

Reflections on Mean Girls: Lauren Lorance, 136

Sticks and Stones Can Break My Bones, but Names
Will Never Hurt Me? Approaches to Language Mis(uses)
in Schooling: Kelly Concannon, 138

The People's Court in a South Bronx
Elementary School: Evelyn Jackson, 142

Creating and Sustaining Positive School Climates:
De Palazzo, 145

Being Out, 152

Confidentiality and LGBT Students:
It's the Law, 154

Our Gender-Nonconforming Youth and
Transgender Youth, 156

Creating a Safe Space for All: Policies, Programs,
and Practices, 156

Federal Law, 158

State Law, 159

Local Policies and Acts, 159

Other Key Ways to Show Allyship to LGBTQ
Youth, 159

Resources, 163

Is There More School Violence Today? A Veteran
Educator Says No: Sarah Raitter, 164

Reflections on PeaceJam and School Violence
in the United Kingdom: Larenda Twigg, 166

Preventing School Violence: Barbara J. Wien, 176

Violence as a Continuum, 176

Shifting U.S. Culture, 177

Ending War and Violence, 179

Cultivating Caring Communities, 183

How to Build Community, 184

Best Practices in Reducing School Violence, 187

Working for a Higher Purpose, 190

The Circle Model, 190

Organizing for Peace in Your Community:
Six Steps for Success, 192

References, 199

Activism against Domestic and Dating Violence:
Stephanie Wong, 200

Turning the Personal into Progress: Robert Spencer
Knotts, 204

4   PROFILES, 211

Part I, 212

Bath, Michigan, School Bombing, 212

Columbine Massacre, 215

Laurie Dann, 219

Kip Kinkel, 222

Adam Lanza, 226

Barry Loukaitis, 228

Patrick Purdy, 229

Evan Ramsey, 232

Charles Carl Roberts IV, 234

Steubenville High School Rape Case, 236

Jeff Weiss, 239

Phoebe Prince, Bullycide, 240

Amanda Todd, Bullycide, 241

Part II, 242

Break the Cycle, 242

Geoffrey Canada, 243

Riane Eisler, JD, 246

Gay, Lesbian & Straight Education Network (GLSEN), 247

Jackson Katz, 249

Paul Kivel, 251

Hank Nuwer, 252

StopBullying.gov, 253

Students Against Violence Everywhere (SAVE), 255

Further Reading, 257

5   DATA AND DOCUMENTS, 265

Data, 265

Figure 5.1 Trends in school-associated violent deaths, 1992–2010, 266

Figure 5.2 Percentage of students in grades 9–12 who reported being threatened or injured with a weapon on school property at least one time during the previous 12 months, by grade: Various years, 1993–2009, 266

Figure 5.3 Percentage of public and private school teachers who reported that they were threatened with injury or that they were physically attacked by a student from school during the previous 12 months, by locale and instructional level: School year 2007–2008, 267

Figure 5.4 Percentage of students ages 12–18 who reported criminal victimization at school during the previous six months, by type of victimization: Various years, 1995–2009, 268

Figure 5.5 Percentage of students ages 12–18 who reported that gangs were present at school during the school year, by urbanicity: 2007 and 2009, 269

Figure 5.6 Percentage of students ages 12–18 who reported being targets of hate-related words and seeing hate-related graffiti at school during the school year, by selected student and school characteristics: 2009, 270

Figure 5.7 Percentage of students ages 12–18 who reported being bullied at school during the school year, by selected bullying problems and sex: 2009, 271

Figure 5.8 Percentage of students ages 12–18 who reported cyberbullying problems anywhere during the school year, by selected bullying problems and sex: 2009, 272

Figure 5.9 Percentage of students ages 12–18 who reported avoiding school activities or one or more places in school because of fear of attack or harm during the school year: 2009, 273

Figure 5.10 Percentage of students ages 12–18 who reported selected security measures at school: Various years, 1999–2009, 274

Documents, 275

Sandy Hook Elementary School Violence Reduction Act, 275

Safe Schools Improvement Act of 2013, 276

Barack Obama's Statement on the School Shooting in Newtown, Connecticut, 281

The Myths about Bullying: Secretary Arne Duncan's
Remarks at the Bullying Prevention Summit, 283

6   RESOURCES FOR FURTHER RESEARCH, 295

Books, 295
        School Violence, 295
        Bullying, 298
        Specific Cases, 299
        Hazing, 300
        Civil Liberties, 300
        Gender, 301
        Dating and Sexual Violence, 302
        Suicide, Eating Disorders, and Self-Harm, 302
        Theories and Explanations, 302
        Responses, 303
        Media, 305

Recommended Journals, 305

Journal Articles, 2010–Present, 307

Websites and Organizations, 309

Films, 316

7   CHRONOLOGY, 323

Glossary, 339
Index, 351
About the Author, 359

It seems as though the United States is in constant recovery from an incident of school violence. In just one week in mid-October 2013, two teachers were killed. On October 23, 2013, an 11-year-old brought a handgun, 400 rounds of ammunition, and multiple kitchen knives to his middle school in Vancouver, Washington. On Monday, October 21, a 12-year-old middle school student in Sparks, Nevada, shot and killed a student and teacher, then injured another student before killing himself. That same day, a student shot at peers with an AR-15, injuring three at a Chico, California, elementary school, and in Danvers, Massachusetts, a 14-year-old was charged with the death of his teacher. He allegedly used a box cutter to murder 24-year-old math teacher Colleen Ritzer. Certainly one could ask, when will we learn?

That young people will bully and harass their peers and teachers, bring weapons to school, engage in dangerous hazing, and abuse their dating partners is nothing new. And although data do not necessarily indicate that the problem is worse now than in previous decades, the availability of more deadly weapons, the use of new technologies to harass and bully at all hours, and the influences of violent media telling youth that this is normal behavior are certainly different today. Because of the nonstop stream of visual, radio, and Internet sources telling us about these horrific incidents, it is not surprising that the majority of the U.S. public believes school violence to be a significant problem warranting dramatic interventions. Indeed, it is, although great care must be taken to ensure that the information on which we base those interventions is accurate.

Schools should be a place in which all children are safe to learn and grow. They are not always that, and thus it is vital that communities continue to examine the scope and extent of school violence, who is most likely to perpetrate and be victimized by it, the forms violence takes, and why it happens. At the same time, it is essential to get beyond stereotypes and misconceptions that suggest only certain groups are responsible for and victims of school violence. For example, we are far more likely to consider today the violence faced daily in schools by uniquely marginalized groups, including lesbian, gay, bisexual, and transgender (LGBT) youth, racial and ethnic minorities, and students with disabilities, and to see that sometimes it is the teacher or administrator who is the perpetrator. Rejecting stereotypical portrayals of boys pushing around other boys for their lunch money, we know that girls too act as bullies and may do so through spreading rumors and gossip and on social media as well as through "traditional" physical means. Educators today recognize that sexual harassment, dating violence, hazing, and cyberbullying are frequent forms of violence experienced by youth in schools. This understanding helps us assist victims and informs our prevention practices.

Perhaps most importantly, it is crucial that we engage in critical reflection and thoughtful dialogue about how we respond to each of these various forms of school violence. Too often, our fear for the safety of our children results in poorly conceptualized and ineffective policies and practices that in many cases do as much harm as good. I taught at the high school level during the spate of school shootings in the 1970s, including the April 1999 Columbine massacre. I remember the horror we all felt when we heard and later saw what was happening at that school, as it was the first such incident to receive immediate and nonstop television coverage. As dismaying as it was to see youth gone so far astray, I was also dismayed, as were many of my peers, at the way that many schools responded. Rather than offering troubled youth additional support and seeking to create more positive and welcoming school environments, many districts, often at the behest of worried parents, responded with punitive measures that made schools look like, and to some students feel like, little more than prisons.

As a professor of sociology and criminology, I believe I have pulled together some of the best and most current data from my field and from others to help readers understand the nature and dynamics of, as well as explanations for, school violence in the United States. Although the focus is indeed domestic, several international incidents are discussed because they too have impacted the landscape and dialogue about the issue. I have also drawn on my own observations as a high school teacher, a position I held for six years prior to entering academia. And, of course, this book is also informed by my role as a parent and volunteer at my daughter's elementary school. As such, the book includes information about school violence in the elementary, middle, and high school levels. More than just an examination of high-profile shootings or school-based bullying, the book also addresses less discussed but no less important forms of violence. In addition to up-to-date information about the scope and extent of various forms of school violence, the book also includes a timeline of significant events, primary source documents, and a list of recommended books, journal articles, websites, and films. Also included is an examination of the major theories in criminology that can be used to explain various forms of school violence and, subsequently, lead to more effective responses. Further, detailed profiles of some of the nation's worst instances of school violence are included, as are profiles of inspirational scholars and activists who are helping create more peaceful schools. Also included are profiles of important organizations doing work to keep students safe. Additionally, the book offers brief overviews of some of the more common responses and prevention initiatives, including zero tolerance laws, installation of metal detectors, dress codes, peer mediation programs, and more. Pros and cons of each, as evidenced in scholarly research, are presented so that readers can assess which initiatives are most effective. Finally, I am pleased to be able to include personal reflections from students, educators, and activists who are making a difference in schools and communities every day. It is my hope that readers will find this an easy-to-use and well-researched tool but also one that inspires more informed and inspired debate about how best to keep children and youth safe in schools and, even more, how to ensure that they are treated with the fundamental human rights of respect and dignity.

Many thanks to the folks at ABC-CLIO who offered me the opportunity to write this reference handbook. As a lifetime educator and the mother of a soon-to-be middle school student, this issue matters deeply to me. Specifically, deep gratitude to David Paige and Robin Tutt at ABC-CLIO for supporting me through this process and ensuring that this book is a timely and useful reference.

I also want to thank all those who contributed to this book, either through research and technical support or through submitting a personal reflection for the Perspectives chapter. Barry University students Korie Happy, Andrew Kappler, and Kelly Moreno were terrifically helpful in finding sources and in compiling data. Contributors Kelly Concannon, Bob Knotts, Larinda Twigg, Evelyn Jackson, Sarah Raitter, Stephanie Wong, Lauren Lorance, Lashanti Jupp, De Palazzo, and Barbara Wien—from the deepest of my heart, I thank you for all that you do and for sharing it with others so that we can all improve.

Finally, I wish to thank my family for their continued support. I really like to write, and as such tend to pour myself into projects in ways that are likely annoying, at best, to those around me. So, Peter and Anya Finley, please know that I appreciate your patience and unconditional love as I immersed myself in this book.

I believe that, as an author, my duty is to do more than just inform. Rather, I feel my task is to use this wonderful platform as a way of supporting best practices in school violence prevention. To that end, I devote the royalties of this book to the Humanity Project, an antibullying and student empowerment initiative described herein that is doing amazing things in South Florida and beyond.

School Violence

While school violence has likely existed as long as have schools, it is relatively recently that adults began to pay attention to the issue. As more children have attended school, something that was far from given in centuries past, so too have there been more reported incidents of harassment, bullying, and assault by peers as well as by educators themselves. This chapter begins with an overview of the types of school violence. It next offers an assessment of the scope and extent of school violence as measured by a number of research tools. In addition, the chapter provides a brief historical overview of significant incidents of school violence, followed by a review of laws and court decisions relevant to the issue.

In order to craft effective prevention programs and responses to school violence, it is imperative that educators, lawmakers, and parents have a realistic understanding of the problem. One of the most challenging aspects of understanding school violence is obtaining accurate data about its scope, the context in which it occurs, and characteristics of perpetrators and victims. While these are seemingly straightforward concepts, they are often complex to measure. One challenge lies in what, precisely, constitutes school violence. Although it is clear that acts

---

Teenager Brenda Spencer leaves court in Santa Ana, California, on October 1, 1979 after she pleaded guilty to two counts of murder in the sniper attack on a San Diego school that left two men dead and eight children wounded. (AP Photo)

3

of overt physical violence, such as punches and assaults with weapons, should be considered school violence when they occur on school grounds, often violence occurs in more subtle ways. Violence can also be nonphysical, as in the violence that occurs through racial or sexual harassment. Additionally, most studies, and typical measurement tools, assess violence perpetrated in schools by and against young people. A growing body of literature, however, shows that educators and administrators also perpetrate violence, both against their peers and against students. Another area of research involves what is commonly called systemic violence. Systemic violence involves more than actions; rather, it includes structural arrangements and methods that result in harm. For instance, disciplinary policies that result in students being paddled (corporal punishment) have been considered by some to be examples of systemic violence.

Another challenge lies in precisely how we define what constitutes "school." While incidents occurring during the school day on school grounds can be easily classified as school violence, what about acts of cyberbullying between classmates? In many cases, both the perpetrator and the victim are not on school grounds, but the bullying is related to school activities or relationships. Legally, schools are liable for any violence that results in an unsafe or ineffective school climate.

Types of School Violence

Most research shows that the most common type of school violence is bullying. While there are many definitions of bullying, most agree that it involves one or more persons trying to obtain power over another through the use of a variety of verbal, social, and physical techniques. Verbal bullying involves harassing, degrading, or threatening remarks. Social bullying occurs when bullies attempt to use peer pressure, rumors, and gossip to demean and degrade victims. Physical bullying includes all types of unwanted physical contact, from pushing to slapping to punching and more. Some forms of bullying can also be categorized as assault, assault and battery, hazing, dating violence, and sexual assault. According to the U.S. Department of Health and Human Services stopbullying.gov website, between one-quarter and one-third of U.S. students report being bullied. The youth-focused organization Do Something features bullying statistics on its website, www.dosomething.org. These statistics show that some 3.2 million students are bullied each year, or an estimated one in seven K–12 students. Rates are highest for middle school youth, with an estimated 90 percent experiencing bullying. Some 56 percent of students actually witness bullying in schools, and each month, 282,000 students report being physically attacked by a bully or bullies while on school grounds.

Certain groups of youth are at greater risk for experiencing bullying in schools. Children and youth with disabilities are victims of school violence at higher rates than their peers. In the United States, children with disabilities—including children with autism, children in wheelchairs, and children with learning disorders—face routine violence in schools at higher rates than do other students. According to a national survey on school discipline conducted by Children and Adults with Attention-Deficit/Hyperactivity Disorder (CHADD), about 32 percent of kids with AD/HD are "egged on" by their peers to act out and get into trouble. The study found that many youth with AD/HD were victims of bullies, but when they reacted to the bully, they were punished for poor behavior and the bully was not. Studies show that students with visible and nonvisible disabilities are subject to more bullying than nondisabled peers. Bullying is frequently a direct result of a student's disability. Students with disabilities are disproportionately likely to face peer rejection, a significant risk factor for victimization. Many students with disabilities have significant social skills challenges, either as a core trait of their disability or as a result of social isolation due to segregated environments and/or peer rejection. Such students may be at particular risk for bullying and victimization. For example, Little's (2002) study of U.S. mothers found that 94 percent of children with a diagnosis of Asperger's syndrome faced peer victimization, with a broad swatch of different types of victimization including emotional bullying (75 percent), gang attacks (10 percent), and nonsexual assaults to the genitals (15 percent).

Other research has indicated that students with a wide range of disabilities face increased bullying victimization, including students with physical, developmental, intellectual, emotional, and sensory disabilities. A 2003 study found that 34 percent of students who report taking medication for AD/HD face bullying victimization at least two or three times a month, a substantial increase over the rate of bullying victimization from other students surveyed. Wiener and Mak (2009) also found high rates of victims among girls with attention deficit and hypertension disabilities. Langevin, Bortnick, Hammer, and Wiebe (1998), in a Canadian study examining the relationship between stuttering and selection as a target for bullying, found that at least 59 percent of students studied were bullied about their stuttering; 69 percent of students who stutter were also bullied about other things and said bullying takes place on at least a weekly basis.

Another group that is victimized at particularly high rates is youth who identify as or are perceived to be lesbian, gay, bisexual, or transgendered (LGBT). The National School Climate Survey, administered every other year by the Gay, Lesbian, and Straight Education Network (GLSEN), has found that homophobic remarks, harassment, and even assault of LGBT students is common in schools. The 2011 survey includes responses from 8,584 students between the ages of 13 and 20. Students were from all 50 states and the District of Columbia and from 3,224 unique school districts. Results indicated that 8 out of 10 LGBT students (81.9 percent) experienced harassment at school in the past year because of their sexual orientation, three-fifths (63.5 percent) felt unsafe at school because of their sexual orientation, and nearly a third (29.8 percent) skipped a day of school in the past month because of safety concerns.

Further, the majority of students in the National School Climate Study study who were harassed or assaulted (60.4 percent) did not report it because they believed nothing would change or that the situation might worsen. Of those who did report, 36.7 percent said school officials did nothing. This finding reinforces research that has continually shown that many teachers and administrators to do little to counteract homophobic attitudes. There has been very little (and in some instances no) improvement in the quality of the learning environment for LGBT youth. Studies have found these same patterns for 15 years, and a study reported in *TES* magazine found that gay teachers are even less likely to respond out of fear for their own job security.

This daily harassment and abuse takes a heavy toll on LGBT youth. The 2011 National School Climate Survey found that almost 30 percent of students skipped a class at least once in the past month because they felt uncomfortable or unsafe, and almost 32 percent skipped a full day of school each month for those reasons. Students experiencing this form of bullying have, on average, lower grade point averages and are less likely to report that they intend to pursue postsecondary education. They suffer from higher levels of depression and lower self-esteem than do their peers. What is more, 50 percent of homeless youth are LGBT, most of whom are homeless because they were kicked out by their family (the others also run away because of an unsafe home environment).

Another common form of bullying is cyberbullying. According to stopbullying.gov, cyberbullying is "verbal and/or social aggression carried out through technology." Do Something statistics show that 43 percent of school-aged youth have been bullied online, with one-quarter of the youth saying it happened more than once. Girls are twice as likely to be both victims and perpetrators of cyberbulling, which youth say is much easier to get away with than in-person bullying.

Hazing is another form of violence that may occur at school. Hazing occurs when groups seek to initiate new recruits by forcing or coercing them to participate in humiliating, degrading, or verbally, physically, or socially injurious acts. Athletic teams and clubs commonly haze rookies as a means of establishing a status order among group members. Hazing experts have identified three levels of hazing. Subtle hazing is typically not physically injurious, as it is simply intended to show that more senior members of the group have power over the newer members. It might involve asking new members to engage in menial tasks or refer to older members using specific reverent terms, assigning embarrassing nicknames to new members, and socially isolating the recruits or pledges. Harassment hazing invokes greater degrees of stress and frustration, as it usually involves more overt verbal harassment, threats, sleep deprivation, and even forcing newer members to engage in simulated sex acts. Violent hazing may cause serious physical, sexual, or emotional harm, as it sometimes involves severe paddling, forcing new members to consume excessive amounts of alcohol, forced sex acts, and other dangerous behaviors. One study by Alfred University researchers found that 48 percent of high school students who belong to some type of group or club, or approximately 1.5 million each year, are hazed. Males are more frequently perpetrators and victims of hazing, and students with lower grade point averages have been shown to be at greater risk of being hazed. Perpetrators and even school officials often defend hazing as an essential form of group bonding and a normal rite of passage. Studies have shown, however, that hazing can leave long-lasting marks on victims' emotional health. Critics maintain that there are other more positive means of group bonding.

Sexual harassment is another form of school violence that occurs with great frequency. There are two types of sexual harassment recognized in U.S. law. Quid pro quo harassment, or literally "something for something," occurs when perpetrators demand sexual favors in exchange for something. Hostile environment harassment involves unwanted sexual comments and behaviors that create an environment which negatively impacts someone's abilities to learn or work. A 2011 survey conducted by the American Association of University Women (AAUW) found that almost 50 percent of 7th to 12th graders had experienced sexual harassment, with 44 percent reporting that the harassment occurred in person and 30 percent reporting online harassment.

Title IV of the Civil Rights Act of 1964 prohibits workplace discrimination based on race, color, religion, sex, and national origin. It was not clear until the 1992 Supreme Court case *Franklin v. Gwinnett County Public School* how this issue was to be handled by schools. In that case, the Court held that the rights of Christine Franklin, a student, had been violated. Franklin had complained about sexually oriented remarks made to her by her teacher and coach, Andrew Hill, which escalated to forcible kissing and coercive intercourse. Although the school district claimed to have investigated Hill, no action was taken and Franklin was discouraged from pressing charges against him. In 1999, the Court further clarified that schools have a responsibility to address sexual harassment in *Davis v. Monroe County Board of Education*, which is discussed in more detail later in the chapter. According to that decision, schools can be held liable for violating Title IX of the U.S. Education Amendments of 1972 when (1) they have actual knowledge of the harassment; (2) they demonstrate deliberate indifference or take actions that are clearly unreasonable; (3) they have substantial control over the harasser and the context in which the harassment is occurring; and (4) the harassment is so severe, pervasive, and offensive that it deprives the victim of access to the educational opportunities provided by the school. Schools have no legal mandate to coordinate sexual harassment prevention programs, however, as the court decision addressed only response requirements.

Although statistics show that girls are more likely to endure sexual harassment, boys too can be victims. According to the AAUW study from 2011, 56 percent of girls and 40 percent of boys reported being harassed, with boys more likely to be the harassers. Further, it is often teachers, coaches, or other adults who perpetrate sexual harassment in schools, either against students or colleagues. AAUW's 2002 survey found that 38 percent of students experience harassment from teachers or school employees, while 36 percent of school employees were harassed by a colleague.

Although dating violence occurs in a number of settings, given that youth spend a large proportion of their time in school, it inevitably occurs there as well. Essentially a form of bullying between dating partners, the Centers for Disease Control and Prevention (CDC) defines dating violence as physical, sexual, or psychological violence within a dating relationship. An estimated 20 to 33 percent of teen relationships are abusive. A 2005 study found that one-third of reporting teens knew someone who had been hit, punched, kicked, slapped, choked, or punched by a partner, and one-quarter knew someone who had been coerced or forced to perform sex acts. Unlike adult domestic violence, studies have shown that boys and girls are almost equally likely to be victimized by dating partners.

Teachers and school personnel may be the perpetrators of what is often called systemic violence. Systemic violence is "any institutional practice or procedure that adversely impacts on individuals or groups by burdening them psychologically, mentally, culturally, economically, spiritually, or physically" (Epp & Watkinson, 1996, p. 1). Teaching methodologies that berate, demean, or stigmatize students and disciplinary practices that result in physical harm or emotional distress in excess of what would be considered normal are also examples of systemic violence. Because they are perpetrated by those in power positions, these incidents and practices are generally not considered violent but instead are deemed normal and necessary for ensuring students' safety. As such, there is little data to quantify the scope and extent of systemic violence in schools. One practice that many consider to be an example of systemic violence is corporal punishment, or the intentional infliction of physical pain with the intent of altering problem behavior. Although the U.S. Supreme Court said corporal punishment is not a violation of the Eighth Amendment's prohibition of cruel and unusual punishment in *Ingraham v. Wright* (1975), research and case studies show that it can be very damaging and that there are likely more effective means of disciplining students. Although some states have banned the practice, at the recommendation of groups like the American Psychological Association, the American Academy of Pediatrics, the American Medical Association, the National Education Association, and the American Bar Association, it remains legal in 20 states. Although likely an underestimate, studies have shown some 200,000 students are paddled in schools each year. Each year, up to 20,000 students who have been paddled seek medical care for injuries they sustain. Further, research has shown that minorities, boys, and students with special needs are paddled more frequently than are others. Others have maintained that demeaning school searches, such as drug testing and strip searches, are also examples of systemic violence.

Students also may target teachers or other educational staff. According to the American Psychological Association, 7 percent of U.S. teachers, or 253,100 individuals, are threatened with injury each year. Fifty-five percent of the incidents occur at the high school level. Far more females are threatened (69 percent of females and 31 percent of male teachers). Approximately 43 percent of teachers are physically attacked each year. Teachers who have unclear or inconsistent rules or are perceived as being excessively harsh are more likely to be victimized.

Although they occur quite infrequently in comparison to other forms of violence in schools, shootings receive the most attention and generate the most debate about how to keep children safe. School shootings are inextricably linked with the other forms of school violence described here. For instance, bullying has been linked to 75 percent of school shooting incidents. Negative school climates have also been linked to an increased risk of school shootings. Further, many have contended that while isolated incidents of violence occurred in urban schools that were heavily populated by nonwhite students, the real focus on school violence came when suburban Caucasian students began assaulting their peers in a very extreme and deadly fashion. Although there are many complex reasons why people have attacked others at schools, a few characteristics are shared by all or almost all of the assailants. First, they are overwhelmingly male. Second, like other mass killings in the United States, most were perpetrated by assailants who acquired, both legally and illegally, arsenals of firearms. For instance, a study published in *Mother Jones* magazine in 2012, which analyzed 62 mass shootings occurring since 1982, found that three-quarters of the guns used were obtained legally. Third, a majority of the school shooters struggled with some mental disturbance, albeit not always a diagnosed mental illness.

The next section of the chapter provides a description of the primary tools used to measure school violence in the United States.

Measuring School Violence

Scholars and practitioners have devised a number of tools that are used to measure the scope, extent, and characteristics of school violence in a variety of forms. The section below discusses some of the primary tools used to measure school violence, as well as the limitations of each.

The Youth Risk Behavior Surveillance System (YRBSS) is coordinated by the CDC. A series of surveys administered every two years in both private and public schools across the nation measures six types of risky health-related behaviors common among youth in 9th through 12th grades, including behaviors that contribute to unintentional injuries and violence; sexual behavior that may result in sexually transmitted diseases, HIV infection, or unintended pregnancy; alcohol and other drug use; tobacco use; unhealthy diet and nutrition; and inadequate physical activity. Additionally, YRBSS measures the prevalence of obesity and asthma among youth. Results are broken down by gender and race and ethnicity.

The 2011 YRBSS found the following related to bullying and violence:

- 16.6 percent of students had carried a weapon (e.g., a gun, knife, or club) on at least one day during the 30 days before the survey.
- 5.1 percent of students had carried a gun on at least one day during the 30 days before the survey.
- 32.8 percent of students had been in a physical fight one or more times during the 12 months before the survey.
- During the 12 months before the survey, 3.9 percent of students had been in a physical fight one or more times in which they were injured and had to be treated by a doctor or nurse.
- During the 12 months before the survey, 9.4 percent of students had been hit, slapped, or physically hurt on purpose by their boyfriend or girlfriend (i.e., dating violence).
- 8.0 percent of students had ever been physically forced to have sexual intercourse when they did not want to.
- 5.9 percent of students had not gone to school on at least one day during the 30 days before the survey because they felt they would be unsafe at school or on their way to or from school.
- 16.2 percent of students had been electronically bullied, including being bullied through e-mail, chat rooms, instant messaging, websites, or texting during the 12 months before the survey.
- 20.1 percent of students had been bullied on school property during the 12 months before the survey.

Rates for all bullying and violence-related measures were either higher for boys or no difference was detected. Black students were less likely to report being bullied, including electronically, than white or Hispanic students. White students were less likely than black or Hispanic students to report being threatened with a gun or other weapon on school property, being in a fight or being injured on school property, and being hit, slapped, or purposely injured by their boyfriend or girlfriend.

The CDC has also, since 1992, coordinated the School-Associated Violent Death Study (SAVD). Developed in partnership with the U.S. Departments of Education and Justice, the CDC collects information annually from media databases, police, and school officials. A case is defined as a fatal injury (e.g., homicide, suicide, or legal intervention) that occurs on school property, on the way to or from school, or during or on the way to or from a school-sponsored event. Only violent deaths associated with U.S. elementary and secondary schools, both public and private, are included. Results show that school-associated violent deaths have been decreasing since 2006 and that most school-associated violent deaths occur during the start of a semester and during transition times, such as passing periods between classes, lunch breaks, and before and after school. In almost half of recorded cases, perpetrators issued some type of warning, such as a note or a verbal threat. When firearms are used, they typically come from perpetrator's homes or from friends or acquaintances. Between 1 and 2 percent of homicides of youth ages 5–18 are considered school-associated.

The Bureau of Justice Statistics and National Center for Education Statistics collaborate to issue an annual report from a number of sources, including the National Crime Victimization Survey, the School Crime Supplement to the National Crime Victimization Survey, the Youth Risk Behavior Survey, and the School Survey on Crime and Safety and the School and Staffing Survey. The report describes the scope, extent, and context of violence in schools on a number of indicators: violent deaths at school and away from school;

incidence of victimization at school and away from school; prevalence of victimization at school; threats and injuries with weapons on school property; teachers threatened with injury or physically attacked by students; violent and other crime incidents at schools reported to police; reported discipline problems; students' reports of gangs at school; students' reports of being called hate-related words or seeing hate-related graffiti; bullying at school and cyberbullying elsewhere; teachers' reports on school conditions; physical fights on school property and anywhere; students' carrying weapons on school property and anywhere; students' use of alcohol on school property and anywhere; students' use of marijuana on school property and anywhere; and students' perceptions of safety at school and away from school. The February 2012 report, which analyzed data from the 2009–2010 school year, found there were about 828,000 nonfatal victimizations at school, which included 359,000 victims of violence (both simple assault and more serious acts). Approximately 74 percent of responding schools reported at least one incident of violence, and 16 percent reported one or more incident of serious violence. Students attending public schools reported being victimized at twice the rate of students attending private schools, although both rates were relatively low (4 percent versus 2 percent). Eight percent of students in grades 9–12 reported being threatened or injured with a weapon, with males more likely to report such threats or injuries (10 percent versus 5 percent). Twenty-three percent of public schools reported that bullying occurred among students on a daily or weekly basis, and 9 percent reported widespread disorder in classrooms on a daily or weekly basis. Sixteen percent of public schools reported that gang activities had occurred during the 2009–2010 school year, and 2 percent reported that cult or extremist activities had occurred during this period. About 9 percent of students ages 12–18 reported being targets of hate-related words at school, and 29 percent of students reported seeing hate-related graffiti at school during the school year. In 2009, about 31 percent of students in grades 9–12 reported they had been in a physical fight at least one time during the previous 12 months anywhere, and 11 percent said they had been in a fight on school property during the previous 12 months. Generally, a higher percentage of students in ninth grade reported having been in fights than students in any other grade, both anywhere and on school property. In 2009, about 27 percent of males carried a weapon anywhere, compared to 7 percent of females, and 8 percent of males carried a weapon on school property, compared to 3 percent of females. In 2009, a higher percentage of students ages 12–18 reported that they were afraid of attack or harm at school (4 percent) than away from school (3 percent) during the school year. In 2009, nearly all students (99 percent) ages 12–18 reported that they had observed the use of at least one of the selected security measures at their schools. The majority of students ages 12–18 reported that their schools had a code of student conduct (96 percent) and a requirement that visitors sign in (94 percent). Approximately 68 percent of students reported the presence of security guards or assigned police officers, and 91 percent reported the presence of other school staff or other adult supervision in the hallway. Metal detectors were the least observed of the selected safety and security measures: 11 percent of students reported the use of metal detectors at their schools.

Monitoring the Future (MTF) is a survey conducted each spring. It is administered in approximately 420 public and private schools in the United States, reaching approximately 50,000 randomly selected 8th-, 10th-, and 12th-grade students. In addition, annual follow-up questionnaires are mailed to a sample of each graduating class for a number of years after their initial participation. In operation since 1975, the survey is able to provide important longitudinal data about trends in drug use and other youth risk-taking behaviors. MTF also breaks down the data to provide important demographic information related to gender, region of the country, and race and ethnicity. Additionally, MTF tracks attitudes toward drug use and other risk-taking behavior, as well as perceived availability of drugs and of social support. MTF is funded by the National Institute on Drug Abuse at the National Institute of Health and is administered by the Institute for Social Research at the University of Michigan.

A limitation of the school-based surveys is that not all students will be present the day that surveys are administered. In fact, it might be that the most vulnerable youth and the youth most likely to perpetrate school violence are the least likely to be surveyed, as both victimization and perpetration are correlated with school truancy. Additionally, a general limitation of self-report surveys is that youth may not remember accurately what they have experienced or may be purposely untruthful. Some assert that young people are likely to lie when they respond to these surveys, yet most research suggests that youth are generally truthful in their responses. Yet survey methodologies do allow for the collection of large amounts of data such that sample sizes are typically generalizable to the wider public. Further, most of these tools help collect data that can provide a longitudinal view of school violence.

In-depth interviews provide an important means of gathering data about school violence. Because interviewees can provide more detailed responses, this qualitative form of research is useful for understanding why perpetrators commit acts of violence, how it has effected various parties, and how schools have responded to school violence. Another form of interviewing involves talking to multiple people in a group setting, called a focus group. The benefit of this is that more data can be collected in one interview session, and the comments from one respondent may trigger additional reflection among others on topics that the researcher did not anticipate. Conversely, it takes a great deal of time to conduct interviews or focus groups; thus sample sizes are typically small. These small samples are thus not typically generalizable to the broader population, which means interviews and focus groups are best suited for case studies.

School-based disciplinary reports can also provide another means of understanding the frequency of school violence and districts' responses to it. Antibullying laws, for instance, typically require that districts report the number of incidents and other details about bullying on campus. The limitation of school-based reports is that not all students who are involved (either as perpetrators or victims) come to the attention of school officials. Victims may not report incidents to school officials, or teachers may elect to handle incidents informally, and thus no official record is made. Further, as evidence grows that there are still biases in the administration of school discipline, it could be dangerous to use these data sources as a conclusive assessment of school violence because certain types of perpetrators and victims may be over- or underrepresented.

The chapter next offers a brief overview of some of the most significant incidents as another tool for understanding school violence. While the young mass shooter is far more likely to attack his or her school in the United States than in other countries, there have been several high-profile attacks that are detailed in the segment below. Unlike the incidents in the United States, many of the mass attacks on international schools were politically motivated. All of these incidents prompted public concern, and many resulted in legislative or significant policy changes. Thus the brief history below highlights some of the incidents, legal changes, and court decisions relevant to understanding school violence.

Brief History of School Violence Incidents

One of the earliest incidents of school violence in the United States, and, incidentally, still the most deadly, occurred in 1927 when 55-year-old school board member Andre Kehoe first killed his wife, set fire to his farm, and then detonated a series of bombs he had planted at Bath Consolidated School in Bath, Michigan. Kehoe's attack killed 45 and injured 58. Kehoe himself died during the attack, which he perpetrated because of a long-standing disagreement with the super-intendent, Emory Huyck, whom he had accused of financial mismanagement. Kehoe's attack stands out for its carnage but also for the fact that most large school massacres are perpetrated by youth. He is not the only adult perpetrator, however.

Although violence in the Middle East had long been a fact of life, the world was astonished to learn about the attack on students from Israel as they were on a school trip. Perpetrated by the Democratic Front for the Liberation of Palestine (DFLP), the attack left 25 dead and more than 50 injured. The team of assailants demanded that Israel release 23 Arab terrorists being held in Israeli prisons. In the end, Israeli defense forces stormed the school in which the attackers had held the children hostage, and the terrorists opened fire. The three members of the DFLP were all killed in the melee.

The next school violence incident to receive significant attention in the United States was the attack on students and staff at a school in California in 1979. Brenda Spencer was 16 at the time that she killed two and injured nine at Cleveland Elementary School in San Diego, California. Since the school was located across from her home, Spencer shot out of a window while students waited outside. She killed Principal Burton Wragg and Head Custodian Mike Suchar as both tried to assist students. In the process of firing 30 rounds, Spencer also killed a police officer. She engaged in a seven-hour standoff and, upon surrendering to police, announced "I don't like Mondays." She later claimed that it was easy, "like shooting ducks in a pond." Spencer was, by all accounts, a strange person who was obsessed with guns. Her father had introduced her to them and even purchased a gun and ammunition for her for a Christmas present. Tried as an adult, Spencer pleaded guilty and was convicted on two counts of murder and assault with a deadly weapon. She is still incarcerated in the California Institute for Women in Chico, California, and is not eligible for parole again until 2014, after having been denied four times. Spencer is one of the few females to perpetrate a mass attack at school.

Throughout the 1980s, several boys committed attacks on school grounds, often killing themselves after their assaults. In 1988, another female, 30-year-old Laurie Dann, perpetrated an odd attack in Illinois before committing suicide. Dann shot and killed one boy and wounded four other children in Highland Park, Illinois, after attempting to poison several family members and friends. She fled the location, taking a family hostage, before killing one man and then herself. Dann had a series of disruptive relationships in which she made allegations of rape and abuse, although no charges were ever filed. In the process, it became clear that Laurie suffered from a variety of mental problems. She received psychiatric help for obsessive-compulsive disorder and had been prescribed clomipramine as well as lithium to address her many phobias. Some have claimed that it was these medications that resulted in her aggression, while others blame the mental illness itself.

The following year, a deeply disturbed man named Patrick Purdy, who had a history of mental illness, abuse of alcohol, and arrests, shot and killed five students and wounded 29 students and a teacher at Cleveland Elementary in Stockton, California. All the students that Purdy killed were refugees from Southeast Asia. Purdy had a rough upbringing and was twice taken from his mother and stepfather by Child Protective Services. Neighbors recall him as quiet, odd, and occasionally violent. Despite telling a mental health professional about his depression and suicidal thoughts, he never received any serious mental health counseling. On the day of the attack, Purdy set fire to his car with a Molotov cocktail, then entered the school, shooting until he ran out of ammunition. He then killed himself with a pistol. Investigations of the hotel room where he had been staying showed a man who was obsessed with the military and who hated minorities, whom he blamed for his horrible life. Purdy's rampage was the catalyst for several legal changes in the state of California and at the federal level. California enacted the nation's first assault weapon ban, prohibiting the sale, production, and possession of certain types of assault weapons. The U.S. Congress passed the federal assault weapons ban years later, but it was this case coupled with some other mass shootings that pushed it forward.

Another school shooting perpetrated by an adult prompted international attention in 1996. Thomas Hamilton perpetrated the worst school shooting in UK history. Hamilton, who was 43, killed or injured 28 of the 29 five- and six-year-old children at Dunblane Primary School. Hamilton was obsessed with guns and with little boys, and he suffered from a long history of rejection. He had previously been rejected as a scoutmaster due to his odd behavior.

For the next decade, school shootings occurred occasionally and tended to involve a relatively small number of fatalities. National attention turned to school shootings in 1996, when Barry Loukaitis, 14 at the time, opened fire at his school, killing one teacher and two students and wounding another student. Loukaitis seemed to differ from the earlier shooters in that he was younger and was an honor student at Frontier High School, a more suburban location than that of most of the previous school massacres. Despite his successes in the classroom, Loukaitis came from a disturbing home life where his parents, who had divorced, tried to pit him against each other. Both parents suffered from depression as well. Loukaitis had also been bullied, with one of his victims repeatedly harassing him for being gay. His case generated attention to the devastating effects of school-based bullying. Additionally, Loukaitis was allegedly obsessed with several forms of violent media, including the film *Natural Born Killers* and the Pearl Jam song *Jeremy*. The video for the song featured a boy shooting classmates who had harassed him. Loukaitis also was a huge Stephen King fan, especially of the book *Rage*, which tells the story of a high school boy who goes insane from being bullied, takes his class hostage, and kills a teacher out of revenge. Loukaitis was tried as an adult. He pleaded not guilty by reason of insanity but was convicted and sentenced to life in prison without the possibility of parole.

Just over a year after Loukaitis' attack, 16-year-old Evan Ramsey killed a popular 15-year-old classmate and Principal Ron Edwards at Bethel Regional High School in the small town of Bethel, Alaska. Ramsey wounded several others and then threatened to kill himself but instead surrendered to police. Like so many other school shooters, Ramsey's family life was difficult. His father was in prison, and his mother an alcoholic who had been in several abusive relationships. Evan and his two brothers were removed from the home when he was in third grade and were separated into different foster homes. As a child, Evan Ramsey lived with 11 different foster families and suffered sexual, physical, and verbal abuse at several of them. By the time he was in high school, Ramsey regularly smoked marijuana, got terrible grades, and had seen a psychiatrist because he appeared depressed and suicidal. He was also teased endlessly by classmates. Also like many of the other shooters, Ramsey was an avid player of the violent video game *Doom.* Ramsey did tell his two friends, both 14 at the time, that he planned to attack the school, but they did not tell anyone else. In 1998, Ramsey was tried as an adult on two counts of first-degree murder. He was convicted and sentenced to 210 years in prison. He deeply regrets his actions and has received many letters from bullied teens to whom he offers support. Ramsey's attack, like Loukaitis's, drew attention to the fact that school violence is not just an issue of urban gangs but instead one of disaffected youth.

Only months later, two more suburban school shootings rocked the nation. On October 1, 1997, Luke Woodham, 16, first killed his own mother and then went on a shooting spree at Pearl High School in Pearl, Mississippi, wounding seven and killing two. Then, on December 1, 1997, 14-year-old Michael Carneal killed three students and wounded five others who were participating in a prayer circle at his high school in West Paducah, Kentucky.

Woodham, too, did not have a great upbringing. His parents divorced when he was young. Luke lived with his mother, who was very controlling and verbally abusive, and his older brother, who tormented him whenever he was around. Luke was also bullied at school for his thick glasses and outdated hairstyle and clothing. The neighbors knew the Woodham boys as odd and aggressive. When he was 15 a new girl moved to town, and Luke fell in love with Christina Menefee, who was nice to him. She broke up with him when he became too controlling, however, which seems to have been a catalyst for Woodham's descent. He twice threatened to commit suicide. Early in 1997 Luke began hanging out with a new crowd of friends he met through his job at Dominos pizza. The group of misfits liked to engage in role-playing games and called themselves "the Kroth." Although the boys all appeared to be good Christians and good students, they lived dual identities, having become fixated on satanism and Hitler. School officials did notice a change in Woodham, who wrote a series of disturbing essays in class, including one that stated he would go on a killing spree. Woodham was prevented from hurting others during the attack when he was subdued by Assistant Principal Joel Myrick. He told police that he had killed his mother and emotionally discussed her lack of love for him. Fueling the community's concern that this was an attack not just by Woodham but by his gang, too, one of the Kroth members, Justin Sledge, pinned a note to the school door stating that the group was still strong. At a candlelight vigil he spoke out in support of Woodham. By October 7, 1997, six of Woodham's friends were arrested for conspiracy. Woodham was tried first for the murder of his mother. His attorney's asserted that he had borderline personality disorder. Jurors rejected his insanity defense and found him guilty of first-degree murder. He was then tried for the school murders, was convicted, and received a life sentence for each of the two murders plus 20 years for seven counts of aggravated assault. Charges were dropped against five of the other boys. The other was tried in juvenile court, but his records were sealed. In October 1998, Kroth ringleader Grant Boyette and Justin Sledge were charged as accessories to murder. Boyette accepted a plea bargain and was sentenced to a prison-based boot camp. Sledge was acquitted (Davis, 2003; Fast, 2008).

Michael Carneal was, in contrast, a seemingly normal young man who earned average grades, was involved in high school band, and had not been in any disciplinary trouble at school. However, he too was bullied by classmates, who accused him of being a satanist (due to his penchant for wearing dark clothes) and called him gay. Armed with two shotguns, two rifles, and a semi-automatic handgun, Carneal fired 11 rounds at the prayer group assembled outside of Heath High School, killing three girls and injuring three girls and two boys. Carneal surrendered to school principal Bill Bond. He was tried as an adult and, despite concerns about his mental health, was declared competent for trial. He pled no contest and was sentenced to three consecutive life terms and an additional 120 years in prison for five counts of attempted murder and burglary. Carneal's case generated even more attention about the role of violent media, as he was said to have been obsessed with the 1995 film *The Basketball Diaries*, which features a scene in which the main character shoots up his school. Parents of the three murdered girls filed suit against Carneal as well as a number of video game companies (including Nintendo and Sega) and Sony Computer Entertainment, two Internet pornography sites, and the makers of the film. Federal courts dismissed all but Carneal from the suit, arguing the link between the media and his attacks was not clear. On August 4, 2000, the court issued a $42 million judgment against Carneal.

In just a four-month period in 1998, the United States saw five school shootings. Starting on March 9 with Jeffrey Lance Pennick II killing one and wounding two at Central Avenue Elementary School in Summit, Washington, the spree ended on June 15, 1998, when 14-year-old Quinshawn Booker shot a teacher and wounded a counselor at his high school in Richmond, Virginia. In between, two very young shooters— Mitchell Johnson, 13, and Andrew Golden, 11—attacked their school, killing a teacher and four students and wounding another 10 in Jonesboro, Arkansas. On April 24, 1998, 14-year-old Parker Middle School student Andrew Wurst killed a teacher and wounded two students at a dance at the Edinboro, Pennsylvania, school. Less than a month later, 15-year-old Kip Kinkel killed his parents and then two students, wounding 23 in the process, at his high school in Springfield, Oregon.

Andrew Golden had asked to use the restroom on March 24, 1998. Instead, he pulled the fire alarm and then joined Mitchell Johnson in the woods outside of the school, where the two had assembled an arsenal that included 13 fully loaded firearms, three semi-automatic rifles, 200 rounds of ammunition, a crossbow, and several hunting knives they had taken from Golden's family. Both boys had grown up with guns, raising issues about youth access to dangerous weapons. The case also generated debate about how to handle dangerous kids. Both were released from juvenile facilities when they turned 21 and have no criminal record. Both boys were described by classmates as bullies, not as victims.

Andrew Wurst is another shooter who generated discussion about violent media and whether teachers and school officials take seriously enough the jokes, writings, and other signs of a disturbed youth. He was a fan of horror writers Stephen King and Dean Koontz and loved the music of heavy metal bands like Marilyn Manson, Korn, and Nine Inch Nails. Like many of the other school shooters, Wurst professed to admire Adolf Hitler and was nicknamed "Satan" by classmates. In advance of his trial, Wurst was seen by many psychiatrists. One concluded that he suffered from psychotic thinking and delusions of persecution and grandeur. Nonetheless, Wurst was tried as an adult and pleaded guilty to third-degree murder. He was sentenced to serve 30 to 90 years in prison.

After murdering his parents on May 20, 1998, Kip Kinkel left a note describing how he heard voices that made him kill. Also at the home was a journal that told how he planned to kill classmates, pictures of classmates he wanted to kill, a sawed-off shotgun and other weapons, and a book on explosives. Kip had previously gotten into trouble for researching how to make bombs and for shoplifting. He was arrested for vandalism and assigned to see a therapist as well as serve some time at a juvenile facility. He began taking Prozac for depression, which seemed to help. Kip was, as were most of the other school shooters, obsessed with guns and could easily obtain them. In fact, his father had encouraged the interest. Defense attorneys described his background and asserted that he was mentally ill. Kinkel was convicted and sentenced to 111 years in prison.

Less than a year after Kinkel's attack, the nation was again shocked by a school shooting in a suburban area perpetrated by two middle-class Caucasian boys. Before the April 20, 1999, massacre at Columbine High School, the columbine was known as Colorado's state flower. Ever after, it has been associated with mass violence, the most deadly attack on a school since Kehoe's bombing at Bath (later surpassed by Adam Lanza's shooting spree at Sandy Hook Elementary). It was the first mass school shooting to receive national media attention. It also highlighted the challenges for law enforcement and school officials in responding to this type of active shooter situation, as by all accounts officials were unprepared and thus failed to respond as quickly as possible. Heavily armed Eric Harris, 18, and Dylan Klebold, 17, killed 12 students and a teacher, wounded 23 others, and then killed themselves on April 20, 1999. Chaos reigned as the two paraded through their school, shooting peers at leisure and saving some. Their initial plan was to bomb the school, but the homemade bombs they had planted failed to detonate, so Harris and Klebold entered Columbine High a little after 11:00 a.m. School video cameras show the two laughing as they mowed down classmates. At approximately 12:02 Klebold and Harris entered the library and, after counting off to ensure it would happen simultaneously, shot themselves. Over an hour later the SWAT team entered the school and, some five hours after the attack commenced, declared the school to be safe. Subsequent examinations of the situation focused on Harris and Klebold's connections to violent media, the fact that they may have endured bullying and abuse at school, and how their parents did not discern that they were planning something. Both boys were avid players of *Doom*, a violent video game, and were even so skilled that they programmed for the game. Initial reports highlighted the fact that the boys identified with a group of outcasts called the Trenchcoat Mafia, which wore trenchcoats and dark clothes and had disdain for the more popular school cliques. Yet later reports showed that neither Harris nor Klebold were really involved with the group, nor was it really an organized, oppositional group at the school. Many criticized Harris and Klebold's parents, as it is difficult to understand how the two were able to assemble bombs at their homes undetected. Years later, the focus has been on the boys' mental stability, with many asserting that both suffered from some mental illness. Motives notwithstanding, it is clear that the Columbine attack spawned both copycat assaults as well as a new wave of concern about school violence. Indeed, just days later, Todd Cameron Smith, 14, shot and killed a student and wounded another in what appeared to be a Columbine copycat attack, while exactly one month after Harris and Klebold's massacre Thomas "T.J" Solomon wounded six people at his school in Conyers, Georgia. Solomon had left a suicide note at his home expressing solidarity with the Trenchcoat Mafia and had previously proclaimed that he was a better marksman than Harris and Klebold.

Less than one year later the nation's attention was again focused on school violence, although this time both the perpetrator and victim were children. On February 29, 2000, 6-year-old Dedrick Owens brought a loaded gun to school and shot his classmate, 6-year-old Kayla Rolland, at Buell

Elementary School in Flint, Michigan. The two first-graders were having a disagreement as the class was lining up to go to computer class when Dedrick pulled out a .32-caliber pistol and pointed it at two other girls, then at Kayla. He said, "I don't like you," to which she might have responded, "So?" Dedrick then pulled the trigger. Teacher Alicia Judd called 911, and Kayla, bleeding profusely, was transported to nearby Hurley Medical Center, where she was pronounced dead. Dedrick had run into the hall and was stopped by school officials. Investigations revealed that Dedrick Owens also had a knife with him at school that day, both of which he had stolen from Jamelle James, a 19-year-old who lived at the house where Dedrick and his eight-year-old brother were staying with their uncle. Dedrick's dad was in prison, and his mother had been evicted from her home. While Dedrick was too young to be criminally charged, James was charged with involuntary manslaughter, contributing to the delinquency of a minor, and gross neglect. Reports showed that Dedrick Owens had been in trouble at school before for cursing, pinching, and hitting. Some said that Owens had tried to kiss Kayla Rolland the day before. Yet it is clear that the school did not respond as thoroughly as possible to prevent tragedy. A student saw the knife that Owens had that morning and told a teacher, who took it away but did not report it to administrators. Immediately after the incident President Bill Clinton urged Congress to enact new gun control measures, none of which came to fruition. Dedrick Owens went on to be enrolled in a private school in Flint, Michigan.

Concerns about the young age of school perpetrators were exacerbated less than a month later, when on March 16, 2000, 13-year-old Nathaniel Brazill killed his teacher in Lake Worth, Florida. It was the last day of classes at Lake Worth Middle School when seventh-grader Nathaniel Brazill, who had been sent home for throwing water balloons, returned to the school with a .25-caliber handgun and demanded to see two female students in his English class. Teacher Barry

Grunow refused to let him in, and Brazill shot him in the face. Grunow died on the spot. Brazill was tried as an adult and is serving a 28-year sentence. It is unclear precisely what prompted Brazill's actions, especially given that he was an honors student with no history of misbehavior or violence, although there were likely a number of factors. His grades had begun to slip that year. Brazill had told others that Grunow was his favorite teacher and had even confided in him that he was being picked on and felt suicidal. Further, one of the two girls Brazill had asked to see was his girlfriend, Dinora Rosales, whom he had told people he was infatuated with. Brazill had also witnessed domestic violence in the home, with his mother enduring abuse from Nathaniel's father as well as a series of boyfriends. While there was much outrage about Brazill's shooting, many expressed dismay that a boy so young was sentenced so harshly. Brazill joined 15 other inmates in Florida who were 13 or 14 when they committed their offenses.

Europe had been generally free of school shootings until 2002, when in just a three-day period attackers killed 17 people before committing suicide. On April 26, 2002, 19-year-old Robert Steinhauser killed 13 teachers, two students, and police officer at Johann Gutenberg Secondary School in Erfurt, Germany. Steinhauser's attack remains one of the worst in history. Steinhauser was a gun enthusiast who legally owned several weapons that he used in the attack. Like many of the U.S. shooters, Steinhauser was also a fan of violent videos and video games, igniting debate about gun control and banning violent video games in Germany. Just days later, Dragoslav Petkovic killed a teacher and wounded another at a school in Vlasenica, Bosnia-Herzegovia.

Two years after Steinhauser's attack, a group of terrorists took hostage a group of schoolchildren in Beslan, North Ossettia-Alania, resulting in at least 368 deaths by the end of the three-day siege. The assailants were intending to direct the world's attention to the situation in Chechnya, a part of Russia that is rich in oil. Chechnyans fought with Russia in what is known as the First Chechnyan War from 1994 to 1996. A peace treaty was enacted in 1997, but the Chechnyans suffered badly. After the fighting ended, poverty and crime increased in Chechnya, and the instability, coupled with an increasingly militant Islamic Chechen separatist movement, lead to the Second Chechnyan War. The rest of the area was virtually destroyed. The terrorists attacked Beslan because many of the Russian artillery attacks were staged from bases there. They chose to attack on September 1, the first day of the school year, as they knew that not only would many students be there but so too would their families, as is customary on what is known as the Day of Knowledge. It is estimated that approximately 32 men and women were part of the assault in which they initially took hostage between 1,100 and 1,200 adults and children. Two hours before a planned negotiation with an adviser to the Russian president, the terrorists allowed two ambulances into the school grounds to remove the dead bodies. As they were approaching, however, an explosion occurred, the gymnasium roof collapsed, and shooting commenced. Because authorities were surprised by the explosion and the shooting, they did not respond immediately. The terrorists began detonating bombs, and Russian troops stormed the building. While there was some increase in the number of Russians citing their sympathy for Chechnya, many others stated they wanted to ban Chechens from major cities.

Over the next several years, severe incidents of school violence occurred sporadically across the country. The next large-scale attack in the United States occurred in March 2005. Jeff Weise, 16, killed his grandfather, his grandfather's girlfriend, and then five students, a teacher, a security guard, and himself at his high school on Red Lake Indian Reservation in Minnesota. Seven others were wounded. Weise seems to have been deeply troubled. His father had committed suicide, and he moved hundreds of miles to live on the remote reservation with his grandfather. There was a history of depression in the family, and Weise had been prescribed antidepressants. He had been in trouble at school and was eventually expelled. Additionally, Weise was obsessed with neo-Nazism, as evidenced by racist blogs he wrote. It appears that Weise had shared some of his frustrations with his cousin, Louis Jordan, who was later charged with conspiracy in the shootings.

While it is shocking when young people perpetrate atrocities like those described here, it is perhaps even more disturbing when the offenders are adults. In just a one-week period in 2006, two adult males killed a total of six young girls in attacks on schools. That same week, a high school student killed his principal in Cazenovia, Wisconsin. On September 27, 2006, 53-year-old Duane Morrison first took six girls hostage and sexually molested them before killing one and then himself at Platte Canyon High School in Bailey, Colorado. Morrison, who had previous arrests for larceny, possession of marijuana, and obstructing police, entered Platte Canyon High School armed with a gun and a backpack he claimed contained explosives. He entered a classroom, fired his gun in the air, and demanded that the students face the chalkboard. He then allegedly let the boys go and carried out his attack on the girls while police negotiators tried to get him to release everyone and surrender. The school was evacuated and reopened one week later.

Then, on October 2, 2006, Charles Roberts, 32, killed five girls in the first attack on an Amish school. He wounded five others before he killed himself in Nickel Mines, Pennsylvania. Roberts was not Amish but did live near the Amish community and routinely went to their farms to pick up milk in his capacity as a milk truck driver. Before killing the girls he tied them up, allegedly with the intent to sexually molest them, although no evidence suggests he did so. Three of the girls he shot died at the school, and the other two died later at the hospital. Roberts called his wife during the attack and admitted to having sexually abused children before. He stated that he was struggling with the urge to do so again. Roberts had also left a suicide note proclaiming that he was seeking revenge on God for having let his baby die in 1997. Co-workers indicated that

Roberts had been acting differently in the weeks before the shooting, although none suspected violence. It is clear, however, that he planned the attack, as investigators found a checklist of supplies that he purchased six days prior, including KY Jelly lubricant and restraints. Because the Amish live simply, they had no security systems in place at the school. This was likely a factor in explaining why Roberts chose that particular school. Eleven days after the attack, the Amish community tore down the school. Morrison's and Roberts' attacks are the only ones in which a sexual motivation has been identified.

Between November 2006 and November 2007, two more European men perpetrated mass shootings on schools. Eighteen-year-old Sebastian Bosse shot five people at his former high school in northwestern Germany, wounding five others. He also set off a series of pipe bombs that did not hurt anyone, although 22 people were treated for smoke inhalation. Bosse was obsessed with guns and violent video games, and classmates thought he was odd. He had written on his website that he planned to do something dangerous and that he wanted to seek revenge on those who had treated him as a loser. Police found him dead when they entered the school.

On November 7, 2007, 18-year-old Pekka-Eric Auvinen killed six students as well as the school nurse and principal at Jokela High School in Tuusula, Finland. He wounded at least 10 others before killing himself. Like Bosse, Auvinen was described as an outcast. He had been taking antidepressants for a year and was the victim of bullying. Auvinen made disturbing comments and drawings before the shooting, but friends thought he was joking. The media called him the YouTube Killer because they found approximately 90 videos in which he expressed admiration for Columbine killers Eric Harris and Dylan Klebold as well as for other mass murderers like Hitler, Timothy McVeigh, and Jeffrey Dahmer. In one video he had described his plan for attaching Jokela High School. Finland considered passing stricter gun laws; although despite having the third highest gun ownership rate for civilians in the world at the time, it had only seen one school shooting prior to Auvinen's attack.

Two years later, on March 11, 2009, 17-year-old Tim Kretschmer, dressed in black combat boots, killed nine students and three teachers at his former high school in Winnenden, Germany. After fleeing the school, Kretschmer killed another person, then took a hostage with him while he engaged in a shootout with the police. Two passersby were killed, and two others wounded. Kretschmer died as well, although it was unclear whether he killed himself or was shot by police. A gun fanatic, Kretschmer trained at a local shooting club. His family reportedly had 18 guns in the home. Reports indicated that Kretschmer was an average student, didn't really get into trouble, and was not bullied. This and the previously mentioned attacks put Germany second to the United States in the number of school shootings.

In the later 2000s, attention was focused on the issue of bullying after a spate of young people committed suicide after being bullied in school and online. One of the first "bullycides" to receive national attention was that of Ryan Halligan, who at age 13 committed suicide on October 7, 2003, after experiencing in-person and cyberbullying from middle school classmates. Halligan was tormented endlessly. Some students accused him of being gay. The last straw was when a girl who had been flirting with him online announced to the world that she had only been joking and that she thought Halligan was a loser. Less than two years later, Jeffrey Johnston of Cape Coral, Florida, committed suicide after experiencing similar forms of harassment at school and online. Months later, 17-year-old Rachel Neblett killed herself after being bullied online, and just eight days later, on October 17, 2006, 13-year-old Megan Meier hung herself after being bullied not just by a classmate but by the girl's mother as well.

On January 14, 2010, Phoebe Prince hung herself from the stairwell in her family's home after enduring months of harassment at South Hadley High School in Hadley, Massachusetts.

Prince, an Irish immigrant, had been verbally and physically harassed by a group of girls who behaved much like the characters in the 2004 film *Mean Girls*. They threw things at her, knocked her books from her hands, sent her threatening text messages, and referred to her as "Irish slut" and "whore" in person and on social networking sites. The girls continued to post mean comments even after Prince's suicide. Just months before Prince's suicide, 17-year-old Tyler Long killed himself as a result of the near-constant torment he endured because of his Asperger's syndrome. School officials did not take the bullying reports seriously, even when Long was pushed down a flight of stairs. Both President Barack Obama and Secretary of State Hilary Clinton have spoken publicly about bullycide.

In another bullying case, a student was killed by a classmate who had been bullying him. Fourteen-year-old Brandon McInerney shot classmate Lawrence "Larry" King, 25, at E.O. Green Junior High School in Oxnard, California. King died two days after the shooting. King, who was small and had difficulties in school, was often bullied. Students teased him about being gay, picking on him for his stature and for the effeminate clothing he often wore to school. King liked McInerney, who was being teased about it. The gay rights community used the incident to draw attention to the daily abuse many LGBT youth face at school, although King's father, Greg, did not approve. GLSEN has dubbed April 25 the National Day of Silence in honor of Larry King.

Between 2008 and 2010, the state of Florida was home to three separate school tragedies. On November 13, 2008, 15-year-old Teah Wimberly shot and killed her friend and classmate Amanda Collette at Dillard High School in Fort Lauderdale. Less than a year later, Michael Brewer, also 15, was attacked by a group of teenaged classmates from Deerfield Beach Middle School, who beat him, doused him with rubbing alcohol, and then set him on fire. Just months later, Wayne Treacy, 15 as well, brutally attacked classmate Josie Ratley after the two exchanged a series of mean text messages. Both Brewer and Ratley suffered tremendous physical and emotional injuries but survived.

Wimberly was friends with Collette but had started to develop more romantic feelings for her. With Wimberly already feeling deeply rejected by her family, who did not support her when she told them she was a lesbian, when Collette rebuffed Wimberly's romantic overtures it was the last straw. Wimberly had a disturbing family life, having been left in grandparents' care when she was just six weeks old, enduring sexual molestation at the hands of a family member at age six, and being severely beaten by both parents. Wimberly's defense attempted an insanity plea, but it was rejected. In court, she wept and apologized profusely to Collette's family. She was sentenced to 25 years in prison. Wimberly is being held in a juvenile facility and is being treated for bipolar disorder. When she turns 21 she will be transferred to an adult prison.

On October 29, 2009, after a dispute about a video game Michael Brewer allegedly did not pay for, four Deerfield Beach Middle School boys nearly killed him when they set him ablaze. Brewer sustained second- and third-degree burns over 65 percent of his body but survived because he jumped into a nearby swimming pool. Although he was in a medically induced coma for many months, he recovered miraculously and began attending another school just six months after the attack. One of the assailants, Denver Jarvis, was sentenced to eight years in prison and 22 years of probation, which was later reduced to 10. Jarvis was the one to throw the rubbing alcohol on Brewer. Two other assailants, Michael Bent and Jesus Mendez, were both sentenced to 11 years in prison. All did not go perfectly for Brewer, however, as he was arrested a few years later for possessing marijuana, crack cocaine, morphine, oxycodone, and drug paraphernalia.

Wayne Treacy, also a student at Deerfield Beach Middle School, assaulted Josie Ratley at the bus stop after school, punching her in the head, slamming her head into the pavement, and kicking her with his steel-toed boots. Treacy's attack was stopped when teacher Walter Welsh pulled him off the girl. The two had exchanged mean text messages, but it was a message Ratley sent about Treacy's brother, who had committed suicide not long before, that made him snap. Ratley was in a medically-induced coma but eventually regained consciousness. Treacy was waived to adult court, where he was found guilty of attempted murder and was sentenced to 20 years in prison.

December 14, 2012, will forever go down in infamy. Twenty-year-old Adam Lanza killed 20 students and six teachers at Sandy Hook Elementary in Newtown, Connecticut. Adam Lanza shot his mother in the face, then drove to Sandy Hook Elementary in Newtown, Connecticut, and killed 26 people, including 20 elementary school students. Four teachers, the school's principal, and a school psychologist were among the victims. The victims were all hit multiple times, some as many as 11 times, with the semi-automatic rifle Lanza used. Lanza committed suicide after his rampage. Lanza used weapons he took from his mother, Nancy Lanza, who legally owned them. The shooting was the most deadly involving elementary school students in U.S. history and might have been worse if some of the Sandy Hook teachers had not acted quickly to usher their students to safety.

Although Lanza's precise motives cannot be discerned, many theories have been circulated. Reports months later showed that Lanza had been researching mass murders for several months before the rampage. Newspaper articles and other documents were found in Lanza's bedroom, including material about Anders Behring Breivik, the Norwegian who was convicted of killing 77 people with guns and bombs in July 2011. Connecticut state police also found evidence that Lanza was very interested in the 2006 shooting at an Amish schoolhouse in Lancaster, Pennsylvania. Based on these findings, some believe Lanza was trying to outdo other school shooters. Indeed, Lanza shot a bullet every two seconds, and the entire incident lasted less than five minutes.

Lanza was a gun enthusiast, a hobby he shared with his mother. Additionally, people close to the family say he played a lot of violent video games, like *Call of Duty*, and that he was very introverted. Some have criticized Nancy Lanza for encouraging her troubled son's interest in guns. When police searched the Lanza home, they found 1,600 rounds of unspent ammunition. They also found samurai swords and a book, published by the National Rifle Association, titled *Guide to the Basics of Pistol Shooting*.

Immediately after the shootings, it was revealed that Lanza had been diagnosed with Asperger's syndrome, a milder form of autism. Experts caution not to read too much into the diagnosis, as persons with Asperger's syndrome are rarely violent. Perhaps more important is the fact that Lanza suffered from tremendous anxiety, so bad that his mother had to rush him to the emergency room when he was 13. Lanza is also said to have suffered from a sensory disorder. He is also described as painfully shy, with few friends. Yet again, experts are quick to point out that these disorders are typically not associated with violent behavior.

The tragedy prompted renewed debate about gun control in the United States. Connecticut passed one of the country's most restrictive laws as a result of the shooting. Since Newtown, however, 44 shootings took the lives of 28 students in schools across the United States, with one shooting every 10 days. Seventy percent of post-Newtown shootings were carried out by minors, and three-quarters involved guns brought from home.

The following section highlights some of the most important legislative and court decisions relevant to school violence, many of which emerged after the shootings discussed here.

Legislation and Court Decisions

On October 12, 1984, President Ronald Reagan signed the Comprehensive Crime Control Act, considered one of the biggest and most important changes in the U.S. criminal justice system. Although there are 23 chapters in the act, the most important segments address bail conditions, the insanity defense, victims of crime and justice assistance, sentencing, and regulation of narcotics. The act authorized courts to consider assessments of an offender's dangerousness when determining bail and allowed pretrial detention if the courts deemed it necessary. Defendants who could prove that they suffered from a mental disease or defect at the time of the offense could now use the insanity defense, but those who were intoxicated or high on drugs were not eligible. The act also established a Sentencing Commission that collects information and recommends sentencing guidelines to federal judges. A Crime Victims Fund was also established in the U.S. Treasury, which includes restitution monies paid by offenders. Relevant to juvenile justice, the act gave the Office of Juvenile Justice and Delinquency Prevention an extension on its operating power, increased federal penalties for many drug offenses, and provided for a missing-children hotline.

The 1990 Gun-Free School Zones Act made it a federal offense to possess a firearm in a school zone. It prompted many districts to enact zero tolerance laws. The act was later invalidated as unconstitutional in *United States v. Lopes* (1995). In 1994, Congress enacted the Gun-Free Schools Act, which took a different approach to addressing weapons on school grounds. States receiving federal funds were required to enact legislation that specified mandatory punishments for specific offenses, typically involving guns, drugs, and acts of violence. While it did not mandate suspension or expulsion, many states included those punishments in their legislation.

The Safe and Drug-Free Schools Act (SFDFSCA) of 1994 authorized federal funding for states to enact safety-related measures and drug prevention programs. State and local educational associations distribute these funds to districts based on rates of drug and alcohol use, gang activity, and arrests and convictions. The SFDSCA also provided districts with a list of evidence-based practices to guide their selection of programs. Among the practices listed were school uniform policies and alternatives to suspension.

Few laws have changed schools as much as the No Child Left Behind (NCLB) Act of 2001. NCLB expanded the 1998 U.S. Department of Education principle-of-effectiveness rule, which required school districts that receive state funding to reconsider their drug prevention and response programs. Schools were required to conduct needs assessments, establish measurable goals and objectives, and implement and evaluate evidence-based practices. While NCLB includes a number of provisions relevant to curriculum and testing, related to school violence it required the establishment of drug- and violence-free school environments and efforts to graduate all students. The Department of Education provided districts with lists of approved programs, which included character education and peer mediation but not Drug Abuse Resistance Education (D.A.R.E.). The list also included hiring school resource officers, conducting drug testing and locker searches, and establishing or expanding alternative education programs. President George W. Bush particularly favored student drug testing, although because it is costly, many districts could not establish testing programs. A very controversial provision of NCLB allowed students enrolled in a school that had been labeled "persistently dangerous" to transfer to another school in the district. Critics noted that rather than address what was making the school violent, this provision would result in flight from the school. It also gave districts a powerful incentive to underreport school violence so as not to lose students. Many others took issue with the list of evidence-based practices, suggesting that it was weak on curricular changes and heavy on punitive and technological bandaids that are incapable of changing the school culture. Further, critics fear that the emphasis on graduating all students would result in districts either promoting youth who had not mastered the required content or ushering them into alternative schools.

After the tragic massacre at Sandy Hook Elementary, many states enacted new gun control laws. While President Obama has pushed for additional federal controls, none have been enacted to date. He did, however, issue 23 executive orders related to gun control. In all, 109 new state laws were passed. In Democrat-controlled states, laws were more likely to mandate background checks for gun purchases from a broader audience. In Republican-controlled states, new gun laws tended to loosen restrictions. In some states, new laws allowed for educators to carry loaded weapons. Some 33 states considered such legislation, but only 5 added laws allowing educators to carry firearms on campus. Prior to these new laws, however, some states posed few restrictions on where someone could carry a licensed firearm, and thus educators were sometimes allowed to bring them on school grounds. For instance, in some states in which rural districts do not have officers on campus, the schools are allowed to train teachers and then provide them with guns to carry. While advocates maintain that this can deter students from acting violently and thereby keep the school safer, critics contend that educators are not amply trained to serve in this capacity. Further, many are concerned that, in the event of a shooter on campus, having more armed persons would complicate the issue for law enforcement, as they might be unable to differentiate the perpetrators from other shooters. Additionally, critics have expressed concern that frustrated educators might use their weapons inappropriately. Court cases also shape school responses.

The following section provides an overview of the most significant Supreme Court cases related to school violence.

Supreme Court Cases

In *Tinker v. Des Moines Independent Community School District* (1969), the Supreme Court did not say that schools were prohibited from limiting student speech or expression, but rather that students in public schools do retain freedom of speech and expression. John Tinker, 15, MaryBeth Tinker, 13, and Christopher Eckhardt, 16, were sent home from school for wearing black armbands to protest U.S. involvement in the Vietnam War. Their action was in violation of a recently enacted school policy prohibiting such armbands. The Court did not prohibit schools from limiting student speech or expression but rather that they could not prohibit legitimate political activity. In later cases about free speech, the Court ruled on the side of the schools. In 1986, the Supreme Court affirmed that schools could set rules related to appropriate speech during school-related activities. Matthew Fraser was nominating a friend for student council, and in his speech before the student body, he made a variety of sexually provocative comments and double entendres, which resulted in students yelling out inappropriately and making sexually degrading and suggestive gestures.

In 1975 the Supreme Court made an important decision regarding students' due process rights during disciplinary procedures. In *Goss v. Lopez*, the Court ruled that schools must hold a hearing before they can suspend a student. The challenge involved Dwight Lopez and eight other students who were suspended for 10 days from Marion Franklin High School in Ohio for destroying school property. The students were protesting U.S. involvement in the Vietnam War. Lopez testified that at least 75 students were suspended that day, which was allowed without a hearing per Ohio law at the time. The students and their parents were invited to attend a conference after the suspension. The Supreme Court's decision was somewhat limited, applying only to suspensions for 10 days or less, but the Court suggested that stronger safeguards than just a hearing should be considered before lengthier suspensions could be assigned.

Just two years after *Goss,* the Supreme Court issued another important case regarding school disciplinary practices. In *Ingraham v. Wright* the Court determined that disciplinary paddling, generally referred to as corporal punishment, does not violate students' Eighth Amendment right to be free of cruel and unusual punishment. James Ingraham, a 14-year-old eighth-grade student at Charles Drew Junior High School, was accused of failing to promptly leave the stage of the school auditorium when asked to do so by a teacher. He was taken to the principal's office, where he denied the accusation. Principal Willie J. Wright Jr. demanded that Ingraham bend over to be paddled. When Ingraham refused, Wright forcibly placed him face down on the top of a table and paddled him more than 20 times while Assistant Principal Lemmie Deliford held his arms and another assistant, Solomon Barnes, held his legs. The paddling resulted in significant injury, with Ingraham sustaining a hematoma that required medical attention. His physician recommended he rest at home for 11 days.

Davis v. Monroe County School Board was a case heard before the U.S. Supreme Court about the liability of school districts in preventing and responding to sexual harassment. LaShonda Davis had complained of repeated sexual harassment by a classmate at Hubbard Elementary in Monroe County, Georgia. The fifth-grader said the boy, known as G. F., would touch her breasts and genitals and make inappropriate remarks. LaShonda reported the abuse to her teacher and her mother multiple times. Her mother reported it to school administration, but no real action was taken by the school. After the boy rubbed up against LaShonda in a sexually provocative way, which she again reported, the boy was eventually charged and pleaded guilty to sexual battery. LaShonda suffered tremendously from the months of abuse; her grades fell dramatically, and her father once found a suicide note. Subsequent investigations revealed that G. F. had been harassing other students as well. In a suit against the district, LaShonda's mother argued that the school district, from LaShonda's teachers to the school administration, had failed to respond in a timely and appropriate fashion, which allowed the abuse to persist. She also noted that the district had not instructed staff on how to respond to sexual harassment and actually had no school policy on the issue. The Supreme Court ruled that districts can indeed be held liable for failing to respond to allegations of sexual harassment. It was a limited decision, however, as the Court did not mandate preventative measures.

In 1995, the Supreme Court heard another case related to school searches. In *Vernonia School District 47 J v. Acton*, the Court held that a suspicionless drug test for students seeking to participate in extracurricular athletics was not a violation of their Fourth Amendment right. Seventh-grade student James Acton wanted to be statistician for the school's football team. He refused the sign the testing consent form and was prohibited from playing. The school had instituted the policy due to concerns about students' drug use. In particular, teachers and administrators had heard student-athletes boasting about their consumption of illicit drugs, and thus the district determined that they were leaders of the school's "drug culture." The policy required students to be tested before the season. A random selection of students was also chosen to undergo a urinalysis test weekly during the athletic seasons. Samples were sent to an independent laboratory to test for amphetamines, marijuana, and cocaine. Results were disseminated only to the school superintendent, principals, vice principals, and athletic directors. Students whose samples showed a positive result were tested a second time. If that test was negative, no further action was taken. If the second test was positive for any of the listed substances, the student athlete could choose between two options: (1) participate in a substance abuse assistance program that mandated weekly drug testing, or (2) be suspended from that athletic season as well as the next season. Students who tested positive for illicit drugs a second time were automatically suspended from participating. In a 6–3 vote, the Supreme Court held that children in schools have less privacy than adults and that because schools are to act *in loco parentis*, or in place of parents, they have an obligation to keep the educational and athletic environments safe and drug free. Although the case did not specifically address school violence, it served to expand school officials' ability to search students. In 2002, the Supreme Court again heard a case about school drug testing. In *Board of Ed. of Independent School District No. 92 of Pottawatomie County v. Earls*, the court again affirmed schools' use of drug testing as constitutional, expanding the target population to include any student involved in an extracurricular activity. Lindsay Earls and Daniel James, both 16, and Lindsay's sister Lacey were all subject to drug testing in 1999 at Tecumseh High School. Lindsay was in the choir, marching band, National Honor Society, and the school's Academic Team. James was seeking to participate on the Academic Team. Lindsay Earls did undergo the urinalysis and tested negative for drugs, but her family decided to pursue a lawsuit against the school because she and others found the process to be degrading and dehumanizing. Much like the policy in the Vernonia case, Tecumseh High School required students to first enroll in counseling if they tested positive as well as to undergo additional drug tests. They were suspended from involvement if they refused or if they again tested positive. The heated oral arguments addressed whether students involved in academic or arts-related clubs were really more likely to engage in illicit drug use and whether doing so posed a threat to school safety. Opponents of drug testing argued that this type of blanket, suspicionless test of youth who seek to engage in activities that are part of the school's curriculum (as band and choir satisfied the school's fine arts requirement) was overbroad and violated student's privacy rights. Earls and others complained that a monitor watched them urinate and that they were called onto a stage when they were selected, which was embarrassing. In a 5–4 decision, the justices upheld the policy, deeming the drug testing to be administrative in nature and therefore not actually a search that is protected by the Fourth Amendment. As in Vernonia, the justices seemed to believe that school-based drug testing is a deterrent to youth substance abuse, although studies show it is not. In 2003, researchers at the University of Michigan conducted a study of 76,000 students across the United States and found that rates of drug use did not differ significantly between schools that had drug testing and those that did not. Justices David Souter, John Paul Stevens, and Sandra Day O'Connor dissented, noting that the extracurricular activities were not necessarily voluntary. Justice Ruth Bader Ginsburg also dissented, arguing that the school could not provide a specific rationale for the policy and expressing concern that rather than deterring drug use it would deter involvement. In the years following these two decisions, the percentage of schools that use some form of drug testing expanded from approximately 7 percent to close to 20 percent.

Seven years later, the Supreme Court heard another school search case, albeit not about drug testing. In *Safford United School District #1 v. Redding*, the Court held that the strip search of a 13-year-old student based on allegations that she had ibuprofen she had not checked in at the school office was an unconstitutional violation of privacy rights. Another student at the school was found with ibuprofen and claimed she had gotten it from Savannah Redding, an honor student. School officials searched Redding's backpack and outer clothing before stripping her down to her underwear and asking her to shake them out so that her breasts and pelvic area were visible. Nothing was found, and Redding described the incident as "the most humiliating experience of my life." The Court decision was 8–1, with the justices expressing grave concern that the school's impetus for the search was so weak, given the allegation that it was a legal substance that Redding allegedly had and that the search so intrusive. The Court did exempt from the liability the assistant principal who authorized the search, arguing that he acted in good faith. Justice Clarence Thomas dissented, maintaining that the search was logical and that the Court's decision would encourage youth to hide drugs in their underwear. Because the Court only considered the narrow issue of strip searches for prescription drugs, they left open the issue of the constitutionality of school strip searches for other purposes. Previous Court decisions had upheld strip searches based on anonymous tips that students had illicit drugs, incriminating letters found in classrooms, and allegations of stolen money. Critics contend that it is deeply problematic that school officials can conduct such invasive searches on youth and that in cases where there is strong evidence that youth have illegal substances, they have the option of detaining the student until law enforcement can arrive with a warrant for a search.

One of the most disturbing strip search cases involved allegations that Brian Cornfield, a student with learning disabilities, was "crotching" drugs because his genital region looked larger than normal and because a teacher's aide had heard rumors that his family was involved with drugs. Although Cornfield was made to strip down to his underwear and hold them out for an administrator to ensure that he was hiding nothing, no drugs were found. The Seventh Circuit Court ruled in 1993 that the search was both reasonable in its inception and not overly intrusive. In one case, two 13-year-old students were strip searched after they were accused of stealing $10 from a wallet they found and turned into their teacher. The school district settled for an undisclosed amount. In another case, *Singleton v. Board of Education*, 894 F. Supp. 386 (F. Kan. 1995), another 13-year-old was accused of stealing money from a woman's car. The assistant principal took Singleton, the student, to his office, reaching into his pockets, turned them inside out, removed and searched his socks and shoes, patted him down, including Singleton's genitals, felt inside his waistband, forced him to hold up his arms while his shirt was removed, and finally searched the coat, books, and papers in his locker. No money or other contraband was found, but the court determined this series of searches was justified because Singleton had been in trouble before. It is not yet clear what age is too young for students to endure strip searching, as previous cases have left standing schools' decisions to strip search eight-year-olds who were accused of taking $7.

On March 25, 2013, the Supreme Court issued a ruling on the use of canine searches that may have implications for schools. In *Florida v. Jardines*, the Court ruled 5–4 that a canine sniff for illegal drugs outside of someone's home is indeed a search and thus is subject to the warrant requirement. Previously, lower courts had called canine indications "administrative" and thus not actually searches that are protective by the Fourth Amendment. On the other hand, Justice Alito noted that the pivotal issue was that the canine was brought to someone's home, not a public place.

Schools often conduct lockdowns in which they search students' lockers. The Supreme Court has never ruled on the constitutionality of such searches, but previous courts have held that such searches are administrative in nature and, because the lockers are actually school property, the students have no privacy right to them. In October 2013, the Supreme Court declined to hear the case *Burlison v. Springfield Public Schools*, which would have addressed random lockdowns, mass searches, and the use of drug-sniffing dogs on campus. The Rutherford Institute had challenged a Missouri school district's policy of locking students down in classrooms while the sheriff's office brought in drug-sniffing canines to conduct mass searches of school grounds, including student lockers and the contents inside them. The U.S. Court of Appeals for the Eighth Circuit found the lockdown policy was a reasonable procedure to maintain the safety and security of students at the school. However, Rutherford Institute attorneys disagreed, insisting that government officials should be required to show particularized suspicion for instituting such aggressive searches and to operate within the parameters of the Fourth Amendment.

Conclusion

This chapter offered an assessment of the primary tools used to understand school violence, beginning with the main types of violence perpetrated in schools, the surveys and other instruments used to collect data about the issue, and a history of the most infamous incidents of school violence. Further, the chapter sought to provide readers with an understanding of the ways that data about school violence has shaped the introduction of legislation and court cases devoted to responding to and preventing school violence.

Further Reading

Adelson, E. (2009, April 24). Did Corporal Punishment Save a Struggling School? *Newsweek.* Retrieved May 27, 2014, from http://www.newsweek.com/did-corporal-punishment -save-struggling-school-77227

Alanazez, T. (2010, March 26). Dillard High School Shooter Sentenced to 25 Years for Classmate's Murder. *South Florida Sun Sentinel.* Retrieved March 31, 2014, from http://articles .sun-sentinel.com/2010-03-26/news/fl-dillard-shooting -sentencing-20100325_1_teah-wimberly-amanda-collette -larry-s-davis

Amnesty International. (2008). *A Violent Education: Corporal Punishment of Children in U.S. Public Schools.* New York: Amnesty International.

Anderson, S. (2008). A Call for Drug-Testing of High School Athletes. *Marquette Sports Law Review, 19*(2), 325–35.

Arnold, T. (1996). Constitutionality of Random Drug Testing of Student-Athletes Makes the Cut. . .but Will the Athletes? *Journal of Law & Education, 25*(1), 190–98.

Aronson, E. (2000). *Nobody Left to Hate: Teaching Compassion after Columbine.* New York: W.H. Freeman.

Associated Press. (2008, May 15). Missouri Woman Indicted in MySpace Cyberbullying Case That Ended in Teen's Suicide. *Fox News.* Retrieved May 6, 2010, from http:// www.foxnews.com/story/0,2933,356056,00.html

Barkley, R., & Murphy, L. (1998). *Attention-Deficit Hyperactivity Disorder: A Clinical Workbook.* New York: Guilford.

Barnes, R. (2009). Supreme Court Rules Strip Search Violated 13-Year-Old Girl's Rights. *Washington Post.* Retrieved May 27, 2014, from http://washingtonpost .com/wp-dyn/content/article/2009/06/25/AR20090625 01690.html

Beger, R. (2003). The "Worst of Both Worlds": School Security and the Disappearing Fourth Amendment Rights of Students. *Criminal Justice Review, 28,* 336–54.

Blenkinsop, P. (2002, April 27). Shootings to Reignite Debate on Gun Control. *Toronto Star,* p. A26.

Brady Center to Prevent Gun Violence. (2004). On Target: The Impact of the 1994 Federal Assault Weapon Act. Retrieved May 27, 2014, from http://www.washingtonpost.com/ wp-dyn/content/article/2009/06/25/AR2009062501690.html

Burns, R., & Crawford, C. (1999). School Shootings, the Media, and Public Fear: Ingredients for a Moral Panic. *Crime, Law & Social Change, 32,* 147–69.

Caistor, N. (2002, April 28). Profile of a Teenage Killer. *BBC News.* Retrieved May 27, 2014, from http://news.bbc.co .uk/2/hi/europe/1956206.stm

Cannon, A. (2000a). The Youngest Shooter. *U.S. News & World Report, 128*(10), 27.

Cannon, A. (2000b). Kayla's Law: Gun Control. *U.S. News & World Report, 128*(11), 39.

Casella, R. (2001). *At Zero Tolerance: Punishment, Prevention, and School Violence.* New York: Peter Lang.

Cathcart, R. (2003, February 23). Boy's Killing, Labeled a Hate Crime, Stuns Town. *New York Times.* Retrieved May 3, 2010, from http://www.nytimes.com/2008/02/23/ us/23oxnard.html

Charles Carl Roberts IV. (n.d.). *Murderpedia.* Retrieved March 31, 2014, from http://www.murderpedia.org/male .R/r/roberts-charles.htm

Chen, S. (2010, October 4). After Student's Death, a Weeklong Look into Bullying. *CNN*. Retrieved October 28, 2010, from http://www.cnn.com/2010/LIVING/10/04/bullying.special .explainer/index.html

Clark-Flory, T. (2010, April 8). Phoebe Prince's Bullies Get Bullied. *Salon*. Retrieved May 5, 2010, from http://www .salon.com/life/broadsheet/2010/04/08/phoebe_prince _bullies_get_bullied

Clete, S., Bailey, C., Carona, A., & Mebane, D. (2002). School Crime Policy Changes: The Impact of Recent Highly-Publicized School Crimes. *American Journal of Criminal Justice, 26*, 269–88.

Cloud, J. (1999, May 31). Just a Routine School Shooting. *Time, 153*(21), 34.

Cloud, J. (2008, February 18). Prosecuting the Gay Teen Murder. *Time*. Retrieved May 3, 2010, from http://www .time.com/time/nation/article/0,8599,1714214,00.html

Clouston, E., & Boseley, S. (2013, March 14). Sixteen Children Killed in Dunblane Massacre. *The Guardian*. Retrieved March 31, 2014, from http://www.theguardian.com/the guardian/2013/mar/14/dunblane-massacre-scotland-killing

Coloroso, B. (2004). *The Bully, the Bullied, and the Bystander*. New York: HarperCollins.

Conn, K. (2004). *Bullying and Harassment: A Legal Guide for Educators*. Alexandria, VA: Association for Supervision and Curriculum Development.

Cullen, D. (2010). *Columbine*. New York: Twelve.

Darling-Hammond, L. (2007, May 21). Evaluating "No Child Left Behind." *The Nation*. Retrieved May 4, 2010, from http://www.thenation.com/article/evaluating-no-child-left -behind?page=0,0

Dautrich, K., & Yalof, D. (2008). *The Future of the First Amendment: The Digital Media, Civic Education, and Free*

Expression Rights in America's High Schools. Lanham, MD: Rowman & Littlefield.

Davey, M., & Harris, G. (2005, March 26). Family Wonders if Prozac Prompted School Shootings. *New York Times.* Retrieved April 14, 2010, from http://www.nytimes.com/2005/03/26/national/26shoot.html

Davies, L. (2009, March 11). "Are You All Dead Yet?"— Teenage Gunman Kills 15 in School Massacre in Germany. *The Guardian.* Retrieved May 28, 2014, from http://www.theguardian.com/world/2009/mar/11/germany-school-shooting-winnenden-albertville

Davis, C. (2003). Dare to Be Different: Luke Woodham. In *Children Who Kill: Profiles of Pre-Teen and Teenage Killers* (pp. 67–79). London: Allison & Busby.

Death from Ritalin. (n.d). Retrieved April 16, 2010, from http://ritalindeath.com/ADHD-Truths.htm

Dejong, W., Epstein, J., & Hart, T. (2003). Bad Things Happen in Good Communities: The Rampage Shooting in Edinboro, Pennsylvania and Its Aftermath. In M. Moore, C. Petrie, A. Braga., & B. McLaughlin (Eds.) *Deadly Lessons: Understanding Lethal School Violence* (pp. 70–100). Washington, DC: National Academies Press.

DeNies, Y. (2012, March 16). Should Your Child Be Spanked at School? In 19 States It's Legal. *ABC News.* Retrieved March 31, 2014, from http://abcnews.go.com/US/spanking-school-19-states-corporal-punishment-legal/story?id=15932135

Devine, J. (1996). *Maximum Security.* Chicago, IL: University of Chicago Press.

Dolnik, A. (2007). *Negotiating the Impossible? The Beslan Hostage Crisis.* London: Royal United Services Institute.

Do Something. (n.d.). 11 Facts about School Violence. Retrieved April 1, 2014 from https://www.dosomething.org/facts/11-facts-about-bullying

Dupre, A. (2010). *Speaking Up: The Unintended Cost of Free Speech in Public Schools.* Cambridge, MA: Harvard University Press.

Egan, T. (1998, June 14). Where Rampages Begin: A Special Report. *New York Times.* Retrieved May28, 2014, from http://www.nytimes.com/1998/06/14/us/where-rampages -begin-special-report-adolescent-angst-shooting-up-schools .html

Eggington, J. (1991). *Day of fury: The tory of the tragic shootings that forever changed the village of Winnetka.* New York: William Morrow.

Epp, J., & Watkinson, A. (Eds.). (1996). *Systemic Violence: How Schools Hurt Children.* London: Falmer.

Fast, J. (2008). *Ceremonial Violence: A Psychological Explanation of School Shootings.* Woodstock, NY: Overland Press.

Fineran, S., & Bolen, R. (2006). Risk Factors for Peer Sexual Harassment in Schools. *Journal of Interpersonal Violence, 21* (9), 1169–91.

Finley, L. (2006). Examining School Searches as Systemic Violence. *Critical Criminology, 14,* 117–35.

Finley, L. (Ed.). (2007). *Encyclopedia of Juvenile Violence.* Westport, CT: Greenwood.

Finley, L. (Ed.). (2011). *Encyclopedia of School Crime and Violence.* Santa Barbara, CA: ABC-CLIO.

Finley, L., & Finley, P. (2004). *Piss Off! How Drug Testing and Other Privacy Violations Are Alienating America's Youth.* Monroe, ME: Common Courage.

Flowers, R., & Flowers, H. (2004). *Murders in the United States.* Jefferson, NC: McFarland.

Former Student Storms German School, Shooting Five People. (2006, November 20). *WHDH News.* Retrieved April 29,

2010, from http://www3.whdh.com/news/articles/world/
BO34580/

Giduck, J. (2006). *Terror at Beslan: A Russian Tragedy with Lessons for America's Schools.* Boulder, CO: Paladin Press.

Goldberg, L., et al. (2003). Drug Testing Athletes to Prevent Substance Abuse: Background and Pilot Study Results of the SATURN (Student Athletes Testing Using Random Notification) study. *Journal of Adolescent Health, 32,* 16–25.

Grenoble, R. (2012, October 10). Amanda Todd: Bullied Canadian Teen Commits Suicide after Prolonged Battle Online and in School. *Huffington Post.* Retrieved March 28, 2014, from http://www.huffingtonpost.com/2012/10/11/amanda-todd-suicide-bullying_n_1959909.html

Gunderson, D. (2005, March 23). Who Was Jeff Weise? Minnesota Public Radio. Retrieved October 22, 2013, from http://news.minnesota.publicradio.org/features/2005/03/22_ap_redlakesuspect/

Guzman, D. (2013, March 21). Teen Burn-Attack Victim Michael Brewer Released after Drug-related Arrest. *Miami Herald.* Retrieved March 31, 2014, from http://www.miamiherald.com/2013/03/21/3298180/teen-burn-attack-victim-michael.html

Harding, T. (2001). Fatal School Shootings, Liability, and Sovereign Immunity: Where Should the Line Be Drawn? *Journal of Law & Education, 30,* 162–70.

Harris, C. (2008, February 21). Lawrence King—Student Who Was Murdered for Being Gay—to Be Honored with National Day of Silence. *MTV.* Retrieved May 3, 2010, from http://www.mtv.com/news/articles/1582039/20080221/story.jhtml

Harris Interactive. (2001). *Hostile Hallways: Bullying, Teasing, and Sexual Harassment in School.* Washington, DC: American Association of University Women Educational Foundation.

Henry, S. (2000). What Is School Violence? An Integrated Definition. *Annals of the American Academy of Political and Social Science, 567*, 123–39.

High, B. (2007). *Bullycide in America: Moms Speak Out about the Bullying/Suicide Connection.* Available at http://www .bullycide.org

High School Hazing. (n.d.) Alfred University Hazing Site. Available at http://www.alfred.edu/hs_hazing/

Hinduja, S., & Patchin, J. (2008). Cyberbullying: An Exploratory Analysis of Factors Related to Offending and Victimization.*Deviant Behavior, 29*(2), 129–56.

Hyman, I., & Snook, P. (1999). *Dangerous Schools.* San Francisco: Jossey-Bass.

Jensen, P., Martin, D., & Cantwell, D. (1997). Comorbidity and ADHD: Implications for Research, Practice, and DSM-V. *Journal of the American Academy of Child and Adolescent Psychiatry, 36*, 1065–79.

Johnston, L., O'Malley, P., Bachman, J., & Schulenberg, J. (2012). *Monitoring the Future: National Survey Results on Drug Use, 1985–2012.* Retrieved March 31, 2014, from http://www.monitoringthefuture.org//pubs/monographs/mtf -vol1_2012.pdf

Kaplan, J., Papajohn, G., & Zorn, E. (1991). *Murder of Innocence: The Tragic Life and Final Rampage of Laurie Dann, the Schoolhouse Killer.* New York: Warner Books.

Kimmel, M., & Mahler, M. (2003). Adolescent Masculinity, Homophobia, and Violence: Random School Shootings, 1982–2001. *American Behavioral Scientist, 46*, 1439–58.

Kleinfeld, N., Rivera, R., & Kovaleski, S. (2013, March 28). Newtown Killer's Obsessions, in Chilling Detail. *New York Times.* Retrieved October 25, 2013, from http://www .nytimes.com/2013/03/29/nyregion/search-warrants-reveal -items-seized-at-adam-lanzas-home.html?pagewanted%253 Dall&_r=0

Kraybill, D. (2011, September 30). Amish Memorials: The Nickel Mines Pasture and Quiet Forgiveness. *Huffington Post.* Retrieved March 31, 2014, from http://www.huffington post.com/donald-kraybill/amish-memorials-the-nickel-mines -memorial_b_982144.html

Langevin, M., Bortnick, K., Hammer, T., & Wiebe, E. (1998). Teasing/Bullying Experienced by Children Who Stutter: Toward Development of a Questionnaire. *Contemporary Issues in Communication Science and Disorders, 25,* 12–24.

Langman, P. (2009). *Why Kids Kill: Inside the Minds of School Shooters.* New York: Palgrave Macmillan.

Larkin, R. (2007). *Comprehending Columbine.* Philadelphia, PA: Temple University Press.

Li, Q. (2006). Cyberbullying in Schools: A Research of Gender Differences. *School Psychology International, 27*(2), 157–70.

Lieberman, J. (2008). *School Shootings: What Every Parent and Educator Needs to Know to Protect Our Children.* Yucca Valley, CA: Citadel.

Lieberman, J., & Sachs, B. (2008). *School Shootings.* New York: Kensington.

Little, L. (2002). Middle-class Mothers' Perceptions of Peer and Sibling Victimization among Children with Asperger's Syndrome and Nonverbal Learning Disorders. *Issues in Comprehensive Pediatric Nursing, 25,* 43–45.

Man Kills Eight at Finnish School. (2007, November 7). *BBC News.* Retrieved May 28, 2014, from http://news.bbc.co.uk/ 2/hi/7082795.stm

Mannuzza, S., Klein, R., Bessler, A., Malloy, P., & LaPadula, M. (1993). Adult Outcome of Hyperactive Boys: Educational Achievement, Occupational Rank, and Psychiatric Status. *General Psychiatry, 50,* 565–76.

Messerschmidt, J. (2000). *Nine Lives: Adolescent Masculinities, the Body, and Violence.* Boulder, CO: Westview Press.

Meyer, E. (2009). *Gender, Bullying, and Harassment: Strategies to End Sexism and Homophobia in Schools.* New York: Teachers College Press.

Moore, M., Petrie, C., Braga, A., & McLaughlin, B. (Eds.). (2003). *Deadly Lessons: Understanding Lethal School Violence.* Washington, D.C: National Academies Press.

Moskovitz, D. (2012, October 22). Wayne Treacy Sentenced to 20 Years in Broward Prison for Beating Girl. *Miami Herald.* Retrieved March 31, 2014, from http://www .miamiherald.com/2012/10/22/3061156/sentencing-for -wayne-treacy-set.html

Mulrine, A. (1999). Once Bullied, Now Bullies, with Guns. *U.S. News and World Report, 126,* 24–26.

Muschert, G. (2007). The Columbine Victims and the Myth of the Juvenile Superpredator. *Youth Violence and Juvenile Justice,* 351–66.

Naughton, K., Thomas, E., & Raymond, J. (2000). Did Kayla Have to Die? *Newsweek, 135*(11), 24.

Newman, K., Fox, C., Harding, D., Mehta, J., & Roth, W. (2004). *Rampage: The Social Roots of School Shootings.* New York: Basic.

Nuwer, H. (2000). *High School Hazing: When Rites Become Wrongs.* New York: FranklinWatts.

Nuwer, H. (2004). *The Hazing Reader.* Bloomington, ID: Indiana University Press.

O'Toole, M. (2000). *The School Shooter: A Threat Assessment Perspective.* Quantico, VA: Federal Bureau of Investigation.

Ollove, M. (2010, April 8). Bullying and Teen Suicide: How Do We Adjust School Climate? *Christian Science Monitor.* Retrieved May 28, 2014, from http://www.csmonitor.com/ USA/Society/2010/0428/Bullying-and-teen-suicide-How -do-we-adjust-school-climateOwens, B. (2001). Governor's Columbine Review Commission Report. Denver, CO: State

of Colorado Governor's Office. Available at http://www
.state.co.us/columbine.

Paterson, T. (2009, March 15). In Europe's League of School
Shootings, Germany Comes Top. *The Independent* (UK).
Retrieved April 10, 2010, from http://www.independent.co
.uk/news/world/europe/in-europes-league-of-school-shoot
ingsgermany-comes-top-1645387.html

PBS Frontline. (2000). The Killer at Thurston High.
Documentary available at http://www.pbs.org/wgbh/pages/
frontline/shows/kinkel/

PBS Frontline. (2008). Growing Up Online. Documentary
available at http://www.pbs.org/wgbh/pages/frontline/kids
online/view/

PBS Frontline. (2010). Digital Nation: Life on the Virtual
Frontier. Documentary available at http://www.pbs.org/
wgbh/pages/frontline/digitalnation/view/

PBS Frontline. (2013, February 19). Raising Adam Lanza.
Documentary available at http://www.pbs.org/wgbh/pages/
frontline/raising-adam-lanza/

Phillips, R. (2009, January 18). Purdy Recalled as Bigot and
"Sick, Sick Man." Retrieved July 19, 2009, from http://
www.recordnet.com/apps/pbcs.dll/article?AID=/20090118/
A_NEWS/901170304/-1/A_SPECIAL0252

Phillips, T. (2007). *Beslan: The Tragedy of School Number 1.*
London: Granta Books.

Piatigorsky, A., & Hinshaw, S. (2004). Psychopathic Traits in
Boys with and without Attention-Deficit/Hyperactivity
Disorder: Concurrent and Longitudinal Correlates. *Journal
of Abnormal Child Psychology, 32*(5), 535–50.

Potter, M. (2001, May 2). Friend Says She Saw Teenager Pull
Trigger. *CNN.* Retrieved May 28, 2014, from http://edition.
cnn.com/2001/LAW/05/02/teacher.shooting.03/index.html

Powers, R. (2010, October 22). Obama "Shocked and
Saddened" by Gay Bullying Suicides. *NBC News.* Retrieved

May 28, 2014, from http://www.nbcnews.com/id/398000 08/ns/us_news-life/t/obama-shocked-saddened-gay-bullying -suicides/#.U4YnmSj6GFg

PR Newswire. (2014, January 15). Twenty Years since a Nightmare: Stockton, CA School Shooting of 35 Led to Strengthening of Gun Laws. *PR Newswire*. Retrieved May 28, 2014, from http://www.prnewswire.com/news -releases/twenty-years-since-a-nightmare-stockton-ca-school -shooting-of-35-led-to-strengthening-of-gun-laws-60948 957.html

Prospero, M. (2007). Young Adolescents Boys and Dating Violence: The Beginning of Patriarchal Terrorism. *Affilia: Journal of Women and Social Work, 22*(3), 271–80.

Ramirez, X. (2011, November 7). National Study Reveals Striking Findings on School Sexual Harassment. *Care2*. Retrieved March 31, 2014, from http://www.care2.com/ causes/national-study-reveals-striking-findings-on-school -sexual-harassment.html

Randall, K. (2001, August 3). Another Florida Teenager Receives Harsh Adult Sentence. *World Socialist Web Site*. Retrieved April 18, 2014, from http://www.wsws.org/ articles/2001/aug2001/flor_a03.shtml

Reinhold, R. (1989, January 19). After Shooting, Horror but Few Answers. *New York Times*. Retrieved July 19, 2009, from http://www.nytimes.com/1989/01/19/us/after-shooting -horror-but-few-answers.html?pagewanted=all

Roche, T. (2001, May 28). Voices from the Cell. *Time*. Retrieved December 18, 2008, from http://www.time.com/ time/printout/0,8816,999966,00.html

Rocky Mountain News. (n.d.) Columbine High School Shootings. Retrieved December 14, 2008, from http://www .rockymountainnews.com/news/special-reports/columbine/

Rollini, G. (2003). *Davis v. Monroe County Board of Education: A Hollow Victory for Student Victims of Peer Sexual*

Harassment. *Florida State University Law Review, 30,* 987–1014.

Rosler, M., Retz, W., Retz-Junginger, P., Hengesch, G., Schneider, M., Supprian, T., Schwitzgiebel, T., Pinhard, K., Dovi-Akune, N., Wender, P., & Thome, J. (2004). Prevalence of Attention Deficit/Hyperactivity Disorder (ADHD) Comorbid Disorder in Young Adult Male Prison Inmates. *European Archives of Psychiatry and Clinical Neuroscience, 254,* 365–71.

The Rutherford Institute. (2013, October 8). U.S. Supreme Court Refuses to Hear Case of Student Subjected to Random Lockdown and Mass Search by Police in Public School. Retrieved March 31, 2014, from https://www .rutherford.org/publications_resources/Press%20Release/ supreme_court_refuses_to_hear_case_of_student_subjected _to_random_lockdown/

Segal, K., Couwels, J., & Brumfield, B. (2013, October 21). Mother of Girl Accused of Bullying Florida Teen Arrested on Unrelated Charges. *CNN.* Retrieved October 24, 2013, from http://www.cnn.com/2013/10/17/justice/rebecca -sedwick-bullying-death/index.html

Sieczkowski, C. (2012, October 16). Amanda Todd's Alleged Bully Named by Anonymous after Teen's Tragic Suicide. *Huffington Post.* Retrieved March 28, 2014, from http:// www.huffingtonpost.com/2012/10/16/amanda-todd-bully -anonymous-suicide_n_1969792.html

Simmons, R. (2010, October 5). Responding to the Bullycides: How We Can Stand Up and Honor Their Memories. *Huffington Post.* Retrieved October 28, 2010, from http://www.huffingtonpost.com/rachel-simmons/ responding-to-the-bully_b_747806.html

Stopbullying.gov. (n.d.). Facts about Bullying. Retrieved April 1, 2014, from http://www.stopbullying.gov/news/ media/facts/.

Survivors Recall 1927 Michigan School Massacre. (2009, April 17). *National Public Radio.* Retrieved May 28, 2014, from http://www.npr.org/templates/story/story.php?storyId=103186662

Teppo, G. (2007, April 19). Experts Ponder Patterns in School Shootings. *USA Today.* Retrieved April 19, 2010, from http://www.usatoday.com/news/education/2007-04-18-school-shooters_N.htm

Twemlow, S., & Fonagy, P. (2005). The Prevalence of Teachers Who Bully Students in Schools with Differing Levels of Behavioral Problems. *American Journal of Psychiatry, 162,* 2387–90.

Uttley, S. (2006). *Dunblane Unburied.* London: Book Publishing World.

Vossekuil, B., Fein, R., Reddy, M., Borum, R., & Modzeleski, W. (2002). *The Final Report and Findings of the Safe School Initiative: Implications for the Prevention of School Attacks in the United States.* Jessup, MD: Education Publications Center, U.S. Department of Education.

Walsh, M. (2013, October 14). Education-related Cases Part of High-Court Workload. *Education Week.* Retrieved March 31, 2014, from http://www.edweek.org/ew/articles/2013/10/16/08scotus.h33.html

Watkinson, A. (1997). Administrative Complicity and Systemic Violence in Education. In J. Epp & A. Watkinson (Eds.), *Systemic Violence in Education: Broken Promises* (pp. 3–24). Albany, NY: State University of New York Press.

Webley, K. (2011, May 5). Teens Who Admitted to Bullying Phoebe Prince Sentenced. *Time.* Retrieved October 24, 2013, from http://newsfeed.time.com/2011/05/05/teens-who-admitted-to-bullying-phoebe-prince-sentenced/

Wiener, J., & Mak, M. (2009). Peer Victimization in Children with Attention-Deficit/Hyperactivity Disorder. *Psychology in the Schools,* 46(2), 116–131.

Wise, T. (2001, March 6). School Shootings and White Denial. *Alternet.* Retrieved May 28, 2014, from http://www .alternet.org/story/10560/school_shootings_and_white _denial

Yamaguchi, R., & Hinkle-DeGroot, R. (2002). *The Legal and Educational Issues behind Drug Testing in School.* Ann Arbor, MI: Institute for Social Research.

This chapter examines the effects of school violence, looking beyond individual victims to address broader impacts. In addition, the chapter highlights the most important criminological theories to explain why school violence occurs. The chapter also offers an overview of the risk and protective factors for individuals, families, schools, and communities, providing an up-to-date compendium of research from various fields. Further, the chapter offers a critical discussion of common interventions and prevention efforts used in school.

Effects of School Violence

The effects of school violence are widespread. Beyond the immediate and longitudinal effect on those who are victimized, there are long-term effects on perpetrators, on educators, and on the school climate. Additionally, fear of school violence prompts parents and law-makers to demand changes that may be helpful or, in other cases, counterproductive.

Individuals who are bullied, harassed, or assaulted in school suffer from a variety of short- and long-term consequences. These youth often feel stressed and report higher levels of

A student pays tribute to his deceased classmates at a makeshift memorial outside the Red Lake Senior High School in Red Lake, Minnesota on March 25, 2005. Jeff Weise, a 16-year-old student at Red Lake High School, killed ten people in a shooting spree. (AP Photo/Ann Heisenfelt)

anxiety, depression, and hopelessness. They are more likely to skip school, tend to report lower grades, and are more likely to drop out of school. School violence victims are also at greater risk for attempting self-harming behaviors, including drinking, using drugs, and suicide. Girls and LGBT youth who are bullied and harassed report poorer mental health than do boy victims. In the late 2000s, the nation began to pay more attention to the issue of bullycide, or when a bullying victim commits suicide, after a spate of high profile incidents.

Often, the lines between bully and bullied are blurred. That is, many bullied youth also bully others. Additionally, those who have experienced repeated victimization by school peers may take extreme responses to protect themselves, to stop the abuse, and to win the respect of classmates. Victims of bullying are more likely to carry weapons to school, increasing the risk that someone will be seriously hurt or killed. According to a report by the U.S. Secret Service, 71 percent of all high-profile school shooters had been bullied at school.

Victims of dating violence also suffer immediate and long-term effects. They may endure bruises, lacerations, and other physical injuries, or they may experience sexual health problems (such as sexually transmitted infections) or unwanted pregnancies. In extreme cases, dating violence can be fatal. The risk that an abusive relationship will become deadly increases dramatically when victims attempt to leave their abusers, with 75 percent of domestic and dating violence fatalities occurring when the victim announces she or he is ending the relationship. Several homicides have occurred on school grounds as well. On March 28, 2003, Marcus McTear stabbed his girlfriend, Ortralla Mosley, in their Texas high school. Mosley, just 15 at the time, died on the spot.

There are lifetime effects of experiencing an abusive relationship as well. Like bullying victims, victims of abuse are more likely to engage in risky sexual behavior, unhealthy or disordered eating, self-mutilation, substance abuse, and suicidal ideation. Dating violence is also a significant predictor of later involvement in abusive domestic relationships.

Even youth who have not experienced bullying or harassment are affected when it happens. Studies have shown that between 5 and 10 percent of high school students skip at least one day of school each year due to safety concerns.

For teachers, incidents of victimization may lead to professional disenchantment and even departure from the profession altogether. Teachers lose almost 1 million paid work days because of actual or fear of harassment, according to the American Psychological Association. Annually, the national cost of teacher victimization to teachers, parents, and taxpayers may exceed $2 billion.

Adults' concern about school violence has prompted many state laws as well as school policies, as detailed in this and other chapters. Many have discussed the fact that while school violence is always a serious issue, disproportionate attention has been paid to the risk of school shootings. That is, there has been far more discussion and debate, as well as policies and laws enacted, to address these relatively rare incidents in comparison to the more frequently occurring forms of school violence like bullying and sexual harassment. Some have called this a moral panic. Moral panic refers to a period in which there is great fear or hysteria about a specific social issue. Coined by sociologist Jock Young in the early 1970s and popularized by sociologist Stanley Cohen in 1973, moral panics generate great concern and a call to "do something." In the case of high-profile school shootings, many parents demanded that districts enact tighter security measures. Critics contend that moral panics reinforce stereotypical thinking about social issues and that reactionary responses can be costly, wasteful, and even damaging. Some adults have even moved their children to different schools as a result of the moral panic about school violence.

Given the many ways school violence affects different parties, it is important to try to explain why it occurs so that the most effective responses and prevention efforts can be created.

The following sections provide an overview of the primary criminological theories that have been used to explain school violence.

Biological Theories

A number of biological theories have been offered to explain the criminal activity of both adults and juveniles. The idea is that genetic and biological factors affect both the brain and the central nervous system, impacting offenders' choices. Some of the earliest biological theories suggested that offenders could be identified because they looked different than did non-offenders. For instance, Cesare Lombroso, an Italian physician considered the father of criminology, maintained that delinquents were biologically inferior, what he called "criminal atavists," and were mentally less evolved. They could be identified by specific physical characteristics, like long arm spans and hooked noses, according to Lombroso. He studied prison inmates, taking scientific measurements of their eyes, ears, teeth, jaws, and arms. Although he advanced the field because he was the first to use scientific methods, Lombroso's work has been discredited because he only studied inmates, not a comparison group of nonoffenders.

Other criminologists picked up on Lombroso's emphasis on intelligence. Charles Goring maintained that inferior intelligence was a heritable trait, and thus those who were "feeble-minded" were prone to criminality. Richard Dugdale and Arthur Estabrook also studied genetics and intelligence, this time focusing specifically on one family that had a criminal record going back decades. Between the 1700s and 1870s, the Jukes family had produced seven murderers, 60 habitual thieves, 50 prostitutes, and approximately 90 other criminals. Again, later scholars took issue with the methodologies employed by these criminologists and asserted that their work was socially or politically motivated. Very dangerous policies have been enacted as a result of this type of thinking. The

U.S. eugenics movement, an effort to maintain "racial purity" by ensuring that people of color, who were deemed feeble-minded, could not reproduce, is an example of the policy implications of some biological theories. Approximately 7,600 women in North Carolina were sterilized as a result of the eugenics movement, which continued until the 1960s. Further, there is documentation that Adolf Hitler read literature from U.S. proponents of eugenics in crafting his final solution.

William Sheldon picked up Lombroso's emphasis on body characteristics. He believed that certain body types made youth more prone to criminal activity. According to Sheldon, there were four basic body types: (1) endomorphs, who had soft, rounded bodies and were often overweight individuals; (2) mesomorphs, who tend to be large, muscular, and athletic; (3) ectomorphs, or those who were thin and fragile; and (4) balanced or "normal" bodies. Calling his theory somatotyping, Sheldon posited that mesomorphs were the most likely to be aggressive and violent, and thus more criminal. Sheldon's theory was also developed from deeply flawed studies that failed to account for important variables. In the 1950s, the husband-and-wife team of Sheldon and Eleanor Glueck compared 500 white male delinquents with 500 white male nondelinquents and agreed with Sheldon that it was mesomorphs who were responsible for a disproportionate amount of the offending. They postulated that it was not that the body type made juveniles delinquent but rather that youth with this body type relieved their tensions and frustrations through socially unacceptable ways. The idea that people can identify offenders by their physical characteristics persists today, in particular in popular culture images that depict demonic-looking offenders. Several of the school shooters, most notoriously Eric Harris and Dylan Klebold in the Columbine massacre, were said to have worn specific types of clothing, what is often called a goth look. Research by a number of scholars and investigators, however, cautions against any such form of profiling, as it can be dangerously biased and can limit thinking, thus failing to prepare educators and others to look for warning signs among youth who look or dress in more mainstream ways.

One of the best ways to study biological links to crime is through studies of identical twins who have been reared apart. In doing so, researchers can account for socialization as a factor that explains criminality, thereby isolating biological factors. Several studies have produced statistically significant results, suggesting some biological links to crime, but biology still tends to explain a small percentage of an individual's behavior. Further, these studies tend to involve very small samples. Indeed, there has never been a study of this kind specifically related to school violence.

Many researchers today are studying biochemical explanations for crime and violence. Studies have focused on the role that sugar and food additives, as well as vitamin and mineral deficiencies, may play in explaining crime. Further, studies have also examined the linkage between exposure to certain toxic chemicals, like lead, copper, and zinc, and criminal activity. A 2000 study determined that gasoline lead exposure between 1879 and 1940 explained approximately 70 percent of the variation in murder rates in that time period (Stretesky & Lynch, 2001). Several studies in the 1980s found that youth delinquency decreased when young people were fed well-balanced diets including protein, vitamins, and little sugar and carbohydrates. For instance, Alexander Schauss, Clifford Simonsen, and Jeffery Bland conducted a study of the diets of juvenile offenders in 1979 and found that compared to a control group, they consumed 32 percent more sugar. A longitudinal study published in 2004 by researchers at the University of South Carolina found that children who were deficient in zinc, iron, vitamin B, and protein at age three were more likely to be irritable and to pick fights at age eight. By age 11, those same youth were more likely to swear, cheat, and get into fights, and by age 17, they were bullies who frequently stole and used drugs. The effects were more pronounced for those with greater nutritional deficiencies ("Poor Diet Linked to Bad Behavior," 2004).

While it is unclear what role dietary and other biochemical factors may have had in the school shooting incidents, there have been links between bullying behavior and inadequate nutrition.

Other biological theories have explored the connection between brain defects and crime. Often called minimal brain dysfunction (MBD), these defects may be caused by the mother's addiction to drugs or alcohol during pregnancy, by trauma to the fetus or to the infant baby, or to birth complications. They may also be heritable traits. To date, however, electroencephalogram analyses are inconclusive in regard to MBD and juvenile offending. Many studies have linked MBD with domestic violence perpetration, again suggesting a possible link with impulse control and aggressive behavior. One expert who analyzed the brain scan of school shooter Kip Kinkel found that he had the same damage to the frontal lobe as did 20 of 31 other murderers whose brain scans she analyzed. She said that these abnormalities might have impaired his ability to learn from social cues and to control his impulses and reflexes. Much concern was raised about the connections between brain abnormalities and violence after reports came out that the Newtown, Connecticut, shooter Adam Lanza had been diagnosed as having Asperger's syndrome, a milder form of autism. Experts were quick to point out that persons with Asperger's syndrome or autism are typically not violent and that it was likely mental illness and other factors that lead to Lanza's attack.

Some studies have examined the link between learning disabilities and delinquency. Studies have confirmed that persons with learning disabilities are overrepresented in prisons and jails. In 1976, Charles Murray posited two potential reasons for the high rate of delinquents with learning disabilities. One is that these youth are impulsive, do not learn from punishment, and thus are more likely to reoffend. The second possibility is that because these youth tend to struggle in school, they act out in frustration. It is clear that several of the infamous school shooters struggled with learning disabilities; however, many did not.

Another major limitation of the biological theories is that they tend to be used to explain an individual's aggressive behavior rather than the actions of those in authority whose policies and practices are themselves a form of violence.

Psychological Theories

Psychology focuses on looking at the individual, or micro-level, mental processes associated with behavior. Psychologist Sigmund Freud's work has been applied to explain delinquent behavior. Freud maintained that crime is the result of repressed and unconscious emotional trauma experienced in childhood. Children who experience and repress trauma develop overactive ids, what Freud described as our self-centered impulses and instincts. They fail to develop effective superegos, which represent social and cultural restraints on the id, or effective egos, which moderate between the id and the superego. Thus the impulses prevail, often accompanied by a deep sense of guilt, which can become abnormal and dangerous. According to Freud and neo-Freudian psychologists, children and youth may misbehave so that they can be caught and punished, thereby assuaging their guilt. The challenge with Freudian analyses is that these concepts are abstract and thus not measureable, and so they cannot be proven or disproven.

Other psychological approaches focus on disorders that might result in a youth acting out. A conduct disorder, which is behavior that repeatedly violates the rights of others as well as major norms for conduct, may be connected with school-based bullying and cheating. To be diagnosed with a conduct disorder, according to the American Psychiatric Association (2000), a youth must exhibit at least three of the following behaviors in a six-month period:

1. Frequent lying
2. Running away from home overnight twice or running away without returning

3. Frequent truancy from school or, for working youth, absence from work

4. Nonconfrontational stealing like shoplifting more than once

5. Vandalism and destruction of property

6. Breaking and entering into houses, cars, or buildings

7. Arson

8. Cruelty to animals

9. Frequent initiation of physical fights

10. Use of weapons in physical fights on more than one occasion

11. Stealing with confrontation, such as muggings, purse snatchings, and armed robberies

12. Forcing another person to engage in sexual activity, such as prostitution or sexual assault

13. Physical violence or cruelty toward people

Critics contend that while this list of criteria is intended to help distinguish those with conduct disorders from those who do not have them, there are still a number of vague concepts. Further, it is unclear why diagnosticians specified that three incidents in six months is the pivotal number.

Some have maintained that most school shooters suffer from sociopathology. Sociopaths are incapable of feeling anguish or guilt and do not learn from experience. They are often charming and manipulative, making it difficult for others to identify their problems. Many sociopaths have above-average intelligence. Reports have suggested that Eric Harris of Columbine infamy was a sociopath.

One concern about the psychological theories as a whole is that the field is what has been called a soft science. That is, diagnostic criteria for the various psychological disorders are not always quantifiable and may be quite subjective. So, if it is unclear whether an individual is properly diagnosed, it is next to impossible to determine that his or her actions are the result of any specific disorder.

Rational Choice Theory

Rational choice theory is one of many choice-related theories. Emerging out of Enlightenment-era thinking, choice theories, often referred to as classical theories, posit that individuals have free will and agency and thus make decisions or choices about their behaviors. According to this viewpoint, people weigh the costs and benefits before deciding which actions to take. Just like any other behavior, then, rational choice theory explains that crime is a choice someone might make when he or she has decided that the benefits outweigh the consequences. There is support for the fact that some kinds of school violence are planned well in advance, which would seem to suggest the offender went through some decision-making process. Many of the school shooters plotted for months. For instance, Eric Harris and Dylan Klebold planned their attack, made videos about what they intended to do, acquired guns, and assembled and planted bombs. Similarly, one could argue that when school officials perpetrate school violence through the use of corporal punishment, it is clearly a decision they have thought about. In 1992, researcher Felix Padilla studied gang members and found that the gang offered the only real economic opportunity for youth. His study, then, suggested that gang members choose to participate because they have weighed their other options and found them not viable.

Critics of rational choice theory maintain that juveniles, whose brains are not yet fully formed, do not necessarily have the mental capacity to weigh costs and benefits in the same way as do adults. Because juveniles engage in short-term thinking, they may not be able to think through the long-term consequences of behaving violently in school. Juveniles notoriously believe they will not get caught for any indiscretions and thus are unlikely to perceive apprehension as a risk or cost.

Additionally, many maintain that the mentally ill do not have the same ability to weigh costs and benefits. Further, each person's understanding of the costs and benefits of a particular action will differ depending on their background, their stakes in conforming to societal norms, and their ability to understand all of the costs and benefits. Critics also contend that these theories are too micro-focused; that is, they look only at the individual's choices and not at the social factors that led to them. Rational choice theory is closely linked with deterrence theory, which explains that an offender can be deterred from committing a criminal act or an act of violence if he or she believes the punishment will be significant. Harsher or longer punishments, then, are supposed to deter an offender from repeating the same behavior (called specific deterrence) as well as prevent others from choosing to commit an offense because they know what will happen if they do (general deterrence). However, critics contend that the tremendous scope of school violence, even given harsh sanctions like zero tolerance laws, clearly shows that youth are not deterred from problem behavior by simple punishments. In sum, the basic premise that youth weigh the costs and benefits before acting may simple be wrong.

Similar to rational choice theory, routine activities theory also posits that crime and violence are behaviors that some people choose after weighing the costs and benefits. This theory adds the notion that opportunity is also a significant factor. Routine activities theory maintains that three things must happen for crime or violence to occur: (1) a motivated offender, (2) a suitable target, and (3) lack of capable guardians. A person motivated to bully others, for instance, is likely to choose a victim who he or she sees as vulnerable and to pick on that person when no authority figures are around. Studies show support for the fact that bullying in schools occurs most frequently at lunch time or before or after school (and increasingly, online), all times when authorities are less likely to see what is happening. Yet critics note that this theory presumes a motivated offender rather than offering any explanation for what made that individual prepared to act out. Advocates of this theory often recommend greater security measures, like increased police presence, video cameras, and metal detectors, as a means of decreasing the suitability of a particular target and increasing the guardianship, and thereby deterring offenders. Called target hardening, the idea is that an offender will not choose to commit an act of crime or violence if it is likely that he or she will be caught. On the other hand, target hardening may simply shift crime and violence, as motivated offenders may move on to another location or another suitable victim.

Another theory that comes from the same set of assumptions about human behavior is called seductions of crime. Jack Katz studied juvenile offenders and determined that most engaged in delinquent acts because of what he called "the sneaky thrill." These offenders chose to commit criminal acts because they enjoyed the risk involved. "Pulling one over" gave these youth a thrill that they considered a benefit of the act. While Katz initially studies minor, nonviolent acts, he found similar logic employed by both youth and adults who engaged in more serious, violent crime as well. The fact that many of the school shooters have seemed to enjoy their acts of violence supports Katz's theory. For example, video recordings of the Columbine massacre show Harris and Klebold smiling and joking as they shot up their school library. Yet again, choice theories do little to explain why offenders are motivated in the first place. In this case, why would a youth choose the "sneaky thrill" of school violence over some other risk-taking behavior, like skydiving or bungee jumping? If the seductions of crime do accurately explain school violence, the logical prevention effort would include involving students in other activities in which they can gain that same sense of thrill.

Social Strain Theories

Strain theories emerged from the work of sociologist Emile Durkheim. Durkheim, a Frenchman, observed that during periods of rapid social change in his country (the French Revolution, industrialization, etc.) suicide rates increased dramatically. He speculated that this was the result of anomie, or a condition in which there are high degrees of confusion and chaos and thus contradictions in a group or society's basic social norms. The norms that usually constrain people from committing socially unacceptable acts are so weakened that individuals do not know what is expected of them. Criminologist Robert Merton expanded the concept of anomie to describe how it leads to criminal offending. Merton defined anomie as a disjuncture between an individual's aspirations and the means he or she has to achieve them. Focusing on the United States specifically, Merton maintained that people are constantly told the importance of "getting ahead" and achieving the so-called American Dream. The emphasis is on attending school, working hard, and saving money. Yet some people's social situation precludes them from achieving these successes easily, if ever. Persons born into lower socioeconomic classes may not be able to attend good schools or get good-paying jobs. Merton maintained that people will respond to this disjuncture in five specific ways. They may conform, which means they simply keep working hard in legitimate, socially acceptable ways. Ritualists respond to the strain by overconforming, or rigidly adhering to the culturally approved methods of getting ahead, despite it being unlikely that they ever will. The remaining three adaptations may be deviant. Some adapt by innovating. That is, they still believe in the ultimate goal of financial success but instead of using legitimate means to achieve it they may engage in illegal or deviant behavior such as stealing or dealing drugs. Retreatists reject both the goal and the means of achieving it. These individuals may run away, become hard-core drug addicts or alcoholics, or otherwise "drop out" of society. Suicide is the ultimate retreat. The final adaptation is rebellion. Rebels seek to replace the goals and socially accepted means with new ones. While some rebels become social reformers, others become neo-Nazis, Satanists, or violent gang members.

Many of the school shooters made comments verbally and in writing to suggest that they were seeking to rebel against a system that had not served them well. Several had also expressed deep admiration of Hitler and other notorious criminals. It is less clear, however, how social strain theory might apply to bullying, hazing, or systemic violence.

Another strain-related theory was developed by Albert Cohen in 1955. Cohen studied lower-class boys and maintained that they experienced "status frustration" because of the perception of blocked goals, which resulted in three specific responses. The "college-boy response" is much like Merton's conformity in that these youth accept the middle-class value system and generally work hard to meet those expectations. The most common response is Cohen's "corner-boy," which suggests that lower-class boys form subcultures in which they can gain status without adhering to middle-class values. These boys often become delinquent, engaging in alcohol and drug consumption, truancy, and other minor acts. Those who respond in what Cohen called the "delinquent boy" mentality become frustrated with their situation and form subcultures that overtly oppose middle-class values. Again, this theory may be useful for explaining gang-related school violence that occurs in lower-class communities, but it does not seem to apply to other forms.

Similar to Cohen, Richard Cloward and Lloyd Ohlin developed a strain theory focused on lower-class boys that they called delinquency and opportunity. Their idea was that, in the same way that legitimate opportunities for success are limited, so too are illegitimate opportunities. Thus, youth may form subcultures around the specific types of illegitimate opportunities that are available in their area. Cloward and Ohlin proposed three types of gangs that form: (1) the crime-oriented gang, (2) the conflict-oriented gang, and (3) the retreatist-oriented gang. Crime-oriented groups respond to their feelings of deprivation and alienation by engaging in theft, fraud, extortion, and other activities in which they can make money. These gangs tend to be largely orchestrated by adults who serve as "apprentice delinquents." Conflict-oriented gangs engage in fighting and violence to secure their status, in particular in neighborhoods, when opportunities for upward mobility are essentially nonexistent. Retreatist gangs demonstrate their contempt for societal norms by engaging in substance abuse. This type of formation occurs in communities in which there is a ready supply of illicit substances.

In the 1990s, criminologist Robert Agnew developed what he called general strain theory. Agnew asserted that it was not just lower-class boys who experience strain but also middle-class boys and girls. Instead of a disjuncture between goals and expectations, Agnew theorized that there are three major sources of stress that lead to strain, which might result in someone acting out delinquently: (1) A discrepancy between means and goals or between expectations and outcomes, much like a sense of anomie; (2) loss of a positive stimuli, such as a parent or close friend or a breakup with a boyfriend or girlfriend; and (3) introduction of a negative stimuli, such as living in slum conditions or experiencing abuse. According to Agnew, a youth will respond differently to these strains based on his or her motivation, self-esteem, social supports, levels of anger, and experience being punished. In a number of school shooting incidents, the perpetrator had just endured some hardship, like breaking up with a girlfriend. Many had grown up in abusive homes, suggesting that these strains may have played a role in their crimes. Research on dating violence has shown that these perpetrators have often been exposed to traumatic abuse in their homes as well. Yet, just like the theories presented so far in this chapter, the strain-related theories seem not to apply to institutional forms of violence.

Walter Miller developed a theory of lower-class culture in 1958. Instead of a lack of commitment to middle-class values, Miller argued that it was an acceptance of different, lower-class values that resulted in crime and delinquency. He identified six lower-class "focal concerns" or values: (1) Trouble, or

the need to avoid confrontations with police or other authorities; (2) toughness, including physical and verbal prowess; (3)
smartness, or verbal agility and quick-wittedness; (4) excite-
ment, including the need for thrill-seeking and risk-taking; (5)
fate, or a tendency to believe that luck is the primary reason
for one's lot; and (6) autonomy, specifically the need to be
independent.

A concern about strain theories is that so many of the theorists studied lower-class cultures exclusively, thereby overlook-
ing the crime and violence perpetrated by youth of other
social classes. Critics also contend that these theories focus too
much on boys and fail to postulate why girls commit offenses
and, even more, why they generally do *not*.

Other strain-related theories focus on communities that
experience anomie and the concomitant impact on formal and
informal social controls. In the 1920s and 1930s, University
of Chicago sociologists Robert Park, Ernest Burgess, R. D.
McKenzie, and others—and later in the 1960s, Clifford Shaw
and Henry McKay—looked at the ways that rapid change in
that city resulted in a state of anomie and how it correlated with
the breakdown of efforts to deter and to hold accountable
offenders. Using maps of juvenile and adult arrests, these theorists found that crime and violence were heavily clustered in
industrial areas. These "disorganized" neighborhoods produced
delinquency, theorists speculated, as new social norms are
created. Further, as people begin to engage in minor acts of
delinquency, such as vandalism and theft, others disinvest in
the community, thereby weakening informal social controls.
Additional community disinvestment reduces funding and support for formal social controls like policing, thereby further
increasing the chance of crime. Although school violence is not
exclusive to traditionally disorganized communities, some have
argued that it might be the schools themselves that are disorganized. These schools fail to set clear prosocial norms and lack both
formal and informal means of reinforcing positive behavior.

Social Learning Theories

Another category of theories to explain crime and violence are the learning-related theories. In general, these theories posit that offenders learn to commit crime and violence just like they learn how to engage in other behaviors. One of the learning theories is called differential association. Developed by Edwin Sutherland, one of the founders of criminology in the United States, differential association explains that people will learn both the motivation as well as the techniques, or the "how-to," from people with whom they have intimate, frequent, and priority relationships. That is, if people we see frequently and value greatly engage in crime or violence, we might learn to do the same. The most obvious place where someone would learn about crime and violence and how to commit it is in their family. This is supported by the mountains of data showing that perpetrators of school violence often grow up in abusive or neglectful homes. In addition, school violence might be learned from watching and interacting with peers who act out. Further, while this theory seems logical, what remains unclear is why and how some people who are surrounded by others who engage in crime and violence still do not follow that path. Is it personal characteristics? Opportunities? Social constraints? The importance of differential association theory lies in the recognition that crime and violence are far from innate. Thus, offenders can "unlearn" them. Prevention programming, then, is a logical application of differential association theory, as the idea is that youth could learn prosocial values and behaviors that would constrain them from offending.

Another learning theory is differential identification. Similar to differential association, differential identification maintains that crime and violence are learned. In addition to those with whom we are close, differential identification theory asserts that people learn crime and violence from those with whom they identify. This could be people we have never met, as in the case of the many serial killers who say that they read about and identified with Jack the Ripper. Many of the school shooters have been infatuated with earlier shooters. Many have also been avid followers of infamous violent figures like Adolf Hitler. Further, differential identification theory implies that the persons with whom we identify need not even be real; that is, some offenders identify with fictional book, television, film, or videogame characters. This clearly has been a factor in a number of school shootings, as many of the perpetrators were heavy media consumers who loved to play violent videogames and to watch hyper-violent films. Although all were eventually dismissed, a number of lawsuits against film production companies and videogame makers alleged that they bore some responsibility for the shooters' behavior.

It is clear that even the worst offenders do not perpetrate crime 100 percent of the time. That is, offenders move between adhering to and violating social norms. As such, criminologists have attempted to explain what allows offenders to drift between offending and not. When they do commit acts of deviance, Sykes and Matza (1957) maintain, juveniles experience a sense of guilt, which prompts them to mentally neutralize or rationalize their behaviors. Techniques of neutralization is a theory which asserts that offenders use five specific techniques: (1) Denying the victim, (2) denying the injury, (3) denying responsibility, (4) condemning the condemners, and (5) appealing to higher loyalties. Like self-talk, offenders tell themselves that no one was really hurt, that the victims deserved what they got, that it was really someone else who was responsible, that authorities are simply out to get them, or that they had to do it because of some other loyalty. Often applied to explain the behavior of gang members, this theory can also help explain why some perpetrators of school violence seem to be "nice kids" from good families. Many believed that because they were picked on, their victims deserved to be targeted. Likewise, perpetrators of dating violence often tell themselves that it is the victim's fault, not theirs. Hazing can also be explained through techniques of neutralization theory, as perpetrators often were hazed themselves, believe that their actions are not harmful, and condemn those who condemn the practice. This theory might also explain why school officials and educators use violent and demeaning punishments and practices, as they typically justify these actions as being "for their own good."

Social Control Theories

Social control theories are unique in that they ask a slightly different question. Rather than wondering why people offend, social control theorists believe that everyone has the capacity to commit criminal acts and thus begin with the question of what factors constrain individuals from offending. One of the first social control theorists was Walter Reckless, who in the 1960s posited that it was both inner and outer containment that resulted in or constrained one from perpetrating crime or violence. Inner containment is a person's internal ability to resist temptations to deviate while outer containment refers to the societal pressures to resist offending, including laws and the punishments of the legal system. Because individuals are subject to push factors (mental conflicts, anxiety, feelings of alienation and frustration) as well as pull factors (societal and peer pressures), there is a constant process of balancing their containment with the internal and external pressures.

The most widely cited control theory is Travis Hirschi's social bond theory. Hirschi focused on social bonds, generally established in early childhood and cultivated throughout the lifetime, that model and reinforce conformity. According to Hirschi, there are four key elements of a social bond: (1) Attachment, or an emotional regard and respect for others; (2) commitment, meaning the development of career and social goals that conform to societal norms; (3) involvement, or investment of time and effort in conventional pursuits; and (4) belief, or one's understanding and commitment to laws and other moral and social norms. It is clear that many school shooters lack positive bonds with others. Most were described as outcasts by peers.

One of the major contributions of social control theories is the recognition that both internal, or micro-level, and external, or macro-level, factors are important. Studies have also shown that youth who commit delinquent acts tend not to be as attached to parents, peers, and teachers. Importantly, Hirschi found that lower-class youth are no more likely to offend than are middle-class youth—the pivotal factors, instead, are the support systems each individual has. Critics note that these internal and external pushes and pulls or social bonds are difficult if not impossible to accurately measure. Further, some people have the four qualities Hirschi outlined but are bonded to a deviant lifestyle. That is, many gang members are deeply committed to one another and have developed their own belief systems. Hazing is allegedly all about bonding to a group or team, yet it is also an act of violence. Likewise, it is hard to argue that school teachers and administrators who paddle students or who demean them through invasive searches are doing so because of a lack of social bonding.

Labeling Theories

Sociological theories emerging from the notion of social constructionism include the labeling theories. The basic idea is that a number of social institutions, ranging from schools to criminal justice and more, label youth as "bad" or "delinquent." This often results in a self-fulfilling prophecy whereby individuals take on a deviant identity. There is a wealth of evidence showing that students who do what they are told, do not question authority, and suppress their own values are more likely to be labeled as "bad kids" in schools. These labels tend to be reified throughout the system as teachers and administrators pass them along, and other students reinforce them as well. Edwin Lemert (1951) articulated the concepts of primary and secondary deviance. His argument was that individuals only progress to secondary deviance after they are labeled. Howard Becker elaborated, showing how a criminal or deviant identity may become one's master status, or an overpowering characteristic of their self-identity. In his classic study "Saints and the Roughnecks," William Chambliss showed that a group of boys who were deemed "good," called the Saints, committed as many deviant and delinquent acts as did the boys who he called the Roughnecks. But because the Roughnecks were labeled "bad," they did not receive the benefit of the doubt from school officials or from local law enforcement. Thus it was the label, not their actions, which resulted in harsher consequences. It is clear that many perpetrators of school violence have been labeled. Some of the school shooters were "known" as outcasts or nerds or had been labeled as "gay." Bullies often seem to take on that identity, exacerbating their abuse. Further, evidence shows that youth who have had any involvement with the juvenile justice system do not tend to fare well in a school setting, which in turn increases the likelihood that they will reoffend. On the other hand, many people who are labeled work extra hard to reject the label rather than take it on. Thus, it is unclear what internal mechanisms, support systems, or other factors allow some to reject a label and others to accept it.

Conflict Theories

Conflict theories are rooted in the work of Karl Marx and were developed by criminologists in the 1960s. According to these theories, crime is rooted in the modern capitalist economy, which creates inequalities. Those who own the means of production, what Marx called the bourgeoisie, tend to also control other institutions, while those who labor, the proletariat, have little social or economic power. Capitalist societies are then characterized by struggles or conflicts between these two groups, as the bourgeoisie seeks to maintain or expand what they have while the proletariat wants more. Richard Quinney, a radical conflict theorist, identified several propositions that delineated the theory: (1) Official definitions of crime are created by the dominant class; (2) crime is defined as behaviors that conflict with the interests of the dominant class; (3) the dominant class is largely involved with the enforcement and administration of criminal law; and (4) the dominant class perpetuates an ideology about crime and who commits it. In essence, Quinney's work suggests that youth crime is perceived as a threat to adults and that minority and underprivileged youth, like adults from those demographics, are most likely to see their actions defined as criminal and to be labeled as such. This very macro-level perspective is more difficult to apply to any individual perpetrator's behavior but might be best at explaining systemic violence. It is those who have power in schools, the administrators and teachers, who make and apply the rules for students.

David Greenberg (1977) drew on the radical/conflict tradition as well as the strain theories to develop the theory of adolescent frustration. He maintained that youth are told that money and material possessions are the key to success, yet are largely unable to obtain them. In particular, youth in a capitalist society experience three basic frustrations that may lead some to delinquency: (1) Lack of money, which is particularly acute for poor youth; (2) lack of respect, as youth often feel demoralized because adults fail to see them as valuable or to solicit their voices; and (3) lack of employment. Many youth are unable to find work and hence cannot make money or feel the dignity of earning for themselves. Males in particular may feel emasculated by these frustrations and may act out in response. This theory might explain why most forms of school violence are disproportionately perpetrated by males. Further, it is also clear that the young males who have perpetrated mass acts of school violence were indeed feeling disrespected by peers as well as school officials; hence they chose to act out in those locations. As Aronson (2000) explained,

> Young mass shooters don't mow down their neighbors or shoot up the local video arcade. They kill their classmates

and teachers, and sometimes themselves, in or around the school building itself. Looking for root causes in individual pathology is an approach that seems sensible on the surface, but it does not get to the root of the problem. What is it about the atmosphere in schools themselves that makes these young people so desperate, diabolical, and callous? (87–88)

Integrated Theories

In the 1980s, several theorists began to develop integrated or developmental theories. These theories tend to include both micro and macro theories. Given that the bulk of youth offenders "age out," or mature and no longer offend, it is important to look at the factors that may make a juvenile offender persist into adult criminality. Robert Sampson and John Laub developed a theory they called turning points in which they explained that juveniles' successful navigation through important life-changing events either encourages or discourages their involvement in crime as adults (Thompson & Bynum, 2012). High school graduation, marriage, parenting, and employment are all markers along this trajectory. Terrie Moffit's life-course theory explains that there are two types of offenders: life-course persistent and adolescence-limited (Thompson & Bynum, 2012). The former are those who begin early and continue to engage in crime, typically perpetrating offenses of escalating severity. Another integrated theory is the general theory of crime, developed by Travis Hirschi and Michael Gottfredson (Thompson & Bynum, 2012). Containing elements of social bond theory and others, the basic focus is on lack of self-control coupled with opportunities for offending. While it is clear that many of the most infamous school shooters had acted out at early ages, many others had not. These theories do not seem very applicable to explaining sexual harassment, hazing, dating violence, bullying, or systemic violence.

Feminist Theories

One important and ever-evolving area of criminological theory is the exploration of feminist perspectives. For a long time, the field has suffered from androcentrism, or the privileging of male perspectives. Indeed, most criminologists were males who studied males to develop theories of male delinquency. While some maintain the dramatic differences between male and female offending is due to biology, other theorists assert that it is sociological factors that explain the discrepancy. One early feminist theory was the liberation hypothesis offered by Freda Adler in 1975 (Thompson & Bynum, 2012). Adler maintained that as women are more involved in every aspect of life in the United States, from politics to the corporate world, they will also be more involved in crime. While some data bears this out, other sources do not. Some have argued that incidents of girl-on-girl bullying and hazing among girls are indicative of the greater involvement girls have in school and extracurricular activities. Deborah Prothrow-Stith has argued that because the United States is still a patriarchal culture in which violence is equated with power, women and girls may act aggressively as a means of obtaining power (Thompson & Bynum, 2012). John Hagan's power–control theory asserts that criminal behavior is influenced by both family structure and societal structure (Thompson & Bynum, 2012). Given that the United States is a male-dominated society, families too are patriarchal in that fairly strict gender norms are still common. Boys are encouraged to take risks and are given greater freedoms, which allow them more opportunities and reinforcement for deviant behavior. In a study of 28 school shooters, researchers found that all were overconforming to masculine norms.

It is possible, however, that besides school shootings, girls commit other kinds of offenses with similar frequency as do boys but are simply less likely to be caught and punished (and therefore not reflected in statistics). The chivalry hypothesis postulates that the deviant behavior of women and girls is minimized by institutions of formal social control, like police and school administrators. There is some support for the idea that women and girls are treated more leniently for minor offenses, such as traffic violations. Further, research on bullying suggests that girls do it differently than do boys and that these differing tactics result in increased likelihood that boy bullies will be caught. For instance, girls are more likely to bully other girls by spreading rumors and hateful gossip or through dirty looks and mean comments on social media. Boys are more likely to act out in front of others, either verbally or physically, and thus may be detected by teachers. Research does show, however, that when women or girls commit serious violent acts, they are more likely to receive harsh punishments, thus presenting a limitation on the chivalry hypothesis.

In sum, all theories have their strengths and limitations. Understanding the various explanations can help practitioners better respond to school violence. Likewise, understanding the risk factors for school violence as well as the factors that serve a protective function can allow for improved prevention efforts.

Risk Factors

Many individual, family, school, and community factors put youth at greater risk for perpetrating school violence. Similarly, research has identified characteristics that make a young person at greater risk for being victimized in school.

Individual

The Centers for Disease Control and Prevention (CDC) lists low IQ, deficits in social–cognitive or information-processing abilities, and history of treatment for emotional difficulties among the individual risk factors for school violence. In many cases, it is exposure to violence that has lowered someone's IQ. Children in early elementary school with a history of exposure to violence or being victims of violence score significantly lower on IQ and reading ability (on average, over 7 points lower on IQ and almost 10 points lower in reading achievements).

A recent study found that fighting between teens may actually reduce young people's IQs. On average, the teens who had been involved in serious fights had a 2-point drop in their IQ score. Although boys engage in physical fights more often, the drop in IQ appears to be greater for female teens who fight.

Some studies have shown that youth who have been diagnosed with attention-deficit disorder (ADD) or attention-deficit/hyperactivity disorder (AD/HD) are overrepresented in incidents of school violence. Youth may be diagnosed with these disorders if they exhibit one or more of these behaviors: attention difficulties or short attention span, restless behavior, impulsivity, motor hyperactivity, irritability or temper outbursts, and distractibility. Youth struggling with these disorders face many challenges in a school setting. They may be chronically truant, have a hard time focusing on school work, and be prone to interpreting others' actions as hostile. This may lead them to respond in aggressive or violent ways. A longitudinal study conducted in Sweden found that 13-year-old boys who were described as restless and who had difficulty concentrating were five times more likely to be arrested for violent crimes at age 26 than were youth who were not described in those ways. Youth with ADD or AD/HD diagnoses are also often diagnosed with other disorders, what is called co-morbidity. Common additional diagnoses include conduct disorders, anxiety disorders, learning disabilities, Tourette's syndrome, personality disorders, and affective disorders. This co-morbidity exacerbates the school and other challenges and thus may increase the risk that youth will engage in risky or aggressive behavior. Many persons diagnosed with ADD or AD/HD also attempt to self-medicate by engaging in substance use.

Others argue that the criteria for these disorders are very ambiguous and thus result in more youth being diagnosed.

It is clear that AD/HD is one of the most frequent diagnoses in child and adolescent psychiatry. One study in 2002 found that approximately 16 percent of school-aged youth in the United States had been diagnosed with ADD or AD/HD. It could be that changes in technology as well as the increasing expectations of youth in schools make it challenging to focus, not that youth suffer from an actual disorder. Others contend that it is slick marketing campaigns from pharmaceutical companies that tell parents and teachers that youth must be suffering from a disorder if they are easily distracted. Because the primary intervention for ADD and AD/HD is the prescription of a psychoactive drug like methylphenidate, typically in the form of Ritalin or Adderall, the pharmaceutical companies that make these substances stand to benefit tremendously when more young people are diagnosed. Prescriptions for methylphenidate have grown dramatically, with the U.S. Drug Enforcement Agency (DEA) noting that in some regions, 15 to 20 percent of young people had been prescribed Ritalin. Similarly, Britain saw a nine-fold increase in Ritalin prescriptions from 1995 to 2000. Stimulants much like cocaine, these drugs can result in dangerous side effects like mood swings and appetite loss. Some youth sell their prescription drugs to others, who use them to get high. Between 1990 and 2000, 569 children were hospitalized and 186 died from Ritalin overdoses. Several school shooters were taking Ritalin at the time of their attacks. T. J. Solomon was taking Ritalin when he wounded six students at his Georgia school in 1999, and Kip Kinkel was taking it as well when he killed his parents and two students, wounding 23 others as he attacked students and teachers at his Springfield, Oregon, school.

Other prescription drugs have been associated with youth violence in general and school violence in particular. Selective serotonin reuptake inhibitors (SSRIs), a class of antidepressants, have been linked to several serious incidents on school grounds. This class of drugs includes Prozac, Paxil, Zoloft, Celexa, Lexapro, and Luvox as well as Remeron and

Anafranil. A similar category, the serotonin norepinephrine reuptake inhibitors (SNRIs), includes Effexor, Serzone, Cymbalta, and Pristiq, while welbutrin, marketed as Zyban, is a dopamine reuptake inhibitor. Although all have been approved by the Food and Drug Administration (FDA), none of these were tested for side effects on youth populations. Known effects include mania, abnormal thinking, personality disorders, hallucinations, agitation, psychosis, amnesia, alcohol craving and abuse, hostility, paranoia, sleep disorders, delusions, confusion, and restlessness. Persons withdrawing from these substances also typically suffer from tremendous emotional and physical challenges.

Many of the school shooters from the last three decades had been prescribed one or more of these substances. A sample includes Laurie Dann, who had been taking Anafranil and Lithium before she killed a child and wounded six at an Illinois elementary school in 1988; Kip Kinkel, who was taking Prozac when he killed four people and wounded 23 others at Thurston High School in Springfield, Oregon, in 1998; Eric Harris, one of the Columbine killers, who had been taking Luvox; and Jeff Weise, who had been taking Prozac before he killed nine and wounded five at Red Lake High School in Minnesota in 2005. These high-profile and deadly incidents prompted the FDA to mandate, on September 14, 2008, that pharmacies provide an Antidepressant Patient Medication Guide to parents or guardians of minors who had been prescribed antidepressants. It also ordered that a "black box" warning be placed on all antidepressants that describes the risk of suicide for users under the age of 18.

Some have identified mental illness as one of the most significant factors in extreme acts of school violence such as rampage school shootings. Most of the assailants had a history of depression, isolation, and suicidal thoughts or attempts, although many had not received a particular diagnosis. In his book *Columbine*, Dave Cullen asserted that it was mental illness, not bullying, that was the main reason for the attack perpetrated by Eric Harris and Dylan Klebold. Cullen asserted that Klebold suffered from depression and was suicidal, while he called Harris a calculating, cold, homicidal psychopath. Another infamous shooter, Jeff Weise (mentioned above), had previously been admitted to a psychiatric facility. He had been banned from entering Red Lake High School just five weeks before his attack due to his erratic and threatening behavior.

Alcohol is the drug most associated with violence as well as the drug most commonly used by persons ages 12 to 20. Associated with both victimization and perpetration, alcohol use impacts the brain development of adolescents, reduces self-control, and inhibits users' ability to process incoming information. Further, alcohol consumption is associated with the carrying of weapons. Studies have documented that youth who admit to using alcohol are three times more likely to carry handguns than are youth who do not drink, and binge-drinking, defined as consuming four to five drinks in a two-hour time period, increases the likelihood that an individual will carry a handgun four-fold in comparison to nondrinking peers.

Students with disabilities, only 14 percent of all students in the United States, make up 19 percent of those who suffer corporal punishment, or abuse by teachers and administrators. Jonathan C., a 15-year-old boy with autism, was repeatedly subjected to corporal punishment at his Florida public school. One day, after he screamed in the cafeteria and ran away from a staff member, a male staff member picked him up and flung him on the tile floor face first. Staff members dragged him to a meeting room, where the male staff member put him in a chokehold. His mother described what happened: "Three or four [staff members] tackle[d] him, and he [was] thrown to the floor again." The staff members used their strength and body weight to pin Jonathan, face down, to the floor.

Studies in the United Kingdom have found similar overrep-resentation of youth with disabilities as victims of bullying, with one study finding 82 percent of students with disabilities to have endured bullying.

Several studies have found that individuals who are heavy consumers of media, especially violent media, are more prone to engage in acts of violence. According to the American Psychological Association (2013), a child who watches two to four hours of television per day will have witnessed 8,000 murders and more than 100,000 acts of violence before he or she leaves elementary school. A longitudinal study conducted by Dr. Leonard Eron found that watching more television at age eight was connected with committing more serious crimes at age 30. Thus, the study implies that the most risky time for viewing violence is when children are under age 10, as they may not be able to distinguish between what is real and what is not. Others have noted that television, film, and videogame violence is often depicted as though it is funny and without consequences. That is, the violence does not appear to really hurt anyone, or at least nor permanently, and is often presented in a way that is supposed to inspire viewers to laugh. This "happy violence" is very common in programming marketed to young people, and it may be the most dangerous for them to see.

Boys are more likely influenced by violent movies, television, and videogames than are girls, and aggressive boys may be drawn to those forms of media. Since the 1960s, studies have shown links between viewing violent media and aggressive behavior. Albert Bandura's famous "Bobo Doll" experiments showed that children learn and imitate aggressive behavior from watching television, as the kids in his experiment repeatedly punched, kicked, and beat a blow-up doll after viewing violence. Studies show that the link between viewing violence and acting violently is strongest when the viewer identifies with the aggressor. Media Education Foundation has produced a number of documentary videos in which they critically analyze the effect of violent media on youth. In *Tough Guise*, Jackson Katz and Sut Jhally document the ways that television and films depict aggressive masculinity as the norm. Violent men are depicted as heroes who are unable to show emotion. Men and boys whose looks or behaviors challenge this norm, what is called hegemonic masculinity, are often harassed and bullied. The same narratives belittle and dehumanize women, making them appear to be little more than sex objects. In Jhally's *Dreamworlds* series, Katz explores the way that music and music videos depict women as sexualized objects and how the storylines in music often feature dangerous themes involving men's and boys' aggression against women and girls. In their 2002 film *Wrestling with Manhood: Boys, Bullying, and Battering*, Katz and Jhally focus on the violence and narratives common in professional wrestling. While the violence itself is problematic, given that it is typically gratuitous and yet depicted as though it is without consequence, even funny, the storylines used to develop the characters are equally problematic. Viewers are told that violence against those perceived as weaker or as gay is acceptable, and when women are the targets it is almost always presented as though "she deserved it."

Rather than directly affect viewers in the form of imitation, some media scholars maintain that viewing, listening to, or playing violent media has a desensitizing effect. That is, people who are consistently exposed to violent media may begin to see it as normal and to feel less sympathy for those who are victims of it. Many studies have provided support for this contention. Bushman and Anderson (2009) found that after playing a violent videogame, people took longer to intervene when they heard a physical fight occurring. In another study, they found that people who had just watched a violent movie were less likely to offer help to someone who was injured. Likewise, Fanti, Vanman, Henrich, and Avraamides (2009) found that people who watched a series of violent movies felt less sympathy towards the victims depicted and actually enjoyed watching the aggression.

Numerous studies have shown that cartoons and children's programming fail to accurately portray the negative or dangerous effects of violence, instead making it seem as though violence is without consequence. Children today grow up with more media than has any generation prior. On average, even children under the age of six consume approximately two hours per day of screen media, as many have a television, VCR, video-game player, or other device in their rooms. Twenty-five percent of children under the age of three have a personal computer. When families leave the television on at home, not surprisingly, children watch more. These children also spend less time outdoors or reading and thus may not be building important prosocial bonds.

In 1985, Tipper Gore, wife of then-senator and later vice president Al Gore, helped found the Parents Music Resource Center, which was devoted to educating parents about what they saw as the dangers of rock music. The group's efforts resulted in mandatory parental advisory notifications on music albums with explicit lyrics. In the late 1990s, President Clinton commissioned the Federal Trade Commission (FTC) to study the marketing of violent media to youth, while Reverend Al Sharpton asked the FTC in 2005 to punish musicians who had been involved in violence by prohibiting radio and television stations from playing their music for 90 days. These critics assert that it is not just the violent lyrics but also the criminal activity of some of the musicians that make the music dangerous for youth. Research is not as clear about the connection between listening to violent lyrics and acting out violently as it is about viewing violence or interacting with it in videogames.

Interestingly, while research is clear that marginalized youth are at risk for being bullied, popular youth may suffer as well. In fact, researchers found that popular youth are often bullied by those who resent their social status and that these youth report more anxiety, depression, and anger than the more traditional victims of bullying.

Family

Family size and birth order are factors that are correlated with delinquency. Large families may lack the financial resources and time to devote to each child. Additionally, less communication, inconsistent discipline and supervision, and simple overcrowding might relate to delinquency. Yet caution is needed, as clearly any specific larger family may be very supportive and able to provide both financially and emotionally. Several studies have also shown that birth order plays a role in regard to delinquency. Thompson and Bynum (2012) found that firstborn children relate well to adults and tend to conform to the societal norms introduced by their parents. Youngest children also seem to fare well, as studies document that parents have gained wisdom from previous parenting experiences, "babies" of the family often receive the most attention, and younger children learn from their older siblings. Thus, it is middle children who may get "lost" in the childrearing process, resulting in a greater propensity for delinquency. Family social class is associated with higher arrest rates for juveniles, although it is important to recognize that this may not be related to greater perpetration but instead to bias in the criminal justice system.

The CDC recognizes that certain types of childrearing techniques can put children at risk for victimization or for criminal involvement. Authoritarian or excessively harsh parenting and lax or inconsistent discipline have both been considered as risk factors. Additionally, parents who are not involved in their children's lives, who do not monitor their children's activities, or who show little emotional attachment are putting their children at greater risk. Further, parental substance abuse is a risk factor.

One controversial aspect of family life is whether youth raised by working mothers are more likely to engage in delinquency. The 2010 Census found that more than 70 million women and over 75 percent of mothers ages 25 to 54 work outside of the home. While some claim that children who are in daycare are more prone to delinquency, research does not seem to bear that out. In fact, some studies find that working mothers make tremendous efforts to spend more time, and more quality time, with their children as a means of compensating for being away. Other studies bear out that experiences in the home have more of an impact on later delinquency than does time spent in childcare.

Children who grow up experiencing physical, sexual, verbal, or emotional abuse are more likely to become either perpetrators of crime or victims. Additionally, child neglect, or when caretakers fail to provide adequate nutrition, clothing, shelter, access to education, or medical care, is also correlated with higher rates of later victimization or criminal perpetration. Families serve as the first role models for children, and when the model is one of abuse or neglect, it is not surprising that children are at greater risk for repeating that behavior. Each year more than 3 million incidents of child abuse are reported in the United States, or an incident every 10 seconds. Nearly five children die every day from child abuse, with more than 75 percent of those being younger than four years old. Additionally, research shows that simply being exposed to domestic violence in the home, even if a child is not actually being abused, increases the risk of later criminal involvement and adds to the likelihood that as adults these individuals will be involved in abusive relationships. While research shows that girls are at greater risk for enduring sexual abuse, boys are more likely to experience emotional neglect and serious physical injuries.

Young people who experience abuse and neglect suffer from higher rates of depression, anxiety, anger, and aggression and are more likely to struggle in school, to engage in risky behaviors such as substance abuse, and to exhibit suicidal behavior. Studies show that youth who have experienced one or more forms of abuse are more likely to end up in juvenile detention or prison than are youth who do not experience abuse. Studies of school shooters have uncovered histories of abuse. Evan Ramsey, who killed two and injured two others at his school in Bethel, Alaska, in 1997, was said to have experienced abuse at the hands of several of the foster parents with whom he lived. Asa Coon, who wounded four at his Cleveland, Ohio, school in 2007, grew up witnessing domestic violence in the home. Approximately 36 percent of women and 14 percent of all men in prisons in the United States were abused as children.

School

School administrators, teachers, and other staff must help ensure that the school climate is not just safe but also welcoming to all. Shafii and Shafii (2000) argue that poor school climate and inadequate or damaging teacher–student relationships are the main reasons for school violence. School climates in which youth feel scared, marginalized, and voiceless create the conditions for other forms of violence to occur. As Aronson (2000) explained,

> It is reasonably clear that a major root cause of the recent school shootings is a school atmosphere that ignores, or implicitly condones, the taunting, rejection, and verbal abuse to which a great many students are subjected. A school that ignores the values of empathy, tolerance and compassion, or, worse still, pays lip service to these values while doing nothing concrete and effective to promote these values, creates an atmosphere that is not only unpleasant for the "losers" but one that shortchanges the "winners" as well (p. 70).

Although administrators have a duty to ensure that school is a safe place for all students, sometimes the rules, policies, practices, and interventions they enact actually make the school climate worse. Research has shown that installing metal detectors in schools with no history of gun-related violence on campus actually makes students more fearful, not less. Similarly, zero tolerance laws that mandate suspension or expulsion for youth who commit specified offenses (like bringing a weapon to campus or fighting) may actually be counterproductive in that they decrease the morale at the school. Metal detectors are a form of target hardening; that is, they make a particular space more difficult to victimize. But research about these kinds of efforts shows that they do not stop crime but rather displace it to different locations.

Schools often use practices that label and stigmatize youth, which has been associated with greater rates of crime and delinquency. Tracking, or using standardized tests or prior grades to place students in a particular classroom, is a way of differentiating those who achieve at higher levels from those who do not. While the practice is often praised by educators who find it easier to teach when the class is more homogeneous, others contend that tracking correlates significantly with social class and is yet another means of distinguishing lower-class students from upper-class students and maintaining the status quo. Students in lower tracks are more likely to be perceived and labeled as less intelligent, and thus teachers may have lower expectations to which those students rise. These students are more likely to skip school, as they believe they do not belong and cannot succeed. Each school day, thousands of youth, especially those who perceive that they are of little value, skip school. Research verifies that juveniles who skip school are more likely to be involved with drugs, gangs, and violence.

Another damaging practice is corporal punishment, or the use of physical punishments like paddling to correct students' behavior. As noted in the previous chapter, corporal punishment is not prohibited in 20 states, and an estimated 200,000 students are paddled in school each year. In their book *Dangerous Schools* (1999), Hyman and Snook describe the dangers of paddling by sharing the stories of youth who were beaten so badly they suffered internal damage simply for being late to class. They also describe the other controlling behaviors educators use that demean and degrade youth, for instance not allowing them to use the restroom or arranging classroom seating so that the students who do well are seated in the front and the ones who do not are stigmatized by having to sit in the back.

Youth who do not like school often strike back. The most typical response is not bringing a weapon but rather engaging in destruction of school property. Yet others retaliate against the teachers they perceive as responsible, with an estimated 250,000 teachers threatened or injured in the job each year. As Thompson and Bynum (2012) explain,

> students who feel they are being treated like numbers rather than people are likely to develop a sense of alienation in the school environment. The assembly line model of education that has dominated our educational philosophy since the industrial revolution has led to viewing schools as analogous to factories. Thus, incoming students are seen as raw materials to be shaped, molded, and transformed into finished products (i.e., productive citizens) by those trained and skilled to do so (the teachers). Students' views of teachers and teachers' views of students are affected by the roles they are forced to fulfill within the bureaucratic structure (p. 232).

Community

One community-level factor that places youth at risk for a variety of forms of violence is the presence of gangs. A 2010 survey found that 45 percent of high school students and 35 percent of middle school students reported that there were gangs or students who considered themselves to be gang members in their school. Rates were much lower in private schools, where only 2 percent of students reported gangs or students who considered themselves to be gang members. Gang members do not leave their conflicts or illegal activities behind when they enter school grounds, and thus the presence of gangs in schools increases the likelihood of violence and other forms of crime.

Youth who grow up in communities with high levels of violence often feel hopeless, angry, and ashamed. Youth who witness violence report higher rates of posttraumatic stress, depression, distress, aggression, and externalizing behavior.

High poverty levels and lack of economic opportunity are also community-level risk factors. School violence is also more common in communities that have high levels of transiency, according to the CDC.

Protective Factors

Conversely, a number of protective factors at each of these levels have been identified. Thus, even youth who have some of the risk factors may be deterred from involvement in violence if there are protective factors in their lives as well. Researchers have developed the list of protective factors described below from studying resilience, or what allows some to adapt positively to challenging conditions.

Individual

Youth with higher IQs and good grade point averages are less likely to be involved in violence at school, according to the CDC (2013). Thus parents', schools', and communities' efforts to help students do well in school pay off in reduced violence. Youth who have skills in conflict resolution fare better than do their lesser skilled peers. Thus efforts to strengthen children's and adolescents' ability to understand conflict and to select nonviolent strategies for handling disagreements serve a protective role.

Strong connections to others can be protective as well. While this is true of families, it is also true of peers who hold prosocial values. Many studies have confirmed that a relationship with a caring adult enables youth to be resilient. Youth who are more religious also tend to be less involved with violence, although it seems to be more related to those connections and the sense of community faith can bring than specifically to the doctrine.

Family

Maintaining clear guidelines for children's behavior and consistent but fair discipline have been found to help nurture youth, who are less likely to be victimized or involved in violence. Students who perceive that their families have high expectations for them in terms of school achievement are less involved with violence, as are those who spend time in quality activities with their caretakers. The simple but consistent presence of a caretaker in the morning, when arriving home from school, during mealtimes, or at bedtime can help protect youth (CDC, 2013).

Thompson and Bynum (2013) have identified eight primary things families can do to prevent youth delinquency: (1) Provide clearly defined roles within the family so that youth feel valuable, not marginalized; (2) make sure that children and youth have opportunities for meaningful discussion and that they participate in family decisions and interactions; (3) supervise children and adolescents; (4) provide clear rules and consistent discipline; (5) provide a stable home environment; (6) offer love, affection, and concern; (7) be aware that socialization occurs constantly and through a number of mediums (i.e., what we say, how we behave, what is in our media); and (8) develop a strong social bond.

Both families and schools can help youth understand the differences between media and reality. Families can limit the amount of screen time of children and adolescents as well as monitor the types of music, videogames, television, and films they are consuming. Additionally, parents and guardians can help engage youth in conversations about media and its effects.

School

Schools that have high expectations for students, provide opportunities for involvement in the classroom, and are supportive and caring can promote competence and protect against the effects of adverse conditions. School-based research indicates that teacher support and student connection and involvement with school can protect against the effects of difficult conditions. Mentoring programs that couple youth with successful older students or community members can reduce misbehavior, enhance students' self-esteem, and increase students' school performance. Schools that help students set realistic and achievable career goals are best suited to remain free of violence.

The safest schools are those in which attention is paid to both physical and affective elements. Safe school climates ensure that LGBT students are supported. One way to do this is to establish a Gay Straight Alliance (GSA). More than 4,000 schools across the United States have GSAs, which have been found to reduce the amount of homophobic comments and decrease the harassment and assault of LGBT students. Allowing youth opportunities for prosocial involvement is an essential component of a safe school climate. Supporting student clubs and extracurricular activities allows youth to share their passions and to develop leadership skills. According to the National Association of School Psychologists (2013), effective school discipline (1) is designed to teach and instruct; (2) focuses not on what went wrong but on how to improve behavior; (3) directly connects misbehaviors to consequences; (4) is coordinated privately rather than as a public means of embarrassment; and (5) never involves name-calling, shouting, berating, or other disrespect.

Schools can include a number of curricular elements that help prevent violence. Critical media literacy helps to engage students in dialogue and reflection about violence in media and about the dangerous and demeaning narratives often used.

Comprehensive school safety plans also include teaching youth about safe technology use, including using privacy protections; always logging out of their e-mail, chat room, and social networking sites; and posting only "PG" photos on social networking sites. Hinduja and Patchin (2010) also recommend that schools remind students about safe technology usage through posters and other signage at computer labs and to ensure that school bullying policies cover this form of harassment. If cyberbullying either occurs at school or originates off campus but has an effect on the learning climate, school districts are legally liable to intervene.

Many schools also incorporate some type of bullying prevention program. One bullying prevention program that is receiving attention from empirical researchers specifically at the elementary and middle school level is the Olweus Bullying Prevention Program (OBPP). The OBPP is a comprehensive, school-wide program that was designed to reduce bullying and achieve better peer relations among students in elementary, middle, and junior high school grades. Studies that have evaluated the OBPP in diverse settings in the United States have not been uniformly consistent, but they have shown that the OBPP has had a positive impact on students' self-reported involvement in bullying and antisocial behavior. The best bullying prevention efforts teach youth about bullying but also inspire them to help disrupt it. Bystander prevention approaches teach young people not as would-be bullies or would-be victims but rather as individuals who will likely witness bullying and thus can play an active role in stopping it. Bystander intervention programs empower both youth and educators to disrupt bullying when they see it. The key is that each individual realizes that he or she is a member of a community and thus must take an active role in ensuring that the community is safe for all. It is an essential component of community building that can ensure that a school climate is welcoming and safe for all students.

Dating violence education, which often discusses sexual harassment as well, is another important curricular addition that can prevent school violence. A number of organizations have developed curricula about healthy relationships that the CDC recognizes as best practices. These are listed in the recommended resources.

A growing body of research shows that schools that have adopted peace education into their curriculum experience less violence. Although it originally emerged as an educational response to war and violence, peace education today involves teaching about the dangers of violence (from interpersonal violence to international conflicts), as well as about what has been called structural violence, or violence that is perpetrated through the way that institutions and societies are structured. This might include addressing poverty as a form of violence. Further, peace education is concerned not just with teaching youth about alternatives to violence but also with inspiring them to apply these alternatives in their daily lives. Carr and Porfilio (2012) explain that peace educators seek to develop "a culture of peace not only to prevent the calamity and devastation caused by war, but also to create more just and sustainable societies where there is some level economic and social security for all citizens" (pp. 5–6). Peace educators typically use alternative teaching methods that are more egalitarian, such as group projects, dialogues, and service-learning. One of the pioneers of peace education was Maria Montessori, known best for the educational philosophy that bears her name, who believed that schools should and could play powerful roles in countering hate. Peace educators also advocate for whole-school approaches in which disciplinary practices, extracurricular activities, and other efforts outside of the classroom also reinforce the importance of nonviolence, respect, and acceptance.

In sum, research has identified five factors that are important in the development of a positive and safe school climate: (1) Collaborative leadership, meaning schools in which administrators work with students, faculty, and the community to determine what is best; (2) teacher collaboration, or the degree to which teachers are afforded opportunities and encouraged to work together; (3) professional development, which involves opportunities for continued educational opportunities for teachers and staff; (4) collegial support, or the degree to which all in the school work towards a common vision and common goals; and (5) learning partnerships, or the involvement of parents and community members.

Community

Although schools cannot necessarily rid communities of gangs, they are ideally suited to incorporate gang prevention efforts into their curricula. One such program is Gang Resistance Education and Training (G.R.E.A.T.), which was developed in 1991. The 13-week school-based curriculum implemented by trained law enforcement officers focuses on life skills as well as myths and realities about gangs. Research has found it to result in lowered levels of victimization, more negative views about gangs, more positive views of police, and reductions in risk-seeking behaviors among students who completed the program.

Other community programs that offer youth a chance to voice their concerns and to be respected and valued can help protect against school violence. This might involve arts-based efforts, service opportunities, and other efforts to allow youth to be active agents in their communities.

Drawing on these risk and protective factors, the next section offers an assessment of some of the most common efforts to respond to and prevent school violence.

Interventions

Anonymous Tip Lines

Many studies have shown that school shooters typically plan their attack and tell others in advance. In a 2002 study that analyzed 41 school shooters, the U.S. Secret Service found that in almost every case the assailants had told someone they planned to attack, typically a peer. Yet these individuals tend not to tell authorities, which could potentially prevent the shooting. Some do not tell because they do not believe their peer is serious, but many do not because they fear repercussions were they to "snitch" on a classmate. Many school districts instituted anonymous tip lines after the 1999 Columbine massacre. While it is not clear how many incidents these lines have averted, authorities believe they have definitely helped. Further, these tip lines can be used to report bullying behaviors in a way that ensures that bullies will not know who reported them and thus cannot retaliate.

Profiling

As a result of the attention paid to the school shootings in the mid-to-late 1990s, many school districts began to wonder whether there was a specific profile of assailants that might prove useful. Indeed, the fact that most school shooters were white males who had been bullied seemed to suggest that a description of the type of student who might commit a major attack at school was possible. After media attention to the notion that Columbine killers Harris and Klebold were members of the "Trenchcoat Mafia," which was a clique that allegedly wore dark clothes and presented as "goths," schools began to target these students as potential shooters. Yet according to the FBI, the American Psychological Association, and other expert bodies, profiling can be dangerously limiting. Instead, they assert that educators and parents should look out for warning signs that a youth is troubled and might act out in school.

According to the Center for the Study and Prevention of Violence (n.d.), the following principles should be followed when seeking to identify early warning signs:

- Develop caring, supportive relationships with students.
- DO NO HARM.
- Understand violence and aggression within a context.
- Avoid stereotypes such as those regarding race, socioeconomic status, academic ability, and appearance.
- View warning signs within a developmental context.
- Understand that children typically exhibit multiple signs (do not overreact to one single sign).

Warning signs include:

- Social withdrawal
- Excessive feelings of isolation and being alone
- Excessive feelings of rejection
- Being a victim of violence
- Feelings of being picked on and persecuted
- Low school interest and poor academic performance
- Expression of violence in writings and drawings
- Uncontrolled anger
- Patterns of impulsive and chronic hitting, intimidating and bullying behaviors
- History of discipline problems
- Past history of violent and aggressive behavior
- Intolerance for differences and prejudicial attitudes
- Drug use and alcohol use
- Affiliation with gangs
- Inappropriate access to, possession, of and us of firearms
- Serious threats of violence (http://www.colorado.edu/cspv/publications/factsheets/safeschools/FS-SC06.pdf)

Dress Codes and Uniforms

Many schools have implemented dress codes as a way to create a safe and orderly school environment. Dress codes range from simple prohibitions on specific logos or inappropriate images and phrases to actual clothing requirements. President Bill Clinton encouraged schools to enact dress codes in his 1996 State of the Union speech. Proponents assert that school dress codes increase student self-esteem, increase attendance, reduce dropout rates, enhance school unity, reduce violence, and decrease discrimination based on social class. Many were enacted specifically to address gang-related violence and thus prohibit certain colors or common gang-affiliated apparel, like bandanas. Some 89 percent of the schools surveyed in a 2006 study (Bureau of Justice Statistics, 2011) stated that the prevention of gang-related activity was their primary motive for implementing a dress code policy. Court decisions have generally supported schools that have enacted dress codes, with the exception of students who are expressing legitimate political views through their clothing choices. In *Tinker v. Des Moines* in 1969, the Supreme Court allowed student free expression that does not create a "material or substantial disruption." Many districts allow parents to vote on whether to implement dress code policies.

Research is mixed regarding whether dress codes achieve the purported results. While some schools have reported fewer disciplinary problems, others have noted an increase in student suspensions for dress code violations but no real change in school atmosphere. Critics also contend that dress codes and uniform policies restrict students' creativity in unnecessary ways and that these may be tied to racial or other biases. For instance, a seven-year-old girl was repeatedly reprimanded for wearing her hair in dreadlocks, which school officials deemed distracting and were explicitly prohibited in the school dress code. Her parents eventually moved her to a different school.

Metal Detectors

After the series of suburban school shootings in the mid-to-late 1990s, many schools added metal detectors in the hopes of identifying youth who were bringing weapons to campus and deterring students from doing so. Many urban districts that had long histories of violence, largely the result of gang conflicts, had been using metal detectors for years. Metal detectors are still most common in urban schools, with about 12 percent of high schools, 9 percent of middle schools, and 2 percent of elementary schools having metal detectors on campus. Schools may install the large walk-through detectors commonly associated with prisons, courthouses, and airports. These are expensive, however, so some schools employ security guards with hand-held metal-detecting wands. Proponents maintain that because people are relatively accustomed to metal detectors they are not excessively invasive. The Supreme Court has never heard a challenge to the constitutionality of school-based metal detectors, but lower courts have tended to affirm them as administrative in nature and thus not technically a search that would raise Fourth Amendment issues. An additional concern is that the installation of metal detectors, as well as other technological measures like video cameras and the hiring of school resource or police officers, makes schools feel more like prisons.

Data do not show that metal detectors are particularly helpful in deterring students from bringing weapons on school grounds. One issue is that there are generally many ways for students to get around being scanned by the metal detector. Most schools do not have them at every possible entrance, which means students who are committed to bringing a weapon to campus can enter where the detectors are not. If students can only access one entrance that does have a metal detector, schools face the problem of having a bottleneck at the start of the day, as students typically arrive to school in a tight window of time before the start of classes. Some schools address this issue by randomly searching students, but generally they resort to searching students via some pattern, such as every third person, which is fairly easy to identify. Additionally, research has shown that in districts that have had problems with weapons, installing a metal detector might be useful. However, when schools install them due to fear and not to actual necessity, research suggests it makes students feel more fearful. Some have also noted that metal detector searches are often the catalyst for more invasive searches due to noncontraband triggers, such as jewelry. Further, several of the school shootings have occurred in schools where there was a metal detector, suggesting it is far from a fool-proof intervention.

Video Cameras

An increasing number of schools, especially high schools, have installed video cameras as a way to both deter offenders who might believe they are being watched as well as a means of apprehending those who have committed acts of crime and violence. Critics contend that the installation, upkeep, and monitoring of these cameras is not cost effective, given that students are quick to find ways around being captured on camera as well as the fact that those students who are most motivated to commit mass atrocities at school care little about being apprehended; indeed, that might be part of their motivation. Further, there is the concern that video cameras might be used to monitor other activities that are not in violation of school rules or state laws, such as the clock-in time of teachers.

Conflict Resolution and Peer Mediation

Conflict resolution in schools often takes the form of peer mediation. In peer mediation programs, schools train student mediators who help peers negotiate the resolution of their conflicts. Key to peer mediation is the respect for all parties' voices and needs, including the commitment to keep all interactions confidential. The first peer mediation program, Teaching Students to Be Peacemakers, began in the 1960s. Today, there are a number of great peer mediation programs, including the widely acclaimed Peace Pals. Generally, peer mediation programs consist of six steps: (1) Disputants agree to meet with a peer mediator; (2) peer mediators listens to all disputants; (3) peer mediators help disputants find shared interests; (4) all parties brainstorm win–win options; (5) all parties evaluate all the options; and (6) all disputants agree to a resolution. Peer mediation recognizes that it is the disputants themselves who need to come to some kind of common ground and that when a mutual agreement is determined it is more likely to succeed. According to evaluation research, schools with peer mediation programs report fewer physical fights among students and reductions in disciplinary problems. Critics contend that peer mediation cannot address all types of conflict and thus is only suited to address the most minor issues. Some claim that the training for these programs is inadequate and that peer mediators are not fully capable of solving many disputes. Some dislike peer mediators, seeing them as "favorites" or "snitches." Some disputants may simply go through the motions of peer mediation as a way to avoid a tougher sanction. In order to coordinate a successful peer mediation program, both teachers and students should receive ongoing training, ideally starting in elementary school.

Peaceable Schools

As noted earlier, peace education is even more effective in creating a positive school climate when it is embraced school-wide. Some have referred to such school-wide efforts as peaceable schools. One such initiative is the Resolving Conflict Creatively Program (RCCP), which seeks to increase students' emotional intelligence, or their self-awareness, self-control, self-motivation, empathy, and social competence. RCCP began in 1985 in the New York Public Schools. It includes curriculum for elementary and secondary schools that focuses on de-escalating violence and promoting respect for others through the use of role-plays, brainstorming activities, and discussion. It also includes a peer mediation program in which students mediate sessions involving conflict between their peers, helping the disputants to reach a mutually agreeable solution. Finally, RCCP includes training for classroom teachers and parent training components. Schools that use RCCP have reported less violence in classrooms, improvements in children's self-esteem, and more caring and accepting behaviors among students. Peaceable schools, then, help build both the intellectual and emotional capacity of students, faculty, and staff. They are schools in which all feel valued and all have an opportunity to share their ideas and concerns.

Restorative Justice

Restorative justice is an alternative to retributive justice. A retributive system, also known as an adversarial system, focuses on punishing offenders. In contrast, restorative justice aims to use cooperative and participatory practices to hold offenders accountable, to give voice to victims, and to repair the harm that was the result of the offense. Through facilitated dialogue, victims, offenders, and community members identify what happened, who was impacted and how, and what should be done about it in a way that will allow the offender to reintegrate into the community rather than be stigmatized and ostracized. Many schools have begun to integrate restorative practices in their disciplinary procedures. Some do so through teen courts in which youth coordinate the disciplinary hearings and collectively determine appropriate sanctions and reparations. Research has shown that restorative practices are effective because they involve all affected parties in identifying solutions.

School Police Officers

School districts have increasingly employed police officers, often called school resource officers (SROs) as a means of increasing school safety. The idea is that not only will officers on campus deter youth from engaging in violent or illegal behavior but that if an incident does occur it can be immediately handled. Further, advocates of SROs maintain that their presence on school grounds can help students see law enforcement as helpful rather than with the animosity that so often characterizes teen–police relations. SROs are typically sworn police officers whose positions are often secured through federal funds. Thousands of schools, mostly middle and high schools but some elementary schools as well, have SROs. In light of the Newtown, Connecticut, school shooting the Obama administration has proposed an increase in the number of officers in schools, pledging $45 million for an additional 356 new officers. Data are unclear as to whether having officers on campus deters students from acting violently. Advocates like the National Rifle Association (NRA) cite examples such as when a Mississippi assistant principal got a gun from his truck and disarmed a student who had killed two classmates in 1997 and when a SRO in 2001 wounded and arrested a California student who had opened fire with a shotgun.

Yet critics say the most obvious effect of having police on campus is that more children and youth are being arrested, often for minor and nonviolent behavior like cursing at teachers. Black students, Hispanic students, and youth with disabilities are overrepresented in those whose minor misbehavior is now being handled by law enforcement instead of schools. In Texas, police officers based in schools wrote more than 100,000 misdemeanor tickets in 2012 alone.

Further, some maintain that law enforcement officers are ill equipped to respond to students in need of mental health attention. Because police are not trained in fields such as education and developmental psychology, decisions such as whether to arrest a student rely solely on legal criteria.

One difficulty lies in differentiating between school discipline and criminal matters. This is particularly problematic in regards to school searches. School police often search students with far less than probable cause, and the evidence of those searches then gets used in criminal proceedings against the youth. TIPS is the general criteria for distinguishing when an officer can conduct a search in school. The "T" stands for the thing or contraband to be seized while the "I" refers to the information that prompted the search. These roughly correlate with the standard for school searches developed by the Supreme Court, which state that searches of students must be justified at their inception. The "P" refers to the place or location to be searched while the "S" is the search method employed. Together, the "P" and "S" relate to the intrusiveness of the search. Countless examples, however, suggest that school-based police officers are using the lesser "reasonable suspicion" standard the Supreme Court upheld for schools and not the probable cause standard that is required outside of a school setting. A 2011 longitudinal study of 470 schools nationwide examined school safety over a period of years (2003–2004, 2005–2006, and 2007–2008) during which police officers were added to some schools but not others over time. The researchers found "no evidence suggesting that [SROs] or other sworn law-enforcement officers contribute to school safety. That is, for no crime type was an increase in the presence of police significantly related to decreased crime rates. The preponderance of evidence suggests that, to the contrary, more crimes involving weapons possession and drugs are recorded in schools that add police officers than in similar schools that do not."

Canine Searches

Schools across the United States rely on random canine searches as a way of detecting contraband, usually drugs but occasionally weapons and bombs. In *United States v. Place* (462 U.S. 696 [1983]), the U.S. Supreme Court held that a canine sniff is not actually a search and thus no probable cause or even reasonable suspicion is required to bring dogs to a scene, including schools. However, a recent Court decision determined that canine detections are indeed searches, although it is unclear whether that decision, which involved an incident on private property, is applicable to schools. While proponents maintain that these random searches serve to deter youth from bringing drugs or weapons to campus, critics contend that the use of dogs accompanied by police in SWAT gear creates fear and disrupts the educational climate more than it helps. Because previous court decisions have established that the canines cannot sniff people, students have learned that if they keep contraband in their pockets it is unlikely to be detected. Most concerning, though, is the fact that the canines are not always effective at identifying illicit items but are a costly investment. Further, use of canines, coupled with video cameras, lockdown searches, metal detectors, ID badges, and the increasing presence of police on campus, has prompted comparisons between schools and prisons. As Mari McLean, cited in *Educate, Medicate, or Litigate?* explained, "When students view schools as prisons and teachers and administrators as guards and wardens, they will begin to behave more like prisoners than students, and violence in the schools will become its own self-fulfilling prophecy" (DiGuilio, 2001, p. 215).

Zero Tolerance Laws

Rooted in the concept known as the broken windows thesis, which states that low-level problems cause citizens to disengage in their communities and thus allow greater opportunity for offending, zero tolerance laws aim to crack down on specific offenses with the idea that it will deter additional acts. The idea became popular in the 1990s as a result of scares about school violence and predictions of a coming wave of "superpredator" teens. Although data does not bear out that there was a surge in violent crime perpetrated by youth, zero tolerance laws remain in effect in many places. The 1990 Gun-Free School Zones Act required students to expel students for no less than a year if they brought weapons to school. Later, the 1994 Gun-Free Schools Act provided funds to schools to enact mandatory minimum policies for specific offenses. All 50 states have since added zero tolerance laws, with most addressing weapons, drugs, and alcohol. Most state laws also have some more vague references to "persistent disobedience" or "disrespect." Lee (2014) argues that thousands of preschoolers are suspended each year for zero tolerance violations and that the overrepresentation of boys, and particularly minorities and those with disabilities, begins as early as preschool.

Supporters contend that zero tolerance laws help keep schools safe and drug-free, allowing educators to focus on teaching. Critics note the many problems with zero tolerance laws, arguing that they disproportionately impact minority youth and youth with disabilities; that they fail to address the root problems that prompt youth to bring weapons, drugs, or alcohol to campus; and that instead of helping troubled youth change their ways, zero tolerance laws simply expel the problem to the community. Further, suspension or expulsion dramatically increase the likelihood that a young person will have some type of interaction with the criminal or juvenile justice systems. This is what criminologists refer to as "widening the net," or expanding the chance that troubled youth will be handled by criminal or juvenile justice instead of school or other informal methods of social control. Many have argued that the "school-to-prison pipeline" begins with zero tolerance laws. The American Bar Association has called on districts to remove their zero tolerance laws and develop alternatives like in-school suspension and counseling.

Many studies have documented the disproportionate impact of zero tolerance laws on youth of color. Most recently, a study by the U.S. Department of Justice and the U.S. Department of Education about racial disparity and zero tolerance led both agencies to urge districts to scale back or repeal their laws. The study found that African American males are three times more likely to be suspended or expelled than white males and that African Americans make up 35 percent of students suspended once, 44 percent of those suspended more than once, and 36 percent of students expelled. Further, more than 50 percent of students who were involved in school-related arrests or referred to law enforcement are Hispanic or African American. Researchers stated that the disparities were not related to disproportionate offending but instead to racial bias.

Other Laws

No federal law specifically addresses bullying. A number of laws, however, are applicable in that they address other forms of discriminatory behavior. Federal civil rights laws require schools to address behaviors like bullying, harassment, and hazing when they are severe, pervasive, or persistent; create a hostile environment at school; or are based on a student's race, color, national origin, sex, disability, or religion. Schools that fail to respond appropriately may be in violation of one or more of these federal civil rights laws: Title IV and Title VI of the Civil Rights Act of 1964, Title IX of the Education Amendments of 1972, Section 504 of the Rehabilitation Act of 1973, Titles II and III of the Americans with Disabilities Act, and the Individuals with Disabilities Education Act (IDEA).

Many states added bullying laws in the 1990s and 2000s. As of March 2014, every state except Montana has some type of anti-bullying legislation, although Montana does have an anti-bullying policy. Bully Police, a bullying watchdog organization, identifies 12 elements of effective anti-bullying laws:

1. Use the word "bully" in the actual text of the bill, law, or policy

2. Clearly prohibit bullying rather than addressing school safety in general terms

3. Explicitly define bullying and harassment while ensuring that anyone can be a victim

4. Include recommendations for making model school policy

5. Involve all stakeholders, including students, educators, administrators, guidance counselors, and parents, in the creation of the law

6. Mandate, not suggest, the implementation of anti-bullying educational programs

7. Include a timeline for implementation

8. Incorporate protection against reprisal and retaliation

9. Protect schools against lawsuits if they implement and follow a good policy

10. Include provision of counseling for victims

11. Require the submission of accountability reports and authorizes consequences for districts that do not comply

12. Specifically include cyberbullying.

Using these criteria, Bully Police assigns states grades for their anti-bullying laws. As of May 2013, three states had C or below grades (Minnesota, Mississippi, and Louisiana), with Montana receiving an F grade for its lack of anti-bullying laws. New Jersey, Michigan, Texas, Virginia, Kentucky, Delaware, North Dakota, Florida, Massachusetts, Georgia, Maryland, New Hampshire, and Wyoming were given grades of A++ for their laws.

The U.S. Department of Health and Human Services has identified 11 key components of anti-bullying laws:

1. A purpose statement that outlines the detrimental effects of bullying on students, teachers, and the overall educational climate and that declares any form of bullying and harassment to be unacceptable.

2. A statement of scope, which delineates that the policy covers conduct that occurs on the school campus, at school-sponsored activities or events (regardless of the location), on school-provided transportation, or through school-owned technology or that otherwise creates a significant disruption to the school environment.

3. Clear specification of which conduct is prohibited in a manner consistent with other state and federal laws. The definition should include a nonexhaustive list of verbal and nonverbal behaviors as well as prohibit retaliation for reporting an incident and perpetuating bullying by forwarding messages or sharing hurtful and demeaning material. It is also important that the definition be written in a way that is easy for students, parents, and educators to understand.

4. Enumeration of specific characteristics, which "explains that bullying may include, but is not limited to, acts based

on actual or perceived characteristics of students who have historically been targets of bullying, and provides examples of such characteristics." Laws should also specify that bullying may not be based on a particular characteristic, however.

5. Development and implementation of local educational administration (LEA) policies. LEAs should work with all stakeholders to create and implement anti-bullying policies specific to local needs.

6. Components of LEA policies, which should include definitions of bullying, requirements and procedures for reporting it, processes for investigating and responding to incidents, the keeping of written records, a graduated range of consequences and sanctions, and appropriate referrals for victims, perpetrators, and others.

7. Review of local policies, including provisions for the state to review local policies regularly to ensure compliance with state and federal laws.

8. A communication plan that details how students, staff, and parents will be notified of policies and consequences related to bullying.

9. Training and preventive education, including a provision for school districts to train all school staff on preventing, identifying, and responding to bullying as well as encouraging school districts to implement age-appropriate school- and community-wide anti-bullying programs.

10. Transparency and monitoring, including a provision for LEAs to report annually to the state the number of bullying incidents and the responses taken and for making aggregate data about bullying publicly available while maintaining student privacy.

11. Statement of rights to other legal recourse, which articulates that victims can pursue legal remedies outside of the school district.

As of February 2014, 19 states still do not specifically include cyberbullying in their anti-bullying legislation. Legislation has been proposed in several other states.

Many states also have legislation requiring dating violence education. As of March 2014, 21 states require some form of dating violence education. Legislation is pending in four other states. For examples, Delaware's Vol. 77 Del. Laws Chap. 357 "Requires school districts and charter schools to establish a policy on responding to Teen Dating Violence and Sexual Assault, including guidelines on mandatory reporting and confidentiality, a protocol for responding to incidents of Teen Dating Violence and Sexual Assault and training on the issue." The law also requires school districts and charter schools to add comprehensive healthy relationship programming as part of the student health classes."

Forty-four states have hazing laws, although many of these laws only specify that hazing is prohibited and that are sanctions for violation. Ideally, hazing prevention would be included as well.

One federal bill under consideration is the Safe Schools Improvement Act (SSIA). The bill was introduced in the House of Representatives by Democratic Representative Linda Sanchez (CA) and in the Senate by Senator Bob Casey (PA). SSIA would require that states and school districts develop comprehensive anti-bullying and harassment policies that include all students. Schools would be required to report incidents of bullying and harassment to their state departments of education so that additional improvements can be made.

Further, SSIA would require that teachers and other personnel receive professional development related to these issues. When educators and administrators know how to create classroom and school climates in which all students feel safe and welcomed, it can only result in a better educational experience, one in which all youth can live up to their true potential.

Conclusion

As is clear from the material presented in this chapter, school violence affects many parties. Further, there are myriad theoretical explanations for why it occurs, all of which can be used by educators, politicians, and others to develop the most effective responses, while a better understanding of the individual, family, school, and community-level risk and protective factors is helpful in devising prevention programs. It is imperative that educators, policy-makers, and parents understand the benefits and limitations of existing approaches as they seek to implement cost-effective measures that affirm the worth and dignity of all.

Further Reading

Ackers, M. (2012). Cyberbullying: Through the Eyes of Children and Young People. *Educational Psychology in Practice, 28*(2), 141–57.

American Psychiatric Association (APA). (2000). *Diagnostic and Statistical Manual of Mental Disorders*, 4th ed., text rev. (DSM-IV-TR). Washington, DC: Author.

American Psychological Association. (2013). Violence in the Media: Psychologists Study TV and Video Game Violence for Potential Harmful Effects. Retrieved May 28, 2014, from http://www.apa.org/research/action/protect.aspx

Aronson, E. (2001). *Nobody Left to Hate.* New York: Holt.

Balfour, S. (Ed.) (2005). *How Can School Violence Be Prevented?* Farmington Hills, MI: Greenhaven.

Bazelon, E. (2013). *Sticks and Stones: Defeating the Culture of Bullying and Rediscovering the Power of Empathy.* New York: Random House.

Bellini, J. (2001). *Child's Prey.* New York: Pinnacle.

Benbenishty, R., & Astor, R. (2005). *School Violence in Context: Culture, Neighborhood, Family, School, and Gender.* Oxford, UK: Oxford University Press.

Blanchard, K. (2003). *How to Talk to Your Kids about School Violence.* New York: Onomatopoeia.

Brady Center to Prevent Gun Violence. (2004). On Target: The Impact of the 1994 Federal Assault Weapon Act. Retrieved May 27, 2014, from http://www.waveedfund.org/sites/waveedfund.org/files/on_target.pdf

Brady, N. (2011). Student Perceptions of High-Security School Environments. *Youth & Society, 43*(1), 365–95.

Brezina, C. (2000). *Deadly School and Campus Violence.* New York: Rosen Publishing.

Bureau of Justice Statistics. (2011). *Indicators of School Crime and Safety: 2011.* Retrieved May 28, 2014, from http://www.bjs.gov/content/pub/pdf/iscs11.pdf

Burns, R., & Crawford, C. (1999). School Shootings, the Media, and Public Fear: Ingredients for a Moral Panic. *Crime, Law & Social Change, 32,* 147–69.

Bushman, B., & Anderson, C. (2009). Comfortably Numb: Desensitizing Effects of Violent Media on Helping Others. *Association for Psychological Science, 20*(3), 273–77.

Carr, P., & Porfilio, B. (Eds). (2012). *Educating for Peace in a Time of "Permanent War."* New York: Routledge.

Casella, R. (2001). *At Zero Tolerance: Punishment, Prevention, and School Violence.* New York: Peter Lang.

Casella, R. (2001). *"Being Down": Challenging Violence in Urban Schools.* New York: Teachers College.

CDC. (2013). School Violence: Risk and Protective Factors. Retrieved May 28, 2014, from http://www.cdc.gov/violenceprevention/youthviolence/schoolviolence/risk.html

Center for the Study and Prevention of Violence. (n.d.). Fact Sheet: Early Warning Signs. Retrieved May 28, 2014, from http://www.colorado.edu/cspv/publications/factsheets/safeschools/FS-SC06.pdf

Chalmers, P. (2009). *Inside the Mind of a Teen Killer.* Nashville, TX: Thomas Nelson.

Chambliss, W. (1988). The Saints and the Roughnecks. In Henslin, J. (Ed.), *Down to Earth Sociology,* 5th ed. (pp. 188–202). New York: The Free Press.

Cianciotti, J., & Cahill, S. (2012). *LGBT Youth in America's Schools.* Ann Arbor, MI: University of Michigan Press.

Clark-Flory, T. (2010, April 8). Phoebe Prince's Bullies Get Bullied. *Salon.* Retrieved May 5, 2010, from http://www.salon.com/life/broadsheet/2010/04/08/phoebe_prince_bullies_get_bullied

Clete, S., Bailey, C., Carona, A., & Mebane, D. (2002). School Crime Policy Changes: The Impact of Recent Highly-Publicized School Crimes. *American Journal of Criminal Justice, 26,* 269–88.

Coloroso, B. (2003). *The Bully, the Bullied, and the Bystander: From Preschool to High School—How Parents and Teachers Can Help Break the Cycle of Violence.* New York: HarperCollins.

Conn, K. (2004). *Bullying and Harassment: A Legal Guide for Educators.* Alexandria, VA: Association for Supervision and Curriculum Development.

Cornell, D. (2006). *School Violence: Fears versus Facts.* Lawrence Erlbaum & Associates.

Dahl, M. (2014, April 1). It's Not Just "Drama": Bullying Happens to Popular Teens, Too. *Today.* Retrieved April 1, 2014, from http://www.today.com/health/its-not-just-drama-bullying-happens-popular-teens-too-2D79463459

Davey, M., & Harris, G. (2005, March 26). Family Wonders if Prozac Prompted School Shootings. *New York Times.* Retrieved April 14, 2010, from http://www.nytimes.com/2005/03/26/national/26shoot.html

Delaney-Black, V., Covington, C., Ondersma, S., Nordstrom-Klee, B., Templin, T., Ager, J., Janisse, J., & Sokol, R. J. (2002). Violence Exposure, Trauma and IQ and/or Reading Deficits among Urban Children. *Archives of Pediatric Medicine, 156,* 280–85.

DeNies, Y. (2012, March 16). Should Your Child Be Spanked at School? In 19 States It's Legal. *ABC News.* Retrieved March 31, 2014, from http://abcnews.go.com/US/spanking -school-19-states-corporal-punishment-legal/story? id=15932135

DeWitt, P. (2012). *Dignity for All: Safeguarding LGBT students.* New York: Corwin.

DiGuilio, R. (2001). *Educate, Medicate, or Litigate? What Teachers, Parents, and Administrators Must Do about Student Behavior.* New York: Corwin Books.

Dupre, A. (2009). *Speaking Up: The Unintended Costs of Free Speech in Schools.* Cambridge, MA: Harvard University Press.

Early Warning Signs. (2000). Center for the Study and Prevention of School Violence. Retrieved April 1, 2014, from http://www.colorado.edu/cspv/publications/factsheets/ safeschools/FS-SC06.pdf

Eaton, D., Kann, L., Kinchen, S., Shanklin, S., Flint, K., Hawkins, J., Harris, W., Lowry, R., McManus, T., Chyen, D., Whittle, L., Lim, C., & Wheschler, H. (2012, June 8). Youth Risk Behavior Surveillance—United States, 2011. Centers for Disease Control. Retrieved March 31, 2014, from http://www.cdc.gov/MMWR/PDF/SS/SS6 104.PDF

Eisler, R., & Miller, R. (Eds.) (2004). *Educating for a Culture of Peace.* Portsmouth, NH: Heinemann.

Englander, E. (2013). *Bullying and CyberBullying: What Every Educator Needs to Know.* Cambridge, MA: Harvard University Press.

Fanti, K., Vanman, E., Henrich, C., & Avraamides, M. (2009). Desensitization to Media Violence over a Short Period of Time. *Aggressive Behavior, 35*(2), 179–187.

Farmer, A. (2011, October 14). U.S: Protect Children with Disabilities from School Violence. *Human Rights Watch.* Retrieved April 1, 2014, from http://www.hrw.org/news/2011/10/14/us-protect-children-disabilities-school-violence

Fast, J. (2008). *Ceremonial Violence: A Psychological Explanation of School Shootings.* Overlook Press.

Fearnley, F. (2004). *I Wrote on All Four Walls: Teens Speak Out on Violence.* Toronto, Canada: Annick.

Finley, L. (2012). *Building a Better World: Creative Peace Education for the 21st Century.* Charlotte, NC: Information Age.

Finley, L. (Ed.). (2007). *Encyclopedia of Juvenile Violence.* Westport, CT: Greenwood.

Finley, L. (Ed.). (2011). *Encyclopedia of School Crime and Violence.* Santa Barbara, CA: ABC-CLIO.

Finley, L., & Finley, P. (2005). *Piss Off! How Drug Testing and Other Privacy Violations are Alienating America's Youth.* Monroe, ME: Common Courage.

Fox, J., & Burstein, H. (2010). *Violence and Security on Campus: From Preschool to College.* Westport, CT: Praeger.

Fried, S. (2003). *Bullies, Targets, and Witnesses: Helping Children Break the Pain Chain.* New York: M. Evans.

Galtung, J., & Udayakumar, S. (Eds.). (2011). *More Than a Curriculum: Education for Peace and Development.* Charlotte, NC: Information Age.

Gerler, E. (2004). *Handbook of School Violence.* Binghamton, NY: Haworth.

Goldberg, L. et al. (2003). Drug Testing Athletes to Prevent Substance Abuse: Background and Pilot Study Results of the

SATURN (Student Athletes Testing Using Random Notification) Study. *Journal of Adolescent Health, 32,* 16–25.

Goodstein, A. (2007). *Totally Wired: What Teens Are Really Doing Online.* New York: St. Martin's Press.

Greenberg, D. (1977). Delinquency and the Age Structure of Society. *Contemporary Crises, 1,* 189–223.

Guynn, K. L., & Aquila, F. D. (2005). *Hazing in High Schools: Causes and Consequences.* Bloomington, IN: Phi Delta Kappa Educational Foundation.

Harding, T. (2001). Fatal School Shootings, Liability, and Sovereign Immunity: Where Should the Line Be Drawn? *Journal of Law & Education, 30,* 162–70.

Hinduja, S. (2008). *Bullying Beyond the Schoolyard: Preventing and Responding to CyberBullying.* New York: Corwin.

Hinduja, S., & Patchin, J. (2010). Cyberbullying: Identification, Prevention, and Response. *Cyberbullying Research Center.* Retrieved May 28, 2014, from http://www.cyberbullying.us/Cyberbullying_Identification_Prevention_Response_Fact_Sheet.pdf

Holtham, J. (2009). *Taking Restorative Justice to Schools: A Doorway to Discipline.* Tulsa, OK: Homestead Press.

Hunnicutt, S. (Ed.) (2006). *School Shootings.* Farmington Hills, MI: Greenhaven.

Hyman, I., & Snook, P. (1999). *Dangerous Schools.* San Francisco: Jossey-Bass.

Katz, A. (2012). *Cyberbullying and E-Safety: What Educators and Other Professionals Need to Know.* Philadelphia, PA: Jessica Kingsley Publications.

Kellner, D. (2008). *Guys and Guns Amok: Domestic Terrorism and School Shootings from the Oklahoma City Bombing to the Virginia Tech Massacre.* New York: Paradigm.

Kimmel, M. (2009). *Guyland: The Perilous World Where Boys Become Men.* New York: Parker.

Kindlon, D. (2007). *Alpha Girls: Understanding the New American Girl and How She Is Changing the World.* New York: Rodale.

King, M. (2014). *School Violence: Crisis and Opportunity.* CreateSpace Independent Publishing Platform.

Klein, J. (2013). *Bully Society: School Shootings and the Crisis of Bullying in America's Schools.* Albany, NY: New York University Press.

Kohn, A. (2005). *Shooters: Myths and Realities of America's Gun Cultures.* New York: Oxford University Press.

Kowalski, R., Limber, S., & Agatston, P. (2007). *Cyber Bullying: Bullying in the Digital Age.* Malden, MA: Wiley-Blackwell.

Langman, P. (2009). *Why Kids Kill: Inside the Minds of School Shooters.* New York: Palgrave Macmillan.

Lawrence, R. (2006). *School Crime and Juvenile Justice*, 2nd edition. New York: Oxford.

Lemert, E. (1951). *Social Pathology: Systematic Approaches to the Study of Sociopathic Behavior.* New York: McGraw-Hill.

Lieberman, J. (2008). *School Shootings: What Every Parent and Educator Needs to Know to Protect Our Children.* Yucca Valley, CA: Citadel.

Lin, J., Brantmeier, E., & Bruhn, C. (2008). *Transforming Education for Peace.* Charlotte, NC: Information Age Publishing.

Lipsett, A. (2007, June 18). Eight Out of Ten Disabled Children Bullied, Report Finds. *The Guardian* (UK). Retrieved April 1, 2014, from http://www.theguardian.com/education/2007/jun/18/schools.children

Messerschmidt, J. (2000). *Nine Lives: Adolescent Masculinities, the Body, and Violence.* Boulder, CO: Westview Press.

Meyer, E. (2009). *Gender, Bullying, and Harassment: Strategies to End Sexism and Homophobia in Schools.* New York, NY: Teachers College Press.

Monaghan, T., & Torres, R. (Eds.). (2009). *Schools under Surveillance: Cultures of Control in Public Education.* Rutgers, NJ: Rutgers University Press.

Moore, M., Petrie, C., Braga, A., & McLaughlin, B. (Eds.). (2003). *Deadly Lessons: Understanding Lethal School Violence.* Washington, D.C: National Academies Press.

Mulrine, A. (1999). Once Bullied, Now Bullies, with Guns. *U.S. News and World Report, 126,* 24–26.

Murray, C. (1976). *The Link between Learning Disabilities and Juvenile Delinquency: Current Theory and Knowledge.* Washington, D.C: National Institute for Juvenile Justice and Delinquency Prevention.

National Association of School Psychologists. (2013). *A Framework for Safe and Effective Schools.* Retrieved May 28, 2014, from http://www.nasponline.org/resources/ handouts/Framework_for_Safe_and_Successful_School _Environments.pdf

Newman, K., Fox, C., Harding, D., Mehta, J., & Roth, W. (2004). *Rampage: The Social Roots of School Shootings.* New York: Basic.

Nuwer, H. (2000). *High School Hazing: When Rites Become Wrongs.* New York: FranklinWatts.

Nuwer, H. (2004). *The Hazing Reader.* Bloomington, IN: Indiana University Press.

Ollove, M. (2010, April 8). Bullying and Teen Suicide: How Do We Adjust School Climate? *Christian Science Monitor.* Retrieved May 28, 2014, from http://www.csmonitor.com/ USA/Society/2010/0428/Bullying-and-teen-suicide-How -do-we-adjust-school-climate

Olweus, D. (2004). *Bullying at School: What We Know and What We Can Do.* Cambridge, MA: Blackwell.

Orr, T. (2001). *Violence in Our Schools: Halls of Hope, Halls of Fear.* New York: Franklin Watts.

Padilla, F. (1992). *The Gang as an American Enterprise*. Chapel Hill, NC: Rutgers University Press.

Patchin, J., & Hinduja. S. (2013). *Words that Wound: Delete Cyberbullying and Make Kindness Go Viral*. Minneapolis, MS: Free Spirit Publishing.

Phillips, R., Linney, J., & Pack, C. (2008). *Safe School Ambassadors: Harnessing Student Power to Stop Bullying and Violence*. San Francisco, CA: Jossey-Bass.

Poor Diet Linked to Bad Behavior. (2004, November 22). *BBC News*. Retrieved May 28, 2014, from http://news.bbc.co.uk/2/hi/health/4032449.stm

Porter, S. (2013). *Bully Nation: Why America's Approach to Childhood Aggression Is Bad for Everyone*. St. Paul, MN: Paragon House.

Raloff, J. (2013). Teen Fighting May Harm IQ. *Student Science*. Retrieved April 1, 2014, from https://student.societyforscience.org/article/teen-fighting-may-harm-iq

Ramirez, X. (2011, November 7). National Study Reveals Striking Findings on School Sexual Harassment. *Care2*. Retrieved March 31, 2014, from http://www.care2.com/causes/national-study-reveals-striking-findings-on-school-sexual-harassment.html

Roberts, S., Zhang, J., Truman, J., & Snyder, T. (2012, February). *Indicators of School Crime and Safety: 2011*. Bureau of Justice Statistics. Retrieved March 31, 2014, from http://nces.ed.gov/pubs2012/2012002rev.pdf

Savage, D., & Miller, T. (2012). *It Gets Better: Coming Out, Overcoming Bullying, and Creating a Life Worth Living*. New York, NW: Plume Press.

Schier, H. (2008). *The Causes of School Violence*. Abdo Publishing.

Sexton-Radek, K. (2005). *Violence in Schools: Issues, Consequences, and Expressions*. Westport, CT: Praeger.

Shafii, M., & Shafii, S. (2000). *School Violence: Assessment, Management, Prevention.* Arlington, VA: American Psychiatric Publishing.

Simmons, R. (2002). *Odd Girl Out: The Hidden Culture of Aggression in Girls.* New York: Harcourt.

Snyder, M. (n.d.). Understanding Bullying and Its Impact on Kids with Disabilities or ADHD. *Great Schools.* Retrieved April 1, 2014, from http://www.greatschools.org/special -education/health/823-understanding-bullying-and-its -impact-on-kids-with-learning-disabilities-or-ad-hd.gs? page=all

Stevenson, L. (2003). *From the Inside Out: A Look into Teen Violence and Rebellion.* Authorhouse.

Stretsky, P., & Lynch, M. (2001). The Relationship between Lead Exposure and Homicide. *Archives of Pediatrics and Adolescent Medicine, 155*(5): 579–582.

Sykes, G., & Matza, D. (1957). Techniques of Neutralization: A Theory of Delinquency. *American Sociological Review, 22,* 664–670.

Thomas, R. (2006). *Violence in America's Schools: Understanding, Prevention, and Responses.* Rowman & Littlefield.

Thompson, W., & Bynum, J. (2012). *Juvenile Delinquency,* 9th ed. Upper Saddle River, NJ: Pearson.

Turk, W. (Ed.). (2004). *School Crime and Policing.* Upper Saddle River, NJ: Prentice Hall.

Twemlow, S., & Fonagy, P. (2005). The Prevalence of Teachers Who Bully Students in Schools with Differing Levels of Behavioral Problems. *American Journal of Psychiatry, 162,* 2387–90.

United States Secret Service and Department of Education. (2002). *The Final Report and Findings of the Safe School Initiative: Implications for the Prevention of School Attacks in the United States.* Retrieved May 28, 2014, from http://www.secretservice.gov/ntac/ssi_final_report.pdf

Vossekuil, B., Fein, R., Reddy, M., Borum, R., & Modzeleski, W. (2002). *The Final Report and Findings of the Safe School Initiative: Implications for the Prevention of School Attacks in the United States.* Jessup, MD: Education Publications Center, U.S. Department of Education.

Webber, J. (2003). *Failure to Hold: The Politics of School Violence.* Lanham, MD: Rowman & Littlefield.

Weill, S. (2002). *We're Not Monsters: Teens Speak Out about Teens in Trouble.* New York: HarperTempest.

Winslade, J., & Williams, M. (2011). *Safe and Peaceful Schools: Addressing Conflict and Eliminating Violence.* New York: Corwin.

Young, J., Ne'eman, A., & Geiser, S. (2011, March 9). Bullying and Students with Disabilities. *National Council on Disabilities.* Retrieved April 1, 2014, from http://www.ncd.gov/publications/2011/March92011

STOP BULLYING.
SAVE LIVES.
GARDEN STATE EQUALITY
.org
STOP BULLYING
SAVE LIVES
WMBC
4 NEW YORK

The essays in this chapter represent some of the best, most current, and most innovative thinking about the issue of school violence. Contributors include college students (Lashanti Jupp, Lauren Lorance, and Stephanie Wong), nonprofit leaders (Bob Knotts and Larenda Twigg), academics (Kelly Concannon), and long-time educators (Evelyn Jackson, Sarah Raitter, and De Palazzo). Each offers a personal viewpoint on the extent of school violence, the forms it takes, and how best we can respond. Further, these essays help shine a light on some of the many creative and effective conflict resolution, peace education, and youth-driven prevention programs.

A Student's Perspective on the Dangers of Bullying: Lashanti Jupp

My brother and I are twins, but we have always been very different. In our first year of high school, I automatically fit in with the "in crowd" whereas my brother was considered a loser and was picked on a lot. Most people simply referred to him as my brother and not even by his name. Some days he would be

---

Steve Goldstein, front left, with Garden State Equality, speaks to a gathering of people holding signs while they stand outside the New Jersey Statehouse on November 15, 2010, as lawmakers hold hearings inside regarding a bill that would toughen New Jersey's anti-bullying laws. (AP Photo/Mel Evans)

walking with his backpack on wheels and classmates would follow him around just kicking his bag because they thought it was funny. My bag had wheels as well, but they never bothered me. After my brother had enough of this, my mother finally got us backpacks. This did not help either; they would simply start tripping him down. They would even follow him down the stairs and "jokingly" push him. Everyone thought this was funny, and no one would say to stop except me. My brother hated that; he would always tell me to stay out of it and that he could handle it himself. I started avoiding my brother altogether, but I would still hear about it and witness the name calling in classes we had in common. The main thing they picked on him for was his crooked teeth, as if their teeth were so perfect (about a year later my mother got us braces). Sometimes I would chuckle at the jokes along with the class. I knew it was wrong, but he had already told me to stay out of it, and everyone else was laughing too. People began to forget that he was even my brother.

One day, a few guys in our grade decided that they would form a group for select male students only. One of my brother's few friends wanted to be in this group of "cool guys." The leader of the pack told my brother's friend that his initiation would be simple; all he had to do was slap my brother in the face. Giving into peer pressure, my brother's friend approached him and told him what was going on. Instead of saying that he wouldn't do it, he tried to ask my brother to just let him do it. My brother would not stand for this. One boy from the group of "cool guys" came over and informed my brother's friend that he was taking too long and decided, just for the fun of it, he would slap my brother to show him how it's done. This was the final straw for my brother. Being made fun of by everyone is one thing, but to be physically assaulted was a completely different story. My brother stood his ground and slapped the boy back. They began to slap each other back and forth. My brother's friend called a teacher, and the altercation stopped. When the principal began handling the matter, no one would come forth as a witness stating what really happened. The only people who would come forth told a story that made their friend look like the victim. The principal was very skeptical, given the reputation of these boys, so he dismissed the case altogether. My brother went down as being a snitch, and everyone in our grade began calling him names like "sissy," "punk," and "gay." Occasionally, they would ask him if he borrowed my underwear because he was such a "pussy" that he could only be my girl twin with short hair. I tried to stand up for him, but there is only so much I could do. He dealt with this until one day these same guys began to mess with his school bag. They would put garbage in it after recess or lunch and even go so far as to take the time to take everything out, turn it inside-out, and zip it back up so that it was impossible to re-open. During gym, they would get back to the changing room before him and try to hide pieces of his clothing. They would try to pants (pull down the pants and boxers of) each other, but my brother was the main target, kind of like the prize. My parents got involved, but that didn't make his life any easier. I recall my mother saying how another boy's mother informed the principal that she taught her son to hit back if he was ever hit—little did she know her son was the bully and not the victim. I think this never helped because everyone began to "see" what the guys were saying about him: that he was soft and couldn't stick up for himself. It always came down to my brother's word against them and the rest of the student body. The principal would never ask for my account because he felt like it would be biased. People began referring to my brother as a snitch. Eventually we all grew out of it; I can never really be sure why. I believe it was because my brother got involved in the sports teams and the other boys began to join after. They must have finally gotten to know my brother because it was almost like overnight there was peace in the corridors. My brother began to do music with one of his new friends toward our last year in high school, so now he's known as Juppo and, by default, I'm known as Juppo's sister. He now gets along with all of the "cool guys," and we choose not to speak about the dark times in high school.

When we reconnect with old school mates today, about nine years later, we are now equally known as the Jupp twins. Faculty members at the school remember us and the issues he went through and always commend my brother for being so resilient whenever the topic is brought up. He doesn't make much of it these days, and I know he doesn't stand for people being bullied, either. Some summer jobs he had would be as an assistant teacher in summer camps, and he inspires kids so much, especially the ones known as "rejects" in the group. He can be in a room full of kids that are segregated and bring them together in a heartbeat. I always think it's really funny how by the end of high school, my brother left being cooler than me.

Lashanti Jupp is an undergraduate student at Barry University, where she is studying marine biology. She serves as a resident assistant and is president of the Caribbean Student Association.

Reflections on Mean Girls: Lauren Lorance

A man once said, "One's dignity may be assaulted, vandalized and cruelly mocked, but it can never be taken away unless it is surrendered." This quote is so true. My story began the day I walked into my freshman year of high school. I was so enlightened and hopeful for all the new opportunities to come. Halfway through the year, though, my optimism changed. My experience with bullying opened my eyes to so much corruption, even within my own high school.

I never thought that I would be a victim of bullying, but I was. Let me give you a preview of my high school—rich, white families. If you did not meet this stereotype, people would judge you. There was clearly an "in" group and an "out" group. I was somewhere in the middle. Not only did students judge each other, but teachers and faculty judged students as well.

This certainly did not help my circumstances when I began getting bullied. It also did not help my circumstances that the bullying was all over a senior boy. I never felt like I brought this upon myself, though some might argue that I did. Victims of bullying should never feel like they deserved what happened to them, because they do not.

This senior boy deceived me. I was young and naive. I began seeing him and later found out that I was not the only one he was seeing. This other girl, a junior at the time who he was seeing, also knew about me before I knew about her. She began harassing me by sending me nasty text messages and voicemails and exposing me on social media. Then she became more aggressive. I remember one day in particular so vividly. She was a softball player. She and a few other girls from the softball team at my high school cornered me by my locker during a passing period. They did not touch me at this time, but they came really close. They were calling me awful names and threatening me. By this time, I knew I had to tell my parents. My mom insisted that we inform the school immediately when I told her, but I knew how stereotypical the faculty were at my school. Disregarding that factor, because my mom was hopeful the school would take action, she informed the school. The bullying still continued, and now even teachers and faculty looked at me differently. It made me feel even worse. I did not know who to turn to for help.

The ultimate bullying occurred at a party near campus. It was the weekend, and I was out with my friends. I knew that one girl and her sister, who was also bullying me at school, could potentially show up at this party, but my friends promised to have my back. But everything happened so fast. One minute I was standing by the stairs talking to one of my friends. Next thing I knew, I looked up and this girl was running towards me. The only place I could turn was to the stairs. I was set up. I turned around, and her sister was behind me. One of them held me down on the stairs so I could not move while the other girl punched me directly in the nose and gave me a bloody nose. My friend who I was talking to kicked the girl off of me and helped me outside.

After this incident, the school still did nothing. They told us that since it happened out of school they could not help—we would have to involve the police. My mom filed a police report and attempted to take these girls to court. All fell through, and the charges were dropped because we were all at a party and they would have to charge everyone with minor consumption. I never wanted to file any charges because it only caused me more struggle at school, but I wanted to share my story because if I had to do this all over, I would have walked away. If you are being harassed and bullied, keep your dignity. Be the bigger person and find the help you need. I did not know who to turn to back then, but now I know that there are many people who are passionate about bullying who would have been there to help.

To prevent bullying in school, most importantly, there needs to be more awareness. Along with more awareness, I think that faculty and staff need to be more available for help when bullying occurs. If students realize there is awareness and they are not alone, then students would see help available and maybe the issue could be resolved before it progresses. To stop this problem we need to come together for a better cause. Having more people involved will create awareness about bullying and stop the problem altogether.

Lauren Lorance is an undergraduate student at Barry University, where she is studying communications.

Sticks and Stones Can Break My Bones, but Names Will Never Hurt Me? Approaches to Language Mis(uses) in Schooling: Kelly Concannon

"You are so gay!"

"No homo."

"You are a pussy."

"What a faggot!"

"She's such a slut."

"She's a bitch."

"He's a douche bag."

"He is acting like a nigga."

These phrases were taken from a series of informal conversations between students that I have heard as I walk from my office to the classroom where I teach at a private university in South Florida. These separate statements each reflect a way to label an individual. More to the point, they represent a method through which to reduce an individual to something, and *someone*, who is not valued in our heterosexist, homophobic, racist, and able-bodied culture. Each individual phrase, when placed on an individual body, represents much more than what we hear on a playground or in the halls of a college building.

Taken together, these phrases create a negative effect. They create a climate that reveals agreed-upon values and assumptions about what is right and good. They create an identity for an individual. They create a map for how an individual can assume a position of *power* to construct an identity for others. They create violence.

The misuse of these phrases solidifies what our culture, as a whole, values and does not value. Words matter.

With school shootings on the rise and increasing incidents of school bullying that emerge in the classroom and manifest through cyberspace, it is imperative that we understand the complexities of bullying and how it is inextricably linked to power and the language that reflects abuse of that power.

According to stopbullying.org,

Bullying is unwanted, aggressive behavior among school aged children that involves a real or perceived power imbalance. The behavior is repeated, or has the potential to be repeated, over time. Both kids who are bullied and who bully others may have serious, lasting, problems.

Thus, we need to ask how to make visible the complex ways power operates in a violent interaction and how those interactions reflect power dynamics embedded in our culture.

According to stopbullying.gov, threats that are enacted by a bully involve the misuse of power (physical strength or popularity in school) to hurt others. The website indicates that "Power imbalances can change over time and in different situations, even if they involve the same people."

Bullying is a massive issue to address. As such, it requires a kaleidoscopic approach—one that is not often reflected through popular culture and initiatives—where we ask students to think critically about how the language that we use reflects our thoughts and actions.

Understanding how larger questions of violence in our schools are connected to bullying and more direct forms of violence requires that we directly address the larger historical and cultural forces that define and shape us. It forces us to engage with larger issues of social (in)justices that are reflected in the language that we use on a daily basis, as language use reflects realities of oppression. Such attentiveness requires development of assignments that establish conditions for students to explore the ethical implications of language (mis)use.

As a professor of writing, I have created a series of assignments that have directly addressed the violences and misuses of language that students encounter on a daily basis. Drawing from work from websites like teachingtolerance.org, I initially ask students to discuss words and phrases that have a negative connotation and association. Often it is a struggle to get students comfortable enough to talk openly about the words that they both use and encounter on a daily basis.

This process requires students to move beyond the individual and the personal and, instead, to get students to understand how their (mis)uses of these words are not necessarily about them individually. Rather, our work in the classroom is to look at how popular culture publicly makes claims about who is and who is not valued in the language that is used throughout the music we listen to, the magazines we read, and the movies that make the most money in the box office.

Students are given assignments where they are asked to delineate where they have heard pejorative terms. They are then asked to directly outline what the word means. To that end, students are challenged to identify the origin of the word. Often this exercise gets students thinking about how limited their knowledge is of the histories that are embedded in the use of particular words. Students are then challenged to engage in the process of inquiry as they examine the ethical dimensions of language use. They describe, assess, and engage in research on the use of particular terms. They ask larger questions about the relationships between intentions ("I did not mean to hurt someone by using this particular word") and the effects of using the word ("How does my use of this word affect attitudes about a particular individual? How does that individual relate to a particular group?") Students are encouraged to understand their active role as language users. They are forced to think about who they are and who they want to become as they construct their realities through words.

What remains hypervisible in our discourses about schooling and violence is the series of school shootings that have significantly impacted our educational system over the course of the past 15 years. Even as there have been several initiatives intended to resist the impulse to identify the events as isolated incidents, often educators need to critically examine the very social fabric of our culture which produces instances of aggression towards individuals based on their gender identity, sexuality, race, ethnicity, and ability. A careful examination of the language that we use can create powerful messages and the links between our thoughts and our actions. The relationship between thoughts and words—as reflected through the language that we use—is a powerful tool to not only ignite violence but to extinguish violence.

Kelly Concannon is assistant professor of communication and rhetoric in the Division of Humanities at Nova Southeastern University in Ft. Lauderdale, Florida. Her work focuses on empowering students to be active agents for social change.

The People's Court in a South Bronx Elementary School: Evelyn Jackson

Third-grade testimony, Latifah: "Herbert was sitting behind me in art class. When Mr. _____ was not looking, Herbert took a scissor and cut off my whole braid."

Second-grade testimony, Delajhi: "I was washing my hands in the boy's room. Tyrone came up behind me and punched me on my left cheek. He said it was because I was not skipping a stall (what boys say you need to do to show you are not gay) and did I want to fight. Then he ran out. He punched me out of the blue."

Fourth-grade testimony, Kevin: "At dismissal that day on March 26 Tyquan was coming toward me. He circled around me and then I felt a fist in my face. He had punched me on my right cheek."

Mother of Kevin: "I was waiting for my son in the car at dismissal. I was wondering why he was late. I saw Tyquan and Melvin across the street beating up another boy. I have seen them do this every day. Tyquon's mother was in the street. She was wearing slippers. I have seen her there often smoking and drinking. My son Kevin can not come to school under this kind of pressure. I can't protect him in this school. He is defenseless. I have to stop what I am doing from my education to try to get my kid out of this neighborhood I have to choose my child's safety. I can't live here with my own people."

These testimonies were taken from the records of 2003—the last year I ran the "People's Court" in the Mott Haven, Bronx,

K–5 school where I was a Project Read teacher. In those years Mott Haven was one of the poorest congressional districts in the United States. Almost 98 percent of the students were eligible for free school lunches. Many children did not have involved fathers; some were being raised by their grandparents. Some came from the large homeless shelter a few blocks west of the school.

When I began teaching in 1987, I soon realized that much of classroom learning was disrupted by violence. Fights in the lunchroom were common. A lesson might be undone because Carlos broke Bernice's pencil and she smashed her book in his face in revenge. Or Brian might have walked past Rosa's desk and scratched her hand hard enough to make it bleed. After such behaviors, it was hard to get the class back to noticing how Curious George was naughty again or comparing the words *not* and *note* and getting them to understand the role of silent *e*.

Too many fights—too much aggressive behavior and outraged victims. I therefore conceived of a program, the People's Court.

The program was open to all those in the fifth grade who wanted to try out to be jury members. I first gave the fifth-graders an information packet to study. They learned about trials, the concept of guilt, the role of a judge, and the jobs of a lawyer and of a witness. I then gave them a "bar exam," asking questions from the packet and requiring them to judge a sample case about two children who got into a fight. The 30 highest scorers—who were also recommended by their classroom teachers—became the jury pool and, taking turns weekly, the prosecutor and the defense attorney.

The two student lawyers then came to my reading room during my lunch hour and, with the help of community volunteers, interviewed the accused, the victims, and any available witnesses. Then every Wednesday, their rough draft of opening and closing statements and witness reports in hand, the student lawyers and the other 28 members of the jury would make the three-block walk to the courthouse.

For this program I had the full support of Robert Johnson, Bronx district attorney. Every Wednesday for over 15 years, DA Robert Johnson made two or three assistant district attorneys (ADAs) available to us for an hour during lunch.

The three ADAs gave up their lunch hour to coach the arriving student lawyers. The students learned to deliver a more polished opening and closing argument and to examine witnesses. They learned to follow the correct procedure of the court. They learned to dress appropriately for the occasion and to speak clearly and audibly. Parents often attended.

Cases were real—they came from complaints filled out by children at the school who wanted to bring charges. It could be that someone had, for example, punched them, pointed a toy gun at them, stolen $5 from their backpack, or kicked them in the knee. Instead of fighting back, they would come to my reading room at all times of the day, politely ask for a complaint form, and fill it out, hoping that their case merited the walk to the criminal court building. All jury members and those involved in the case had permission slips from their parents.

Those students found guilty by the People's Court jury— those who were not chosen that week to be the prosecutor or the defense attorney—were given sentences ranging from writing essays to "doing time" with a "mean but strict" fifth-grade teacher.

After a few successful years of the program, I was able to get grant money for shirts for the jury members. They quickly became identified as "winners" and role models.

The violent behavior of many in my South Bronx elementary school is, unfortunately, not unique. A project such as the People's Court can be implemented school-wide or in an individual classroom. If courts are nearby, visits are useful in introducing children to the criminal justice system. Teachers can contact the district attorney's office in their area for information and assistance.

Luis was in the People's Court class of 2002. I hope he spoke for many on the jury and in the school when he wrote, "Thank you for teaching us what we know. I hope I carry it in my mind forever. And if there ever is a problem, I will try to solve it with my mouth, not my hands."

Evelyn Jackson is a retired teacher who helped develop a school-based violence prevention program.

Creating and Sustaining Positive School Climates: De Palazzo

Two students are texting one another. One is a middle school student who identifies as gay, the other a sympathetic though unskilled middle school friend:

Middle-schooler who is gay:	"I'm tired of all the harassment taking place day in and day out at this school. No one at this place ever wants to stop the bullying. I think it would just be easier if I end it all."
Friend:	"Dude, life sucks. Hey, what did u get on yr algebra qz?" No text back.
After 5 minutes, Friend:	"U there?"
Middle schooler who is gay:	"Not 4 long." (sad face icon). Isn't it time I just make myself scarce. . .everyone I know will be better off."
Friend:	"Hey, u there?"
Middle schooler who is gay:	(no response)

How do we help school-based professionals become more aware of and sensitive to the unique challenges lesbian, gay, bisexual, transgender, and questioning (LGBTQ) youth face in today's elementary, middle, and high schools?

When we take a sober look at harassment and bullying in school communities, we know that antigay bullying is rampant and, concerningly, often unchecked. A 2011 survey by the

Gay, Lesbian, and Straight Education Network (GLSEN) of 8,584 middle and high school students that identify as LGBT from across the United States tells us that nearly 9 out of 10 LGBT students experienced harassment at school in the past year, and nearly two-thirds felt unsafe because of their sexual orientation. We also know that high levels of harassment and bullying correlate with poorer educational outcomes, lower future aspirations, frequent school absenteeism, and lower grade point averages. This is only one of the many finding about anti-LGBTQ language and bullying in schools.

Personally, I know that bullying and harassment do not happen in a vacuum. As an elementary and high school educator for 20-plus years, and more recently a diversity specialist in Broward County Public Schools, the sixth largest school district in the nation, I have the well-timed opportunity to design programs that help to ensure the well-being of LGBTQ youth. Broward County Schools is one district that exemplifies care, forward thinking, and a safety-focused culture. That said, we also know culture and climate begin in our hallways, classrooms, and cafeterias. Schools that exemplify a strong and healthy culture and climate have a higher sense of connectedness among and between students and staff and a lower level of mistreatment and violence. Connectedness is when youth have their developmental needs for safety and belonging met.

What is a positive school climate? A positive climate means that youth and adults feel valued and "connected" at the school. It is the feelings and attitudes elicited by a school or organization's environment. They include but are not limited to a sense of belonging that everyone feels or does not feel within a school community and the physical and psychological aspects of a school, which both influence us and are influenced by us.

It is our professional, ethical, and legal responsibility to value the worth of every person from every background and identity and to do our best to ensure their physical, mental, and emotional safety. Our students who identify as LGBTQ are no exception. We know this group of marginalized youth has many unique needs, issues, and challenges due to societal stigma about their identity.

The challenges that students and people who identify as LGBTQ face and the resiliency necessary to circumvent the challenges are present and palpable in all of our nation's schools. The school district that is my home, Broward County Public Schools in Fort Lauderdale, Florida, is not an exception. Being an educator and social justice advocate for numerous years, I know the population of students and adults in our schools is simply yet powerfully a microcosm of our larger community, including South Florida, Florida, the United States, and our world. We do not live in a vacuum, and we are aware of that every day as we maneuver and negotiate our day-to-day life happenings and responsibilities.

The "face" of Broward County Public Schools in the 2012–2013 school year echoed South Florida's diversity. In that school year, our school population came from 171 countries, spoke 53 languages, and represented 261,000 students, of whom almost 10 percent were English language learners (ELLs).

Gary Howard,[1] the well-respected antibias educator, makes a provocative comment when speaking about diversity in our school systems. He shares, "Rather than experience the discomfort of interracial dialogue, people often put an emphasis on how we are all alike instead of addressing our obvious differences."

Sexual orientation and gender identity and expression are layers of diversity. For some of us, accepting that there are people that identify as LGBTQ may be counter to our beliefs, values, or personal faith. Honoring one's beliefs does not have to run counter to accepting a person's LGBT identity as one of

---

[1]Howard, G. (2006). *We Can't Teach What We Don't Know: White Teachers, Multiracial Schools.* New York: Teachers College Press.

our human diversities. It does, however, align with caring about the physical, mental, and emotional well-being and safety of LGBTQ people and the importance of ensuring a safe school environment for all.

Some educators have stated that it seems we are hearing about LGBTQ youth violence more in the last decade, and even more so recently. If LGBT people and students have always been a part of society, why is there more interest in LGBTQ support, well-being, and safety now than before?

There has been a long and slow curve of support for youth who identify as LGBTQ in our school communities. If we take a historical perspective, support for young people who identify as LGBT first began within the gay community. Diversity clubs and gay–straight student alliance clubs then began to spring up in the late 1990s and early 2000s. The Internet made a strong debut about that time as well, and more information, both good and not so good, was accessed by people who wanted to learn more about either themselves, if they identified as LGBT or were questioning their sexual identity (Q), or if they were someone who simply wanted to know more for whatever reason.

Research points to why adolescents have not realized their orientation in the past and are now doing so as being due to "cognitive isolation"—meaning there simply was very little or no means to aggregate support, role models, and dialogue in the past. Add in the intersecting marginalities of race, ethnicity, socioeconomics, language, and faith, and the challenges become even more palpable. Now, with the emergence of support programs for LGBT youth, the Internet, the change in public perceptions, the increase in positive media images and coverage, and the expansion of community support groups, LGBTQ students are emerging, along with their unique needs, issues, and challenges. As a society, perhaps we may be behind the curve when acknowledging our diversities and identities.

In addition, here are some other reasons why there has been a "call to action" to become more aware of and support our schools' youth who do not identity as straight:

- The U.S. government issuing an imperative regarding the safety of LGBTQ youth in our schools
- An increase in biased language in our schools across the nation and also in our district
- Sobering documentation about personal experiences of harassment and assault
- The emergence of gender nonconforming youth and LGBTQ youth
- A significant increase in gay–straight alliance (GSA) clubs across the country

From October 2010 to February 2011 there was a highly disturbing spate of suicides in our nation by mostly middle school students who took their lives because of antigay harassment, bullying, or lack of acceptance of their identity. Thirteen young people took their lives. Since then there have been many more, locally in South Florida, in our state, and in our nation. Following the 13 suicides, a national campaign was initiated by Dan Savage entitled "It Gets Better."

So what might it be like for a young person in our school system who identifies as LGBT or who is questioning their sexual identity? Here is a quote from a South Florida student who identifies as gay: "Where I was brought up . . . there's that island culture that is strongly against homosexuality. I would feel like I would want to kill myself. I felt like I was a mistake. I wanted to be someone else."

There are three primary places young people go either for support, to socialize, or both—home, place of worship (church, temple, mosque, etc.), or school. We know from research that LGBTQ youth often feel disconnected from their places of worship when faith communities believe that being LGBT is wrong or a sin. In addition, a sobering reality is that many children have had conflictual experiences with their parent(s) or caretakers ranging from disbelief to nonacceptance or being told to leave home. Students spend more than seven hours a day in school, and if we consider before- and after-school programs, clubs, athletic events and practices, service work, and other activities, many children spend much longer than that. Recently, it was reported that only approximately 15 percent of school districts nationally do any type of staff sensitivity training about LGBTQ needs, issues, and resiliency.

In order to understand the day-to-day experiences of LGBTQ students, it's important to educate ourselves about the facts pertaining to safe climate, personal safety, and physical, mental, and emotional health and life support systems that are present or not present in an LGBTQ youth's life.

We are beginning to become more aware that, due to societal stigma, it can be a great challenge to identify as lesbian, gay, bisexual, or transgender. It is important to note that as we learn and understand more about how to ensure the health and safety of LGBTQ students, we know that someone's orientation does not cause challenging situations and difficult circumstances, including bullying or rejection. Instead, it is the hurtful reaction of society, based on people's beliefs, assumptions, and misperceptions, that can create great stigma and pain for the LGBT population.

An analysis of the key findings from empirical research sheds light on sobering realities and the clear and urgent need for school environments that nurture and promote respect and dignity for students of all identities. For instance:

• LGBT youth are at increased risk for suicidal ideation, attempted suicide, and depression. This increased risk appears to be consistent across age group, gender, race, and self-identified orientation.

- Compared with other students, LGBT youth are more likely to report feeling unsafe at school.

- LGBT youth report experiencing elevated levels of harassment, victimization, and violence. School-based victimization due to known or perceived identity has been documented.

- Rates of substance use, including smoking and alcohol consumption, are higher among LGB youth than heterosexual youth. Almost no research has examined substance abuse among transgender youth.

- The homeless youth population comprises a disproportionate number of LGBT youth.

- The few studies that have examined protective factors for LGBT youth suggest that family connectedness and school safety are two possible areas for intervention, and family acceptance among LGBT youth is a protective factor against depression, substance use, and suicidal ideation and attempts.

- LGBT youth may lack access to health care professionals who are able to provide appropriate care to LGBT patients.

- Youth who report high levels of family rejection in middle and high school are 8.4 times more likely to report having attempted suicide and 5.9 times more likely to report high levels of depression.[2]

Disturbingly, a 2012 survey of 50 Broward County, Florida, youth at an LGBTQ youth support group mirrored most of the above findings, with 55 percent of the youth group reporting that they have engaged in self-harm.

---

[2]Ryan, C., Huebner, D., Diaz, R., & Sanchez, J. (2009). Family Rejection as a Predictor of Negative Health Outcomes in White and Latino Lesbian, Gay, and Bisexual Young Adults. *Pediatrics, 123*(1), 346–352.

It is important that all students and staff look forward to coming to school and to work. Yet, for youth who identify as LGBT, environmental stressors, parental conflict, and in some cases parental or caregiver rejection as well as social stigma can have disturbing effects.

Being Out

*Bring harmony to this world, one at a time. One at a time—
with a teacher, a parent, I know it will work, it has to...*
    —19 year old Haitian-American youth of gay identity

For a variety of social and societal reasons, LGBT people are more comfortable being "out" to their peers, families, and communities in 2013, even though it is still not always safe to be out. Recent research tells us that LGBT people are anywhere from 8 to 13 percent of our world's population. Also, the preponderance of research about sexual formation and human development supports the belief that sexual orientation is not a choice. Even though many people are still not out for different reasons, it is reasonable to say that more than likely each of us knows an adult who identifies as lesbian, gay, bisexual, or transgender. It is also quite possible you know a student or students who identifies as LGBTQ or a young person who is not a student at your school who is out. He or she may have even found you a safe person to talk to and came out to you personally.

We know that adolescents and even younger students are engaged in an ongoing process of sexual development, and many young people may be unsure of their sexual orientation, while others have been clear about it since childhood.

Interestingly, the development of sexual identity in lesbian, gay, and bisexual people is a unique process that has been widely reported in the scientific literature and popular culture but has received surprisingly little empirical attention.

First, we should understand what "coming out" means. There are varying definitions of coming out, but all definitions center around the fact that coming out is a means to publicly declare one's identity, whether to a person in private or a group of people. In our society, most people are generally presumed to be heterosexual or straight, so there is no need for a heterosexual person to make a statement to others that discloses his or her sexual orientation. A person who is LGBT must decide whether or not to reveal to others her or his sexual orientation or gender identity.

"Outing" occurs when someone else tells others that a particular person is LGBT without that person's permission. Even though we often do not know what someone's beliefs are or reactions might be, outing someone may have large repercussions for students. It is an unfortunate reality that LGBT students commonly experience parental rejection because of their sexual orientation or gender identity or expression. Studies have shown that approximately one-third of LGBTQ youth are victims of physical violence by a family member after the student comes out or their sexual orientation is disclosed. Students have had their emotional and physical safety jeopardized when school staff outed them to other students and even family members.

A disturbing reality is that students who identify as LGBTQ often face serious homophobia in their families, schools, and communities and are widely understood to be at serious risk. It is important that schools be a place where they can learn, thrive, be safe, and graduate. That said, young people are coming out in larger numbers and at younger ages, seemingly becoming more active by empowering themselves through clubs, interests, and activities; more vocal about their identity; and more resilient, and they are often leading social change. Research has also found that self-awareness, self-labeling, and disclosing an LGBT identity to others is happening at younger ages, and if we are employed at a middle or high school, we have seen the increase and know this to be so.

If you have had or will have an LGBT student choose to come out to you—congratulate yourself! More than likely this person has noticed qualities and ways of being about you that made her or him feel that you would be an appropriate and safe person with whom to share an important and, before that day, quiet or secret part of her or his identity.

Interestingly, a significant number of LGBT youth share their identity with teachers because they spend a good deal of their waking hours in an educator's or support staff's presence at school. Actually, friends are the first sphere of support that LGBT youth turn to in the coming-out process because they often feel the most accepted or safest with their like-aged peers. Next young people often come out to other people at school, either adults or other youth. Third, it is often but not always siblings or extended relatives, and often last are an LGBT student's parents because their acceptance is critical to the child.

When a student tells you he or she is lesbian, gay, bisexual, or transgender, your initial response is important. The student has likely spent time in advance thinking about whether or not to tell you and when and how to tell you. The following are some tips to help you support her or him:

- Recognize the importance of this process for the LGBT student. Recognize the choice to tell YOU.
- Respect the risk the student is taking by coming out to you and ensure confidentiality.
- Show your appreciation for the student's courage.
- Honor your religious beliefs if they are counter to the LGBT identity, and at the same time show that you value, respect, and support the student who has come out to you. Both can be done with grace, compassion, and tolerance.
- Help to make it a happy occasion. (Smile and relax!)
- Listen, listen, listen—and listen some more.

Confidentiality and LGBT Students: It's the Law

The U.S. Supreme Court has recognized that the federal constitutional right to privacy protects not only an individual's right to bodily autonomy but also the right to control the nature and extent of highly personal information that may or may not be released by that person. This right to privacy extends to students in a school setting. They have the right to share or withhold information about their sexual orientation or gender identity from their parents, teachers, and other parties, and it is against the law for school officials to disclose or compel students to disclose that information. This means that teachers, school staff, and administrators cannot discourage a student from being out at school, but they also cannot force a student to be out at home. It is up to the student—and the student alone—to decide where and when to be open about her or his LGBTQ status.

It is important to note that—even when a student appears open about his or her sexual orientation or gender identity at school—it is that student's right to limit the extent to which, and with whom, the information is shared. Failure to follow these guidelines and policies could place a student in a hostile, dangerous, or even life-threatening environment or circumstance.

School officials or teachers may think they are doing the right thing by revealing a student's sexual orientation or gender identity to his or her parents. However, doing so not only violates the student's rights but can negatively impact a young person's life. Young people whose schools have outed them to their families often report subsequent rejection or verbal, physical, or emotional abuse at home. Experts on homelessness have determined that family conflict over a youth's sexual orientation or gender identity is a significant factor leading to homelessness.

It is important to know that the Supreme Court has ruled that students do not shed their constitutional rights at the schoolhouse gate. Furthermore, the only time schools may restrict an individual student's free speech is when it causes *significant disruption* in the classroom, according to *Tinker v. Des Moines Independent School District* of 1969.

The Fourteenth Amendment to the U.S. Constitution guarantees all people protection under the law, and public school officials and employees may not single out a student for negative treatment based on prejudices against LGBTQ students. Nor may they discriminate against students just because they feel uncomfortable around those who do not conform to traditional gender stereotypes.

Our Gender-Nonconforming Youth and Transgender Youth

Finally, transgender students, coming to the forefront more and more in our schools and at younger ages, face extreme harassment in schools and at home. In a nation-wide study[3] of transgender youth, almost all transgender students had been verbally harassed at their school. More than half of transgender students have been physically harassed (pushed or shoved) in school in the past year because of their orientation or gender expression. Deeply concerning is the finding that less than one-fifth of transgender students said that school staff intervened most of the time or always when hearing homophobic remarks about gender expression—and school staff also contributed to the harassment, with the study noting that a third of transgender students heard school staff make homophobic remarks, sexist remarks, or comments about someone's gender expression in the past year.

Creating a Safe Space for All: Policies, Programs, and Practices

There are many ways to be an ally to all students who may need support or encouragement. As good educators, we know

---

[3]Grant, J., Mottet L., Tanis, J., Harrison, J, Herman, J., & Keisling, M. (2011). *Injustice at Every Turn: A Report of the National Transgender Discrimination Survey.* Washington, D.C: National Center for Transgender Equality and National Gay and Lesbian Task Force.

the myriad personal and professional ways to show a young person that you care, value their identity, and will do your best to ensure both your classroom, working environment, and school community is a safe place to be who they are, learn, and grow.

One key way to create a welcoming and affirming place for all students and staff is to stop any sort of bullying or harassment in its tracks. Research points to the fact that as young people watch everything we do and say because they desire to see us as role models to them, they also pay deft attention to how we as professional educators handle bullying and harassment by students to one another, students to adults, adults to students, and even adults to each other. Close to home, in a 2012 survey of 50 Broward County LGBTQ youth, 83 percent said they heard homophobic remarks from other students in school frequently or often. Disturbingly, 42 percent reported that they heard homophobic remarks from teachers or schools staff sometimes, often, or frequently. We know every student and staff, regardless of their culture, their background, their identity, or their race, deserves to feel valued, respected, and safe in our school communities.

So just what is an ally? There are numerous definitions, but each points to the same "spirit," that of being someone who is supportive, tries to understand, listens, expresses value, and watches out for the well-being and safety of another person who may be marginalized or at risk. Therefore, allyship is "walking the talk" by being someone who generously supports, values, and demonstrates genuine care about another's well-being. Allies are of all ages, backgrounds, life experiences, genders, orientations, personalities, races, and religions. We can find allies within a school community, a family, a neighborhood, a place of worship, a circle of friends, or the broader community, state, or country, to name a few.

An ally for the needs, rights, and resiliency of LGBTQ youth should be aware of the legal landscape and how it protects or does not protect students. Our founding fathers, state legislators, and local school board members have given us the tools and the resources to empower all students; now it is up to us to use them.

Federal Law

The Fourteenth Amendment of the U.S. Constitution

The U.S. Constitution guarantees all people equal protection under the law. This means public school officials and employees may not single out a student for negative treatment based on prejudices against a certain culture or identity. The Constitution's equality also means that public school officials may not turn a blind eye to anti-LGBTQ harassment or treat it less seriously than other forms of harassment.

Title IX of the Education Amendment Acts of 1972

Federal civil rights statutes reinforce antidiscrimination principles as well. Title IX of the Education Amendment Acts of 1972 prohibits discrimination based on sex in education programs and activities that received federal financial assistance. Although Title IX does not expressly apply to discrimination based on sexual orientation, it does prohibit gender-based harassment, such as harassment on the basis of student's failure to conform to stereotyped notions of masculinity and femininity.

In 2011, a key policy letter was sent to every school district in the nation by Secretary of Education Arne Duncan, underscoring the serious problem in our schools pertaining to harassment and bullying, with acknowledgement of LGBT students as the disproportionate targets of bullying in schools.

The secretary of education also distributed to all school superintendents a "Dear Colleague" letter and a "Guidance" letter and specified that youth who identify or are perceived to be LGBT are included under the antibullying policies stated in the letters.

State Law

Florida Statute 1006.147

The Jeffrey Johnston Stand Up for All Students Act was passed in 2008. From this, Florida Statute 1006.147 was enacted, creating a statewide prohibition of the bullying and harassment of any students or employee of a public K–12 educational institution, whether at a school, on a school bus, or via electronic device. What bullying law has your state legislated on behalf of all students?

Florida Department of Education Code of Ethics 6B-1.006

As a professional educator in the state of Florida it is our charge to abide by the Florida Professional Code of Ethics, which states that every educator will value the worth and dignity of every person, and essential to the achievement of these standards are the freedom to learn and to teach and the guarantee of equal opportunity for all. Does your state have a professional code of educational ethics?

Local Policies and Acts

Pay attention to your school board's policies and guidelines. For example, the School Board of Broward County policies and guidelines prohibit bullying and discrimination, which includes sexual orientation and gender identity and expression, under Anti-bullying Policy 5.9 and Nondiscrimination Policy 4001.1. Does yours?

Other Key Ways to Show Allyship to LGBTQ Youth

Establish Guidelines in Your School and Classroom or Office from Day One and Revisit Guidelines Regularly

From day one of the school year, establish clear guidelines about respect for all types of diversity in your environment. Youth know that levels of safety and inclusion can vary from person to person, leader to leader, teacher to teacher—even though every classroom and hallway should be safe. Ensure that your space is one in which name-calling, mistreatment, or cruelty of any kind, whether jokingly stated or a clearly hurled epithet, with not be tolerated. Be certain to review your guidelines regularly throughout the school year for the betterment of the entire school community.

Meet with Your Leadership

Professional educators know that classroom or offices must be affirming to all people. It is our ethical and legal obligation to ensure that all students are emotionally and physically safe, valued, and respected so that they may learn, thrive, and develop their educational and personal aspirations. We also know that leadership in our school community is an integral part of an intact, expansive, and sustainable school climate and culture.

Ensure that school leadership is "on board" with understanding the significance of LGBTQ student and staff safety and well-being. Plan to meet with leadership, and the following tips may help you. Note: These are suggestions, and the context of your school environment may lend itself to varying ways of ensuring leadership is ahead of the curve regarding LGBTQ safety.

Markers

Markers or cues are ways in which at-risk youth can decipher if one is supportive of their identity. One clear, simple, and very telling method of allyship for LGBTQ students is markers. A marker is a method of acknowledgement or display widely recognized by LGBTQ youth and adults.

Both subtle and overt markers or cues that let lesbian, gay, bisexual, transgender, or questioning youth know that they have someone who values them. They let youth and adults know that you are an easily identifiable LGBTQ ally. It also lets them know that they can presume your basic awareness of and concern for LGBTQ youth and that you have basic issue knowledge and are willing to provide resources and support. Be aware of and exhibit markers youth "read" that subtly say "I am safe; you are safe with me!"

Visibility Markers

- Make yourself a visible marker as an ally
- Let other educators know you are an ally: speak up for LGBTQ youth and adults
- Post safe-space stickers and posters
- Display LGBT supportive materials

Action Markers

- Make no assumptions: Remember that approximately 10 percent of our population identifies as lesbian, gay, bisexual, or transgender. In a school of 2,000, do the math and you may be surprised about how many youth are LGBT, are questioning their sexuality, or have an LGBT father, mother, sibling, extended relative, or good friend.
- Use inclusive language: Be aware of using pronouns or nouns that are always of the opposite sex when speaking with youth and adults. LGBT students hear when an educator is being inclusive and appreciate the effort to be broad minded when speaking about day-to-day happenings, events, and other issue in a student's life.

Respond to Anti-LGBT Behavior

Interrupt anti-LGBT behavior in the same manner you would stop any negative comment related to appearance, race, income, ability, language, and so on. Make certain that the interruption is directly followed by why you stopped the mistreatment or negative comment.

Safe Space Items

Knowing that an adult is supportive of LGBT students is very important to all students of varying identities, and safe-space stickers or posters indicate that this is a safe place for all.

Curriculum

GLSEN's National School Climate Survey consistently finds that students with inclusive curricula have a greater sense of belonging in their school community, hear fewer homophobic remarks, and are less likely to be bullied, harassed, or feel unsafe at school than those without inclusive curriculum. All school districts should desire for all youth to stay in school and feel welcomed and valued, including this at-risk minority of students.

What does a diverse curriculum that includes LGBT persons as active contributors to history, literature, and events look like? Include positive representations of LGBT people, history, and events. For example, when teaching about history include the persecution, struggles, and resiliency of marginalized groups, include the challenges that people who identify as LGBT have experienced.

GSAs

> *Just the mere presence of the GSA at my school helped me feel like I was not alone. I gotta say, it helped me to survive in school and made being at home and closeted more tolerable. Please let teachers and principals know how much my GSA helped save me.*
>
> —Broward LGBT student, 2010

Research tells us that the presence of a GSA at a school is one of the most powerful indicators for youth of varying identities that the school is affirming of diversity. Our student quote at the beginning of this GSA section underscores this fact.

Resources

Even though LGBT youth turn to their friends first as allies for support, it is to teachers that youth look next as models of safety and connection. The next step to ensure youth support and safety are connection to resources by allies. Many students may inquire about where they can go for help, whether the help be emotional, intellectual, physical, or social. Many may also want to be educated about where in the community at large there is support or assistance for a variety of concerns so that they may be resilient when coming out or living as a lesbian, gay, bisexual, or transgender student or where to go socially to interact in a healthy environment with other LGBT youth or youth allies. Youth may also want to know about national resources that specialize in LGBT support, safety, GSA involvement, and so on.

A final and important note to remember is to be aware that some students have LGBT parents and some educators identify as LGBT in our schools. Be aware that some parents and educators are not visible. For some parents, only one may be registered with the school. It is important to provide opportunities for LGBT parents and their children to get together (identify, support, and network). Providing these opportunities for LGBT teachers, support staff, and leadership is also important to maintaining a healthy school culture where all people are valued and feel safe and connected. Encourage teachers to check with LGBT parents about how they want to handle class activities and projects around Mother's Day, Father's Day, and other holidays, and ensure that LGBT issues are part of antibullying training for teachers, staff, and students. Last, remember the markers and cues discussed earlier that let LGBT students, as well as educators or parents, know that they are welcomed by you.

In conclusion, as an educator and ally to all at-risk or marginalized students in our school communities, I hope that you will join me as I strive to work, live, and play by the words of one of our great world leaders. He professed, as a hopeful mantra to us all,

"Be the change YOU wish to see in the world."
—Mahatma Gandhi

De Palazzo is a conflict resolution educator and president of Perspective Unlimited, which provides training and consultation to schools and community groups. She also works with the Broward County, Florida, school district to help train teachers and students on issues faced by LGBT youth.

Is There More School Violence Today? A Veteran Educator Says No: Sarah Raitter

Nineteen years ago, I graduated from Western Michigan University and set out for Fort Myers, Florida, to begin my career as a special education teacher. My first teaching position was in a classroom for kindergarten, first, and second graders with emotional impairments. While my teacher preparation program gave me all of the tools to design curriculum and meet the academic needs for my students, it did not really prepare me for the biggest surprise I encountered that year—violence among the students. Granted, these were students who had exhibited problem behaviors throughout their young lives, or they would never have been placed in my program, but the level of violence I witnessed that year was something that continues to shock me to this day. One student was suspended on multiple occasions for throwing a pair of teacher scissors at another student. Another student was expelled from the special education bus for throwing rocks at the school bus as it approached the bus stop in the morning. And almost all of my students that year had no other strategy for dealing with their frustrations than to use their fists to punch, legs to kick, or teeth to bite the perceived offender. Academic instruction that year became less important. Teaching this young group of students how to deal with frustration and disappointment without resorting to violence quickly became the driving force in my classroom instruction.

Fast-forward 19 years, and I am still teaching special education, although now in a middle school setting in Reno, Nevada. When asked to reflect on whether school violence has increased in the years I've been in the education profession, my automatic response was "Of course it has!" After all, school shootings have increased dramatically and unfortunately seem almost like an everyday occurrence. There was even a school shooting close to home, in the neighboring town of Sparks, Nevada. In response, school districts have been charged with using increased safety measures in their school buildings and on school campuses. All schools in my district are required to practice a "code red" drill twice a year, which puts into place emergency safety procedures should a violent act occur on campus. While I have not taught in such a district personally, I know that some places have instituted metal detectors to prevent students from bringing potentially lethal weapons onto the school campus. In addition, most schools have some level of surveillance cameras so that potential violence can be prevented or halted in a timely manner.

But upon further thought, I really do not believe that school violence has increased. There is still a level of violence that shocks me at the middle school where I currently teach. There is still a group of students who seem not to have learned how to use their words to prevent arguments that lead to violent attacks. There are still students who lack strategies for dealing with problems besides resorting to some sort of violence. We still have fights in the hallways, cafeteria, and outdoor areas. However, I truly believe that this violence involves a very small percentage of the student population.

So why does it seem as though school violence has increased? I believe that the media has a great deal to do with this perceived increase. A violent attack in a school is no longer dealt with "in house" by school administrators and the students involved. Instead, it is immediately broadcast all over local media stations along with various social media sites. Parents, community members, and other students are understandably horrified that violent acts are "allowed" in schools, so they continue to discuss the issue of school violence, which, in turn, keeps the problem in the forefront of people's thoughts. I believe that social media sites, such as Facebook, inadvertently lead to the perception of increased school violence. Whenever a fight occurs in my school, it is immediately posted about on Facebook and not allowed to blow over quickly and quietly. I believe that schools and school districts are doing all they can do to prevent violence from happening. Many schools, including most in the school district where I teach, have implemented school-wide positive behavior supports to reinforce students for doing the right thing and dealing with problems and conflicts in appropriate ways. While school violence is never an okay thing, I truly believe that there has not been an increase throughout the past two decades. Rather, we all need to keep this in perspective and continue to do our best to help all youth succeed.

Sarah Raitter is a special education teacher at Swope Middle School in Reno, Nevada. She has been teaching special needs students for 19 years. In addition, Raitter is a highly competitive runner, having been asked to compete with the elite runners at the 2014 Boston Marathon.

Reflections on PeaceJam and School Violence in the United Kingdom: Larenda Twigg

Although in the rural and suburban schools I attended as an adolescent we never spoke of school violence, from the ages of

11 to 13, I faced bullying, teasing, and name-calling on a regular basis. I dealt with these issues at school, through fights with my family, and through constant tardiness to school. I was lucky to have inspiring teachers, and opportunities to participate in numerous activities helped me gain confidence in myself and develop different peer groups. By the time I turned 14, I was able to ignore the bullying and negativity with the support of a new group of friends. My own personal experience created a desire to work with young people on peace education programs helping to address various types of violence in their own lives. Of the various programs I have participated in, one I discovered as a graduate student at the University of Bradford, called PeaceJam, has provided some of the most remarkable inspiration to address these issues by empowering young people to take action in their own communities.

The idea for PeaceJam began in Denver, Colorado, in 1994 when Ivan Suvanjieff, a long-haired, leather-clad rock-and-roll musician challenged some teenage gang members who were hanging out on his street. To his astonishment, these young men, who were clearly dealing drugs and toting handguns, sang the praises of Archbishop Desmond Tutu when the conversation veered to South Africa. Although they had no interest in the president of the United States, who they did not see as relevant to them, these gang members believed Archbishop Desmond Tutu was "cool" for having stood up— nonviolently—to apartheid. Seeing the potential power that an influential nonviolent role model might have if brought together with young people, Ivan recruited his friend Dawn Engle, who had a contact in the Dalai Lama's office, to find a way to bring together young people and Nobel Peace Prize recipients to inspire them to take positive action in their own communities. After a trip to Dharamsala where they convinced His Holiness that young people needed positive role models such as himself and his fellow Nobel Peace laureates, PeaceJam was born. A group of 13 participating laureates form the board of the PeaceJam organization and decide its vision, educational curriculum, and strategies built around three core pillars of inspiration (the laureates), education (the curriculum and classroom), and action (student-led service projects).[4]

In 2006, the PeaceJam program was brought to the United Kingdom based on the desire of the late Sir Joseph Rotblat, one of the participating PeaceJam Nobel Peace laureates, with the help of Sally Milne of the Pugwash Foundation and Dr. Fiona Macaulay at the Peace Studies Department at the University of Bradford. From 2006 to 2012 the University of Bradford hosted one of the annual PeaceJam Youth conferences—and the only PeaceJam conference located in Europe. The history of the city of Bradford made it an ideal location to introduce this innovative curriculum-based peace education program in the United Kingdom. Bradford, in West Yorkshire, England, is a city with an industrialized past from wool mills and a diverse population due in large part to the multiple waves of immigration to work in those mills from Germany, Estonia, Poland, India, Pakistan, and the Caribbean to name a few. More recently refugee groups from places such as Somalia, Iraq, and Zimbabwe have joined the growing minority ethnic groups in the city.

Long past are the days where poets like T. S. Eliot in *The Waste Land* would make reference to "a silk hat on a Bradford Millionaire." When I was first moving to Bradford many I spoke with in other parts of England knew Bradford only for its economic deprivations, social tensions, and issues of race relations between the city's large Asian community and white working-class community. These tensions were highlighted in

---

[4]More information on the story behind PeaceJam and some of the projects young people around the world have started due to their involvement in the program can be found in Ivan Suvanjieff and Dawn G. Engle (2008), *PeaceJam: A Billion Simple Acts of Peace,* New York, Puffin Books.

the nation's consciousness by riots in the city in 1995 and 2001. But along with the rise and decline of the city's wool mills is also a proud history of philanthropists, social reformers, and activists for social justice and peace—including Sir Norman Angell, the 1933 Nobel Peace Prize recipient (who was the member of Parliament for Bradford North).

"What better way to teach empathy, intercultural under-standing and community cohesion to young people than by using the inspiration of Aung San Suu Kyi?" the head of an all-girls school in Yorkshire asks. "I would argue that by using twelve Nobel Peace Laureates, of whom Aung San Suu Kyi is one, in our curriculum, we can inspire a new generation of pupils to look at the world around them, and help create criti-cally conscious young women who are ready to make a differ-ence in the world." When I first heard the story of the founding of PeaceJam I agreed with this teacher and was inspired to become part of the program, but why would teen-agers respond to a president of an island nation like José Ramos-Horta or a middle-aged Iranian lawyer such as Shirin Ebadi, especially when facing difficulties and violence in their own lives every day?

Within Bradford, PeaceJam is one of several programs that have attempted to address issues around communication and dialogue in a city where it was felt, pre-riots, that no-one was talking. Forums that have provided space for sharing knowl-edge and addressing the importance of community engagement have had the most lasting impact across the city, and PeaceJam has been one those. Young people participating in the program never have the sense that they are not worthy because the teach-ers, university staff and students, and the Nobel laureate give them their full commitment—whether or not the student may go on to attend a university. There is a huge impact on young people to enter a lecture theater on the university cam-pus and not be patronized. It raises aspirations and provides a new sense that things are possible and a belief that students and their voices will be taken seriously by people who know what they are talking about—creating meaningful engagement and allowing meaningful engagement with other young people from different backgrounds. This neutral territory also provides a freedom to express feelings with less fear and to begin to question.

Jody Williams provided a great example of not underestimating young people at the 2007 PeaceJam UK conference hosted in Bradford. Having just spent an exhausting and traumatizing month interviewing refugees in Darfur for the United Nations, Jody talked of the endless testimonies she had heard of the rape of women refugees by the janjaweed militias. The response by the youth at the conference was to engage and challenge her with well-informed questions about the apparent inaction of the United Nations and the Sudanese government, her capacity to deal with stress and trauma in her work, and her views on international justice issues. Jody Williams then discussed with them and listened to the students' own problems of bullying and racism in their schools and communities.

This not only can help students speak about the idea of peace or conflict resolution as a theory but provides real inspiration for putting it into practice. John,[5] who lived outside of Bradford and attended the first PeaceJam conference held in the United Kingdom in 2006 with Máiread Corrigan Maguire, provides an excellent example of this. The school John attended had faced constant turbulence, especially in staffing, with the majority being in their position for two years or less. Almost every day after classes ended, John and his friends used to go and fight with the kids from another nearby school which they considered "snobby." These fights were what one did to be part of the group, and none of them spent much time thinking of the implications or consequences of this constant fighting. "But now that I've been to PeaceJam with some of

---

[5]For anonymity the names of students and schools have been changed.

them, well, it seems really silly to do that now." PeaceJam provided a space for the students to speak and work alongside each other in small groups, changing the way the students saw each other and themselves. By 2008, John, who had previously had no expectation of attending university, had started to spend his summer working as a counselor in youth camps, and in 2010 John enrolled in university with the plan to be a youth worker.

This sharing of stories with the laureate, in their youth or school group, and with their mentor groups is an empowering feature which can bring together people from an incredibly wide range of backgrounds: liberal middle class, white British working class, Asian British Muslims, gang members, and asylum-seekers and refugees. It can be surprising that whatever their background, everyone can relate so passionately and directly with the laureates. In 2012 a student commented, "I was really surprised how everyone got on so well and I enjoyed listening to Adolfo [Pérez Esquivel] talk about his life experiences and how he overcame what he went through." For another student engagement with the stories of Betty Williams made her realize "life doesn't have to be like this" despite the abuse she faced at home, which had led to bad behavior at school. After listening to the laureate, she realized she had control over her own behavior and became very active in multiple projects at school. After another conference a participant related, "I realized through hearing [Máiread Corrigan Maguire] speak [about her response to the death of her sister's children in the violence in Northern Ireland] that I was hanging out with some mean people. We were always looking for other girls to pick on and bully. But I didn't like them really. So I changed my group of friends, they like me, and now I do my homework and don't get into trouble; my parents are much happier too."

The diversity of the laureates themselves helps them as a group appeal to the diverse audience of young people, but what resonates is that all the laureates manage to communicate their absolute conviction that when facing injustice everyone can, and should, make their voices heard and make a difference. This conviction is carried over by the university student mentors and by the teachers and youth workers who facilitate the local PeaceJam groups. As one participant summarized, "[PeaceJam] inspired and encouraged me to stand for what I believed. It also taught me that staying silent and doing nothing is not the answer. Doing something about an issue might not solve it 100% but at least you can do something that makes it a bit better than it was at first."

The program is also about having an ability to speak about issues and life in a meaningful way, especially in one's own community. In 2011 Betty Williams's engagement with a group at a community in the center of Bradford inspired the young people who had been previously been reluctant to participate in PeaceJam, but Betty's ability to talk with them about gun and knife violence on a personal level gave them the encouragement they needed to begin taking an active role in some community projects. The group was then able to work on two projects (painting at a community center and working in a community garden) with young people from Armenia and Azerbaijan. During the project the groups were able to speak with each other about their experiences with war and violence. This inspiration from the laureate and the action of the volunteering provided support and validation to both their individual experiences of violence and their ability to make a change in their own communities.

This encouragement that, as an individual, as a young person, one can do something is empowering. Unfortunately, many of our participants have voiced a feeling that they are often seen as the problem rather than as a solution to issues in their community or school. We need to find ways to help young people find identity and status in what they actually do or think rather than, for example, in the things they own or wear. "Listen, shopping is not a human right," Jody Williams tells the youth. For some of our youth these issues of identity and consumerism link directly to the bullying and other school violence they face. The celebrity nature and energy of someone like Jody Williams telling them, "instead of hanging out in the mall for hours every Saturday, go do some volunteer work, raise money, do some campaigning," helps to make peace and activism cool, allowing for the possibility for some of the young people to begin to make new choices in the face of the violence they face at school—or at home.

This personal transformation, in my anecdotal experience, is a result not only of their encounters with the laureate but also their interactions with each other. Shirin Ebadi stressed, "Listen, I don't want to be your role model. Your life will have different challenges from mine. Look around and learn from lots of different people that you admire and find your own path in life," a path which will be different for all the participants. Those from comfortable backgrounds gain the chance to share life experiences with those far removed from their own. For those struggling with their behavior, school work, or home life, involvement in PeaceJam may provide an anchor in a chaotic life. "I am sure that many of the young people I bring would have been excluded from school by now, were it not for PeaceJam," one teacher explained, "And best of all, especially as far as the boys are concerned, it's made peace cool in school."

Depending on the way participants are selected for the PeaceJam in schools, the effect of the PeaceJam program may be a large factor in reducing overall violence in a school. As violence in a school is typically centered on a small group of students with influence, if these students stop their behavior and model a new pattern based on peace and empathy being "cool," then not only does the school violence decrease but the nonviolent message spreads as well. This has been the case for one of our participating schools from the Midlands. Over half the school's students are from a minority ethnic background, and over a third speak English as a second language. A high proportion of the students receive free school meals, and the school has an above average rate of students who join or leave school in the middle of the year. The teacher coordinating the program has reported spending less time stopping conflicts as a result of her choice to send certain young people to PeaceJam.

The school first became involved in PeaceJam in 2006 when it was invited to bring students to Bradford to a conference at a time when the school had several girls who were involved in a school-wide maelstrom of conflict within their year group. It was a miserable school environment with constant rows and fisticuffs over who was going through a door first, countless detentions, girls in isolation, and constant exclusions. A teacher explained that when "Sally Milne invited me to bring students to a conference I thought—OK—we've tried everything else, let's try this. So I took 8 girls who were heavily involved in problems—five in danger of exclusion, to the first UK PeaceJam."

There was a dramatic effect on those eight students who participated, as Alice, who was 13 years old at the time, relates:

> Going to PeaceJam totally changed my life. In March I was excluded from school for fighting and was constantly falling out with my friends. A group of three of us was going to attack another girl after school which I now sincerely regret. What I learnt at the conference really helped. I remember what Mairead said—that there is no need for arguing. She changed her life and other peoples' lives by being peaceful. Life is too short to waste it fighting. Since then, instead of fighting I stop fights! I have stayed out of trouble and at home I get rewards for being good in school instead of punishments for being excluded! I just stopped going around with violent people so much and chose to spend my time with peaceful people. I find this easier because I don't have to be scared to say the wrong thing. I like myself more now being a peaceful person.

Of the eight students taken to the conference in 2006, only one of the eight has since been excluded for violence. Of the others, five were the first in their family to make it through to a final assembly in year 11. Of these, four went on to further education, and one has a job with training. And one of the students has managed to keep her younger siblings out of violence and encourage them to go for further education as well. Although some staff complain about rewarding the "villains," due to the success of participation in the PeaceJam program among students most in danger of exclusion for violence, the school continues to select young people to participate because of need rather than solely as a reward for good behavior. Strong interest in the PeaceJam program within the school means there is a waiting list for students wanting to attend any PeaceJam conference weekends.

Finally, transforming a violent school environment is not only about personal transformation but also needs to be linked to school and community transformation. PeaceJam uses the stories of the laureates within the curriculum and at conferences to provide the inspiration and a bit of the education, but it is the action the students take through volunteering or service projects developed themselves that is a main component of this transformation and may range from issues of poverty to the environment to racism and human rights. By basing the program within the community of the school, PeaceJam aims to teach young people about wider issues in society and root causes of problems, and then to introduce skills to enable the students to tackle practical projects within their own community to address the issue with which the students are most concerned. One student summarized the impact of PeaceJam: "It has taught me that we need to get everybody together to work together to make things better in our community. Everybody needs to support each other—like the fingers of a hand working together like the dude [Adolfo Pérez Esquivel] said—parents really need to support their children to make things better."

Larenda Twigg is a Ph.D. student at the University of Bradford in the United Kingdom. She is an active member of the United Kingdom's PeaceJam team.

Preventing School Violence: Barbara J. Wien

Violence as a Continuum

Micro aggressions, from the playground to college campuses, from battles in Congress to international relations, are part of our acceptance of too much violence in our culture, how we raise our children, and broader societal values. But how? Why?

Violence is a continuum. The more we accept micro aggressions at the interpersonal level, the more we accept and allow violence at all levels of our lives. Bullying is violence, whether it is on the playground or on the world stage when powerful nations invade and occupy other countries. Such bullying on the world stage causes tremendous values confusion among youth. Why do adults lecture youth not to fight yet support war? Why do national leaders spend vast amounts of money preparing for war if violence is not a valid method of resolving conflicts? Who are the action figures and heroes children are encouraged to adore? What types of values are the media exalting and glorifying? Are military power, masculinity, and material wealth celebrated? Who benefits from this? Are simplicity, basic human kindness, and humility rewarded in our society today? Why? Why not? Who benefits from this? Are peaceful responses perceived as weak? Are nonviolent responses applauded and glorified? What kind of messages are we sending youth? How can we counterbalance unhealthy societal values? What choices can we make in our lives? We have the power to choose. What have we learned from the campus tragedies at Virginia Tech, Howard, and Bowie State? What could have been done differently by parents, national leaders, educators, and teens?

Youth violence is largely a reflection of adult society. When youth commit violence, they are holding up a mirror to adult conduct, showing us the values we embody and foster in our own homes, neighborhoods, and society. When adults and national leaders endorse war and violence to resolve conflicts, children absorb such values, practices, and images into their belief systems and psyches. Many children are also raised with the premise that the human race is inherently violent and war is inevitable. When combat and fighting are the only solutions shown in popular media and glorified in our textbooks, our children learn this lesson only too well. TV violence influences behavior. If it did not, big corporations would not invest billions of dollars in advertisements.

This premise is further reflected and embedded in U.S. economic policies, with the highest level of war spending in the world, more than our top five adversaries combined. "Children who are brought up to believe in the inevitability of war are much less likely to work for peace" (UNESCO, 1986). Conversely, research studies show that children who see adult role models actively working for peace and the rights of others believe they will have a more extended, secure future; learn greater social responsibility; and are more likely to respond to violence with skills such as negotiation (Harvard University Medical School, 1984).

Shifting U.S. Culture

According to leading psychologist and adolescent expert Dr. Ofer Zur, Ph.D., an outstanding resource for parents, educators and citizens, numerous research studies "established the undeniable relationships between militarism, sexism, racism and violence within a culture." He writes:

- Principally, there is no difference between the state of mind that seeks to resolve international conflicts by force and the state of mind that seeks to resolve interpersonal or familial conflicts by force and the misuse of power.

- There is a direct link between the way in which we use power with our children, our significant others, our neighbors, and our environment and what we teach our children about violence.

- Cultures in which young children regularly receive loving touch have lower incidents of violent crimes.

- Research done with psychiatrically hospitalized adolescents demonstrated a significant reduction of violent and sexual acting out when staff increased the use of nonsexual, affectionate touch with the teens.

- Fear and violent behavior have a direct correlation. Monitor media news presentations that capitalize on creating fear through undue sensationalism and manipulative means.

Dr. Zur writes in summary: "The misuse of power through violent action is taught through and supported by culture. The United States is one of the most violent cultures in the Western world with more crimes being committed with guns and through violent force."[6]

Dr. Martin Luther King Jr. proclaimed this same thesis when he said in his famous "Beyond Vietnam" speech in New York City on April 4, 1967, that "A nation that continues year after year to spend more money on military defense than on programs of social uplift is approaching spiritual death," and the "U.S. is the greatest purveyor of violence in the world."

How can we expect our schools and children to be nonviolent when the United States has militarily intervened 180 times

---

[6]Zur, O. (2014). *Teen Violence, School Shootings, Cyberbullying, Internet Addiction, T.V. and Gaming Violence and Teen Suicide: Facts, Ideas, and Actions.* Zur Institute. Retrieved June 3, 2014, from http://zurinstitute.com/teenviolence.html.

since the 1890s, currently maintains 1,000 military installations and bases around the world, and has been a nation at war for decades in Central America (1980s), the Middle East (since the 1990s), Asia (1950s, 1960s, and 1970s) and Europe (1940s)?

Couple these national military policies with the mass availability and lethality of guns in the United States thanks to the National Rifle Association (NRA), and it is astonishing that we do not have *more* school violence. Just imagine: On a daily basis, teachers and school administrators must seek to counter the full weight of warped values, parental apathy, television violence, the gun lobby, militarism, and national leaders resorting to the use of force, all without the equivalent financial resources! Schools and educators are held to an impossible standard in this regard.

Ending War and Violence

The good news is that resistance to war is building worldwide and may be reaching critical mass in the near future. This seems like an outrageously insensitive and foolish claim when so many people are dying in armed conflicts. Yet there is increasing evidence. We can hasten the demise of war by spreading peace education in every possible setting, by transforming the role of soldiers and military institutions for a *global environmental recovery race*, and by supporting nonviolent struggles unfolding around the world for economic equality, human rights, and democratic participation.

Thomas Kuhn first suggested in 1962 that a set of ideas, theories, or schools of thought (known as paradigms) can become dominant, self-reinforcing, and self-perpetuating. In his book *The Structure of Scientific Revolutions*, Kuhn posits that paradigms are born out of a society's structures, such as race, gender, and class. These paradigms become a system of logic unto themselves, although they may be fundamentally flawed. Research then stems from these paradigms and produces flawed outcomes. Such was the case when people thought the world was flat. People and societies come to believe in or depend entirely on the flawed paradigms, which serve only the interests of a narrow few. This is true of today's war system.

But what was once enshrined and celebrated can be reconsidered. Contradictions or flaws in the theory may emerge. A group comes along and challenges the dominant views and turns the whole notion on its head. A revolution in thought, or a *paradigm shift*, occurs. Such people change forever the way we view history, societies, and ourselves. This happened with the institution of slavery, the divine right of kings, women's roles in society, and many others.

We are in the midst of such a paradigm shift at this political moment in history. Here are three of the promising trends that are gaining traction and creating a paradigm shift:

1. *Peace education is growing everywhere* in formal and nonformal settings, in kindergarten through 12th grades, colleges, universities, preschools, refugee settings, after-school programs, inner city gangs, summer campuses, church and Bible study circles, labor unions, and thousands of other contexts in many countries. (See the Global Campaign for Peace Education website, http://www.peace-ed-campaign .org/newsletter/archives/77.html).

2. *Resistance to military intervention among soldiers and officers* is growing, even inside the military academies. They have been to Iraq and Afghanistan. They know war is not making us safer and is creating greater and more lethal threats. Iraq Veterans Against the War, Vietnam Veterans for Peace, Captain Paul Chappell, Lt. Colonel David Grossman, Josh Steiber, and countless other soldiers are speaking out and teaching peace.

3. *Nonviolent revolutions are increasing exponentially.* Since 1974, over 60 countries have transitioned from dictatorships to democracies using Gandhi's nonviolent principles

and strategies.[7] The spring of 2011 saw massive, tectonic paradigm shifts in the Middle East. The outcome is unclear in Yemen, Bahrain, Egypt, and of course Syria, but the people have spoken and waged nonviolent struggle to change their conditions.

The Seville Statement on Human Violence debunks the myth that the human race is hard-wired for war and violence. It is the work of hundreds of social scientists, archeologists, anthropologists, primate specialists, political psychologists, and peace researchers. Additional contributions from West Point professor Lt. Colonel David Grossman or Captain Paul Chappell concur. They posit that there is a greater preponderance of evidence that the human race is naturally cooperative *or our species would not have survived this long*, and war is a social construct that serves the interests of war profiteers. War is not fixed in nature like gravity in the cosmos; otherwise why would so many people go insane during war? Why have 500,000 soldiers come back with posttraumatic stress disorder if war is normal?

The Seville Statement challenges us to evolve to a higher stage of human development. Millions of young people are graduating from peace and conflict resolution programs rejecting racism, violence, and economic inequality. They do not believe in war anymore. Start a peacemaking program in your community or a peace education course in your local school system today and start the paradigm shift!

Resistance to war is coming from surprising circles indeed. Indeed, Andrew J. Bacevich, a former military colonel, now a professor of history and international relations at Boston

---

[7]See "How Freedom Is Won," a report by Freedom House, 2007, or "Why Civil Resistance Works: The Strategic Logic of Nonviolent Conflict" (2008), *International Security*, 33(1), 7–44.

University and author of *Washington Rules: America's Path to Permanent War*, wrote, in an article called "No Exit" (2010):

> The impetus for weaning Americans away from their infatuation with war, if it comes at all, will come from within the officer corps. It certainly won't come from within the political establishment, the Republican Party gripped by militaristic fantasies and Democrats too fearful of being tagged as weak on national security to exercise independent judgment. Were there any lingering doubt on that score, Barack Obama, the self-described agent of change, removed it once and for all: by upping the ante in Afghanistan he has put his personal imprimatur on the Long War.
>
> Yet this generation of soldiers has learned what force can and cannot accomplish. Its members understand the folly of imagining that war provides a neat and tidy solution to vexing problems. They are unlikely to confuse Churchillian calls to arms with competence or common sense...[8]

For further inspiration and hope, Harry Targ writes in his blog...

> [Howard] Zinn demonstrated that participants in people's struggles were part of a "people's chain," that is the long history of movements and campaigns throughout history that have sought to bring about change.... [Zinn] wrote in his autobiography, *You Can't Be Neutral on a Moving Train: a Personal History of Our Times:* "What we choose to emphasize in this complex history will determine our lives. If we see only the worst, it destroys our capacity to

---

[8]Bacevich, A. (2010, February 1). No Exit. *The American Conservative.* Retrieved May 28, 2014, from http://www.theamericanconservative.com/articles/no-exit/

do something. If we remember those times and places—and there are so many—where people have behaved magnificently, this gives us the energy to act, and at least the possibility of sending this spinning top of a world in a different direction.

And if we do act, in however small a way, we don't have to wait for some grand utopian future. The future is an infinite succession of presents, and to live now as we think human beings should live, in defiance of all that is bad around us, is itself a marvelous victory.[9]

Military force is an outdated paradigm. Young people are striving and starving for peace. There may always be a greedy or frightened few who push for violent solutions out of selfishness and fear of the unknown, but they are the minority. Most of us are tired of war draining our purses and treasuries, while vast human needs remain unresolved. The world is rapidly moving beyond the old model of violence and war as an instrument of foreign policy to a richer, deeper sense of human security, to a higher humanity. We are aching for cultures of human dignity and peace. The day is near when a child will ask, "Mommy, what *was* war?"

Cultivating Caring Communities

Strong, caring communities can help prevent adolescent isolation, teen suicides, bullying, shootings, and school violence where young people lack a sense of belonging, acceptance, respect, and love. A vast body of evidence across dozens of disciplines based on 40 years of youth surveys, research, and evaluations shows that strong communities are a highly effective deterrent to violence. Youth of color, in particular, feel that

---

[9]Rothschild, M. (2010, January 28). Thank You, Howard Zinn. *The Progressive*. Retrieved May 28, 2014, from http://www.theamericanconservative.com/articles/no-exit/

adults are waging war on them with surveillance, detention, suspension, expulsions, and incarceration. In the name of discipline or security, punitive policies in poor neighborhoods often destroy young people's futures, sending them from the school into juvenile detention centers or, worse, adult prisons. Instead, communities based on respect, civic engagement, listening to youth, connection, caring, responsiveness, positive adult role models, peaceable relationships, peacemaking circles, community conferences, and empathy are a key building block for well-balanced, healthy, nonviolent adolescents and children and a major indicator for an absence of school violence.

How do we reweave and strengthen the fabric of U.S. culture and society to become more closely knit, just, fair, equitable, loving, respectful, joyful, and kind? How do we redirect and counterbalance all the violent consumerism and militaristic influences bombarding our youth? One of the most important methods is to listen to youth themselves. If we sit down with young people most affected by violence, we will learn some surprising insights and find that youth hold some of the greatest promise for resolving the crisis.

Unfortunately, media ask the wrong questions about youth violence and harshly scapegoats and stereotypes young people. The media avoid looking at the deeper questions of adult responsibility, the role of the gun lobby in spreading lethal weapons, and social structures and rampant inequality. Media framing of violence leaves the public without a handle on what to do and lacking a sense of agency or hope. According to the famous nonviolence scholar Dr. Michael Nagler (2007), the more a person watches the news, the more depressed she or he becomes. This may be one reason so many young people opt for independent media.

How to Build Community

We can foster respectful relationships with youth so that they truly feel heard. We can create a sense of community where insults and violence are unacceptable, while mutual respect prevails instead. But what are the signs of such healthy communities? What are the dynamics? Moreover, how can we ensure that everyone stands up and speaks out when violence occurs, both structural violence (poverty, hunger, and injustice) and direct overt violence (school shootings, bullying, and so forth)? How do we overcome the "bystander effect" where people feel paralyzed and no one acts to de-escalate the situation?

Specific, practical, documented proof of what works to create safe communities and childhoods can be found through the Search Institute's national surveys of over a million youth during the last five decades. They analyzed the data and results to understand why some kids struggled, while others grew up with ease; why some were endangered and prone to violence, while others contributed to society; why some are trapped in humane conditions, while other "beat the odds." While many factors influence young people's success in life—including economic circumstances, genetics, and trauma—*they are not the only things that matter.* They alone do not determine the outcome of teens' lives. Rather, healthy, productive youth are affected by the presence of what are known as developmental assets. The Search Institute has been able to identify 40 such assets for 12- to 18-year-olds as the essential building blocks for strong communities and young people. The assets are cumulative, increasing in value over time, and provide a sense of well-being and security. They are the best deterrent to violence in schools. Although a complete listing cannot be provided here, the following is a sample: Support, including from family, other adults, caring neighbors, and a supportive school climate; empowerment, such as being given useful community roles, being valued by adults in the community, serving others, and feeling safe at home, in school, and in the community; appropriate boundaries and high expectations provided by families, other adults, peers, school officials, and community members; constructive use of time, or spending time in arts, music, theater, sports, faith, family, and youth-driven programs;

commitment to and enjoyment of learning; positive values, such as helping others, belief in equality, integrity, honesty, responsibility; social competencies, such as help making positive choices, developing friendships, comfort with people from different backgrounds, the ability to resist, and positive forms of conflict resolution; and positive identity, or high self-esteem, sense of purpose, and a positive view of the future.

Sadly, the Search Institute finds that most U.S. children report having only 18 of the developmental assets in their lives. When these indicators are present, I have personally witnessed the effectiveness of the developmental assets model in turning around the lives of endangered youth in Harlem, New York; Washington, DC; and Arlington, Virginia, since 1981. The teens I know who survived and thrived in tough situations were those linked to community centers, neighborhood groups, Big Brother and Big Sister mentors, congregations, and scouting. We practiced respectful, inclusive, and humane treatment with three key ingredients: (1) tackling the root causes of violence in our area so people's needs are met and grievances are addressed; (2) listening to teen voices for creative solutions that gave everyone a role in banding together; and (3) responding to violence with skills of compassionate listening, advocacy, conflict resolution, and nonviolent action. Letting youth articulate their reality and working for social justice as a whole community made a huge difference. It was an important reality check for the children to know they were not always at fault or to blame for the conditions found in their schools and neighborhood. They were able to step back and see the big picture of how conditions were affecting them but also taking responsibility for their own behavior and how they might be contributing to violence through community accountability and peacemaking circles. It took a communal approach to turn rage and anger about the lack of resources, opportunities, and infrastructure and unmet human needs into nonviolent, grassroots organizing strategies for social change to nurture and safeguard our youth. A holistic approach is required.

Feeling isolated, many youth seek companionship and community on the Internet. This is not something adults should automatically condemn. These youth are seeking a form of community, after all, and frequently feel misunderstood, condemned or judged by adults, and neglected by their parents. Parents may be distracted and emotionally or physically absent due to work or the care of an elderly relative. Too few families share a daily meal to talk about their lives. Families are scattered and disconnected. According to Dr. Ofer Zur, Ph.D,, an expert on bullying and school violence, "Youth are using the Internet for a wide range of activities. These include: homework, communication, fun, gaming, social connection and interaction, information gathering, to view videos, listen to music, post photos, blog, chat, etc." (http://www.zurinstitute.com/teenviolence.html). Parents, guardians, and adults, therefore, should share, review, monitor, discuss, and enjoy together to understand their children's Internet usage, not just condemn it. Internet use should not be excessive. It is no substitute for authentic community and face-to-face relationships. Exposure to violence on the Internet is rampant and desensitizes youth to the real effects of killing. Spending countless hours a day, every day, on gaming or perusing the Internet can interfere with young people's emotional, physical, intellectual, and spiritual development (Young, 2014). *So unplug and talk with youth.*

Best Practices in Reducing School Violence

Another big problem in youth violence is the *bystander effect* when bullying occurs. Studies show that the most effective intervention program to stop bullying and psychological violence is to transform the environment and shift the culture in the school *by activating everyone to play a role*. A groundbreaking study conducted by the University College London (UCL) and U.S. researchers in 2009 with 1,345 third to fifth graders (8–11 year olds) in nine U.S. elementary schools found the most effective method to end bullying focuses more on the bystander, including the teacher, than on the bully or the victim. Creating a Peaceful School Learning Environment (CAPSLE) is one of the few *controlled trials* of school antibullying programs, and it exposed about 4,000 children to the protocols in the end. It assumes that everyone feeds into the power dynamics of bullying. It addresses the co-created relationships among bully, victim, and bystander. Rather than just targeting aggressive children, the CAPSLE program worked to develop empathy, awareness, responsibility, and skills across all populations in the school and gradually recruited bullies over time into helping roles. And it demonstrates that *everyone* in the school has a role in ending bullying and school violence. This means having a genuine community where everyone is engaged and paying attention.

The study published in the *Journal of Child Psychology* and *Science Daily* (January 27, 2009) aims to improve the capacity of all community members to counteract bullying, which has an extensive impact on children's mental health, leading to depression, social withdrawal, substance abuse, anxiety, disruptive and aggressive behavior, dropout, and academic failure. The percentages of children victimized at CAPSLE schools were substantially lower compared with schools receiving no intervention and those using only school psychiatric consultation, particularly at a time when the school district had numerous socioeconomic problems, making the results of the study even more remarkable. The study shows that adults (from the librarian to the janitor) and all the other children must model solidarity, compassion, and leadership and interrupt *unequal power relationships*.

Another highly effective model of violence prevention since the 1980s can be found in the Parenting for Peace and Justice Network, begun in 1981 at the Institute for Peace and Justice as an interfaith, interracial, transnational association of families of all descriptions who seek "Shalom"—well-being, wholeness, peace, justice—in their own living situations and in the broader community. On their website, www.ipj-ppj.org, they state,

> We recognize that the well-being of our families is tied to the well-being of our global family and the earth itself.

Moreover, as both Elise Boulding, the famous peace scholar, and Gloria Steinem, the famous feminist leader, have written, peace and democracy must begin in the home with equitable gender relations. If we do not model a just society in our households, we cannot expect our children to either. Gender equity is a key ingredient in solving poverty, violence, illiteracy, and overpopulation. It is a huge untapped solution across the world. The solution is right under our noses if we would seek gender equity.

A further model to help with school violence can be found in Kindness Clubs, started by Kellie Guinan, a Nebraska peace educator. Such clubs have spread to more than 60 countries now. Teachers say that children are hungry for these kinds of after-school activities in the face of so much television violence and mean-spiritedness in U.S. society. Find a school that adopted the model: http://teachersites.schoolworld.com/webpages/ACummings1/kc_club.cfm.

As a result of the mass shooting at Columbine High School in Colorado on April 20, 1999, parents of the first victim, Rachel Joy Scott, sent out a challenge to schools, families, and communities across the country to stop the social isolation of many youth, the widespread availability of guns, bullying, violent video games, the excessive use of pharmaceutical anti-depressant prescriptions for teens, and unmonitored Internet use. The Scott family began a network to create more caring communities in schools. From their website, they explain that Rachel's Challenge is designed to empower students and equip them to combat bullying by working with adults to create cultures of kindness and compassion.

Working for a Higher Purpose

I have supervised hundreds of interns at eight nonprofit organizations since 1984 and taught hundreds of college students since 2002. Too many expressed to me they felt "lost," "adrift," or "morally confused." Rarely had adults spoken to them of ethics, values clarification, and character development. Finding wisdom, guidance, and meaning in peace and social justice work led the youth I mentored to a larger ethical purpose: to be part of something greater than themselves. National statistics show increasing number of high school and college students seeking such volunteer opportunities to serve others and work for human rights and social justice. All adults who know youth in their neighborhoods, area parks, schools, or congregations thus have a role to play in showing concern for them, getting involved in their lives, and offering them opportunities to "get outside themselves," which can to lead to a sense of greater purpose, community, involvement, caring, trust, nurturance, and a ultimately a curb on media and school violence.

Further, research shows that visits to young people in juvenile correctional facilities can have a significant positive impact on their recidivism rates (Annie E. Casey Foundation, 2012). Many of my Georgetown University students are now trained in the Alternatives to Violence process and the Help Increase the Peace curriculum. They travel to prisons to visit with inmates. It has made them so appreciative of their lucky lives being on the outside and has given them a whole new outlook on working for social justice and change. Visiting and tutoring juveniles in detention is not a pity party but rather a partnership and two-way exchange of mutual respect for the conditions inmates have confronted growing up and the support my students provide.

The Circle Model

All of us have, within us, a tremendous capacity for empathy and compassion. Early child development specialists have found these characteristics again and again in research studies. Our earliest childhood impulses are to help others, animals, and the disadvantaged. Tragically, the economic reward system in our society discourages such qualities. Competition, rugged individualism, and survival of the fittest have been encouraged much more than cooperation.

However, according to the economist, political theorist, and social commentator Jeremy Rifkin, we are moving toward a more global "empathetic civilization." He predicts the new global economy will be based upon *renewable energy*, such as wind power, solar energy, and geothermal energy. New forms of power, in turn, will create more human-scale, decentralized communities because these energy sources are dispersed rather than centralized. They are best controlled by smaller communities. This will entail a very different power structure from fossil fuels and financial capitalism. This new structure is networked and decentralized and an inherently much more democratic form of globalization. There is increasing evidence that a "sharing economy" is emerging in different parts of the world as wealth becomes more and more concentrated in the top 1 percent and the mortgage crisis, financial meltdown, and debt forced people to cooperate and pool resources. We witnessed such a spirit of caring and cooperation at the 1,600 Occupy encampments. Such a sharing economy was also on display during the Arab Spring in the number of nonviolent struggles in city squares and roundabouts in Yemen, Egypt, Tunisia, and Bahrain while people banded together nonviolently to share medicine, food, music, and political debate. This mass group spiritual collective uplift is known as the effervescent affect, and it gives people great inner peace and strength.

In my own neighborhood, we swap outgrown clothes among the 28 children, organize block parties and yard sales, shop for each other at area farmers markets, share veggies from our gardens, offer our homes if someone needs extra housing, and provide free childcare for one another during long work days, school closings, and other events. We all help the elderly on the block, shoveling their driveways and sidewalks. Teens rake leaves for the seniors, mow their lawns, and help them clean out their attics. The senior citizens support the youth in myriad ways. The neighborhood operates almost like a commune.

Such models work in schools too. Talking circles, school "speak outs," and community conferences show kids respect, hold youth accountable through formal agreements to make amends, foster greater communication and active listening, and keep students safer. Talking Circles demonstrate an egalitarian interaction that gives each person a place on a shared footing with others in the circle.

As Native American leader Dr. Martin Brokenleg says, "Youth of any status are not likely to be treated with respect in North American. The legacy of youth as property and commodity has existed since the time of Charles Dickens. The talking Circle format advocated as peacemaking Circles provide a new environment for youth of any ancestry to be understood and treated with the innate dignity that is their birthright" (Boyes-Watson, 2009). La Roca (The Rock) is a community center that works for justice in one of the most broken and dangerous neighborhoods in Boston, using the circle model as a strategy to build positive connections among marginalized youth and families. Using the circle model, La Roca has decreased violence and transformed dozens of schools, neighborhoods, and residential facilities, even the social service systems in the Boston area. In 2013, the Peace and Justice Studies Association, a binational network of Canadian and U.S. professors, gave La Roca their Outstanding Peacebuilding Award.

Organizing for Peace in Your Community: Six Steps for Success

A Curriculum Module for Parents, Community Animators, and Educators by Barbara Wien

(A) Learning objectives for this module:

1. To build trusting, respectful relationships in your neighborhood or community

2. To explore alternatives to violence and war in an open, friendly manner

3. To encourage positive action and move the world toward a nonviolent future

(B) Skills you will gain in this module:

1. Active listening and appreciative inquiry

2. Grassroots community organizing and coalition-building

3. Creative responses to de-escalating violence and hostility

(C) Concepts and terms you will learn in this module:

1. Militarism and the war system

2. Nonviolence

3. The beloved community

(D) A few strategies and tools for building peace in your community:

1. Living-room dialogues and study circles

2. Community peace fairs, art shows, and festivals

3. Peace toys and curricula in schools and stores

4. Candle light walks, vigils, and public "speak outs"

5. Door-to-door visits

6. Training workshops and summer peace camps for kids

Background

My reflections are based on 30 years of organizing for peace in my neighborhoods of Harlem, New York; Washington, DC; and Arlington, Virginia, and introducing peace studies on over

200 college campuses around the world. Each community is unique and diverse. You will find your own style and comfort level wherever you reach out. No one size fits all situations, and you know your own backyard best.

Things to Keep in Mind

- The first lesson to remember is that you are a teacher of peace. You must be patient, model respect, and not be dismayed when people disagree with you. You are introducing new ideas, and many people may be uncomfortable. Some people are reluctant to talk about difficult issues, and people are afraid of change. They may not be accustomed to sharing their views on topics like war and peace. That is OK. You are simply opening up a dialogue. There is nothing to fear. Be reassuring. If some people do not wish to share their views, do not be pushy. Find others in your community more open to fresh thinking and whom reluctant folks may admire and trust. Build relationships from there. "Each one, teach one," as the Quakers always say.

- Second, you are a farmer planting new seeds of peace, kindness, and compassion. You may never know how the seeds you plant today will benefit future generations. Most importantly, we are trying to spread beauty in the world, and this is much more positive and attractive than all the destruction caused by war. Emphasize the aesthetic aspects of peace through art, songs, imaginative activities, and much more. Cultivate cultures of peace. Do not exhibit anger and hostility.

- Third, most people are raised to believe that war makes us safer, and they have not been exposed to the concept of non-violence or how it works. They are accustomed to the idea that we can only solve big, bad conflicts with force. You are spreading new notions and strategies, so be prepared to be labeled as a trouble-maker. Some folks may label you are as unpatriotic, but dissent and contending points of view are valuable in a democracy. In the earliest years of the United States, political dialogue and discourse were practiced all the time. Remember that people of good will can disagree, and that does not make us enemies.

- Be bold. Never be apologetic or defensive about organizing for peace. There is a great deal of evidence that people are waking up to the fact that war does not make us safer. More people agree with us then we realize. They see for themselves in their villages and towns that 500,000 soldiers have returned from Iraq and Afghanistan with severe post-traumatic stress disorder. They know war is not working and disadvantages the poor. We have a long and rich tradition in the United States dating back to the 1600s of non-violent means of change. It is a proud history, too little taught and shared. People have stood up time and time again using peaceful means to challenge wrongdoing and injustice. Our nation's history is replete with such examples. Own that history. Do not shrink from the challenge. Find your voice.

Finally, keep in mind that you are not alone in your efforts. There is a huge worldwide movement to end war, and it is growing. Here is a list of fabulous websites to give you a sense of the larger global movement to abolish war and connect you with others:

- http://www.popularresistance.org/building-a-global-movement -to-end-all-war/
- http://aboldpeace.com/. Spark your neighbors' creativity and imagination by showing people a different way to organize society.
- https://www.youtube.com/watch?v=tIDe_uPe67I. Neva Shalom —Wahat al-Salam.
- http://www.peaceoneday.org. A short video clip about a global cease fire (which the Taliban honored in 2009).

Click on the tags and be sure to review the curriculum Peace Once Day is distributing to thousands of schools.

There are millions and millions of micro-level efforts going on for peace every second of every day in almost every community all around the world. It is just a matter of time before we tip the scales and a child asks, "Mommy, what *was* war?

Six Steps to Success

Step One Start small. We are not going to end war tomorrow, but each step we take brings us closer to that goal. Simply questioning violence and war has a cumulative effect and impact. I once asked the manager of an amusement park to remove a mock electric chair which executed customers with fake jolts and smoke. He laughed and told me it was his biggest money maker. I then asked other parents to complain and wrote a letter to the local newspaper. The next year when I returned to the boardwalk, the electric chair was gone. Countless kids will not be exposed to the idea that it is funny to kill people, even if only pretending. Ask the manager of your local toy store to put violent toys up high on the shelves so small children cannot see or reach them. Better yet, ask them not to sell them at all! Open up a dialogue with others about the issue. I have seen this work many times.

Step Two Stay local. Do not begin with distant issues of foreign affairs. Start with pocket-book concerns and meal-ticket issues at the local level. Learn how much your community is being affected by excessive military spending. Explore what arms industries may be operating in your area and how many people they employ. Ask your neighbors to identify how much they think they are contributing to the war budget. Research what they are actually spending per capita using the website of the National

Priorities Project in Amherst, Maryland: www .nationalpriorities.org. Work with others to calculate how many jobs could be created if green, peaceful technologies to heal the planet were developed in your region. Depending on the industry, 10 times more jobs could be generated than for the same amount of money spent on war. Spread the idea that we need a global environmental recovery race rather than a world arms race. Set up study circles on these issues at the local library or in your living room.

Step Three Use the metaphor of addiction or a parasite to explain militarism and war. War is actually a system of interlocking institutions which reinforce and perpetuate themselves. The war system has its own logic and takes on a life of its own. Militarism is a disease or addiction that saps our national strength. Somehow the logic goes that the more weapons we build, the safer we will be. Just as an addict needs more and more alcohol or drugs to satisfy the craving, our country has built a vast infrastructure for war, which requires more and more resources and propels us to use force. War then becomes a self-fulfilling prophecy.

Step Four Create lasting images of beauty and random acts of kindness in your community. It is contagious. I promise! We cannot create a future we first cannot conjure in our mind. We must first try to imagine a peaceful future and how the world would work if we did not use violence and weapons. How would we resolve our differences and defend our rights? Use all kinds of tools to get people to think creatively about this question. One of the most important visions for what our society and the world would look like comes from Dr. Martin Luther King Jr. He called it the Beloved Community. Check out Martin Luther King's Vision of the Beloved Community at http://www.religion online.org/showarticle

.asp?title=1603. Organize film festivals showing how societies used nonviolent means to overthrow oppressive rulers and dictators, such as *A Force More Powerful*. Sponsor festivals, songs, concerts, dances, sports, nonviolent games, nature, playgrounds, food, displays, and exhibits. Distribute 198 methods of nonviolent action, which can be found at the following website: www .aforcemorepowerful.org/resources/nonviolent/methods.php.

Step Five Study and learn about nonviolence as much as you can. There is a rich and deep, yet hidden, history of nonviolence in the United States. Check out this very important video online. It is free to the public and may be used for any type of program: http://www.archive.org/details/ The American Tradition Of Nonviolence. It offers great hope for the world. Today, more than ever before, people are turning to methods of nonviolent action to fight for democracy and human rights. Around the world, groups are discovering that they do not have to simply submit to injustices and that nonviolent struggle is a more effective alternative to violence. People armed with "nonviolent weapons"—such as economic boycotts, mass demonstrations, strikes, political noncooperation, and civil disobedience—brought down racism and segregation in the United States, defeated communist regimes in eastern Europe, undermined the legitimacy of the Chinese government, dismantled the system of apartheid in South Africa, toppled Marcos in the Philippines, and much more. "People power" is transforming the global political landscape in unprecedented ways. Share these inspiring trends with your neighbors.

Step Six Find out who else in your community is working for nonviolence. Take stock of any allies out there. Build coalitions in your region. There may be men's groups against rape. There may be synagogues, churches, and mosques working to stop torture and genocide such as in

Darfur. Teachers in your schools and professors in nearby universities may be teaching conflict resolution and alternatives to war. If they are not, ask them to start offering classes! Do a survey of the public's views about war and military intervention. Ask survey research experts in the private sector to help you design the survey pro bono or local universities to help write the questions to ensure objectivity and accuracy. College students under supervision from their professors often have to conduct such projects. What you learn from the survey will help frame your organizing work and inform your messages so they resonant with the public in your region. Issue a media release and hold a press conference to publicize the results of your survey. When people read about a poll conducted in their own town questioning military force, maybe they will think more deeply and get involved. You just never know what it can lead to!

Last, have fun! Be joyful. Exude serenity and optimism. Do not be negative. Engage others and their ideas in a thoughtful, attentive manner with care and respect. Dare to dream! Encourage children especially to dream of a world without bullying and war. Good luck!

References

Annie E. Casey Foundation. (2012). "No Place like Home: Reducing Juvenile Incarceration."

Boyes-Watson, Carolyn. (2009). *Peacemaking Circles and Urban Youth: Bringing Justice Home.* Minnesota: Living Justice Press.

Harvard University Medical School. (1984). "Fear in the Nuclear Age."

Nagler, Michael. (2007). *The Search for a Nonviolent Future.* California: Berkeley Hills Books.

United Nations Educational, Cultural, and Scientific
    Organization (UNESCO). (1986). *Seville Statement on
    Human Violence.* http://www.unesco.org/cpp/uk/declarations/
    seville.pdf

Young, Kimberly. (2014). The Center for Internet Addiction.

*Barbara J. Wien is a long-time peace educator. Since 1981, Wien
has worked to stop human rights abuses, violence, and war. She has
protected civilians from death squads in conflict zones, led eight
nonprofit organizations, taught alternatives to war and violence
at six universities, and delivered peace seminars in 58 countries.
She is the author of 19 articles, study guides, and books and the
winner of numerous awards for her activism.*

Activism against Domestic and Dating Violence: Stephanie Wong

Domestic violence continues to be the United States' dirty little
secret. The media tends to deal with it as separate events rather
than as a dangerous trend. I believe that domestic violence is at
the heart of many societal ills. The emotional damage it causes
cannot be fully measured. I have volunteered at abuse shelters
and had face-to-face contact with victims. I attended a high
school that went through the traumatic experience of a school
shooting. I consider myself to be an activist. I participate in
community outreach projects such as the College Brides Walk
and Peace in Every Relationship (P.I.E.R.) mentoring. My
passion to raise awareness about dating and domestic violence
has come from different sources, and my overall perspective of
domestic violence has evolved over the years.

I was raised by a mother who has been an activist against
domestic violence. I first became interested in activism while my
mother worked as the executive director of Safe Space
Foundation, a women's shelter in Miami, Florida. I remember
spending Thanksgiving serving food to women and children
who were victims of violence. I also recall helping out with toy

drives for kids and their mothers at Christmas, trying to support those who were going through difficult times. I learned that something as simple as a toy could brighten up their holiday season. I must admit, at 10 or 1 years old I did not always understand why I was a part of these charity events, nor could I clearly see the difference between myself and the little girl to whom I was passing a plate of food. Eventually, my work as a volunteer helped me to understand that everyone has the right to live a life free from physical and emotional violence. Although many abusers were themselves abused, there is never any justification for harming another human being, especially those who we say we love.

During my sophomore year in high school, my friend Amanda was killed in our school hallway by another student, Tia. I had known both girls since the sixth grade. Although we were never close, about a month before the incident Amanda had asked me for dating advice, and I told her what I could. According to reports, Tia was in love with Amanda, but Amanda was not interested. It was reported that Tia then stole her grandfather's gun and shot Amanda at our school. Just an hour before the shooting occurred I saw my friend Nicole was sitting in our English class staring at her phone with a dazed look on her face. I asked her if she was okay, and she just brushed me off and said she was fine. I later found out that Tia had been texting Nicole saying that she wanted to hurt someone and that she was very angry. Tia had a history of sexual abuse, and though it may not be directly related to the incident, I believe it played a part in her unhealthy way of dealing with rejection. Nicole never spoke up or did much to prevent the violence from occurring. It is this type of situation that makes raising awareness about dating violence even more important to me. Too many people are still reluctant to take action when they know that someone is in danger of abuse. I have found that the lack of open discussion about abuse is what perpetuates the silence and fear of speaking out.

Speaking out was not a problem for my mother. I was eight years old when I was told she was donning her wedding gown and walking along the East Coast of the United States to spread awareness about the evils of domestic violence. My mother, Josie Ashton, who was 28 years old, had been a victim of domestic violence at the hands of her first boyfriend when she was 17. My mom committed to do the walk after learning about the horrific story of a woman named Gladys Ricart. Like my mother, Ricart was of Dominican descent. Ricart had been shot and killed on her wedding day by an abusive former boyfriend named Augustin Garcia. Because of the lack of understanding in many communities about dating and domestic violence, many began to blame Ricart for her own victimization. Outraged, my mother decided to wear her own wedding gown while raising awareness about domestic violence. The movement she began 12 years ago is still going strong. I have organized events with my mother as educational tools for high school and college students who are concerned about domestic violence. What is known as the College Brides Walk is an annual event held at Barry University in North Miami. Every year I have the amazing opportunity to see how the College Brides Walk allows the topics of dating and domestic violence to be discussed openly with the goal of finding solutions. As our annual event continues, more and more people I know disclose their experiences with dating violence and share how happy they are that the walk takes place. To me, abuse in our society has been the elephant in the room. It has become too big to ignore. It is only when we finally confront this cancer that will be able to work together to formulate practical and effective strategies to decrease and, eventually, eliminate domestic violence.

P.I.E.R. mentoring is a comprehensive program that has been teaching students in North Miami how to address the problem of domestic violence. I, along with other mentors and students from Barry University, facilitate workshops for students from 4th to 12th grade about dating violence. Not only do we inform students about how to recognize signs of abuse, we also promote and explain what healthy relationships should look like. As our flyers state, "Our P.I.E.R. presentations are used to educate our youth using interactive projects that are age appropriate such as, storytelling, video clips, and class discussions." In my experience teaching at various schools in North Miami, I have seen how desperately children need to receive the information we teach. I am often asked, "What would be the way to solve this problem?" When hearing this question, some children say something along the lines of, "well I would just go take a gun and shoot them." Many children who hear this response laugh and agree. It is disappointing to see how many children have become comfortable with the culture of violence. The idea that more violence is as a solution, whether jokingly or not, is very alarming to me. If young people are not taught that violence is never the answer the cycle of abuse will continue. It is impossible for our P.I.E.R. mentoring program to uncover everything that goes on in the personal lives of each individual student, but by the way they interact with me and other peers during the presentation, it is clear that many are suffering in silence. I am excited to be a part of the mentoring program, and I see the continuing need in these schools for education regarding domestic violence. It is a satisfying feeling to provide assistance and see the results of hard work. It is truly a labor of love.

The problem of dating and domestic violence must not be ignored. In the last few years, I am proud to say that my skills in addressing situations about abuse among friends and family have improved. Being a budding activist has allowed me to be more comfortable talking about domestic violence. I am happy to be a voice that spreads positive alternatives to resolve any issue. There will be no change if we do not teach the children that everyone has the right to live in peace and safety.

Stephanie Wong is a junior psychology major at Florida International University. She is also an organizer of the College Brides Walk and a mentor for a dating violence prevention program called P.I.E.R.

Turning the Personal into Progress: Robert Spencer Knotts

As a child, I was bullied. As an adult, I work to stop bullying. There is, believe me, a direct correlation between the two experiences.

Though the 501c3 nonprofit organization I founded in 2005, the Humanity Project, now offers a variety of programs with a common philosophical thread among them, our Anti-bullying Through the Arts program was the group's first and remains our signature effort. It is presented live by a two-person team that includes myself, given to kids in grades K–5 at no cost to the schools.

So far more than 14,000 students have benefited from Anti-bullying Through the Arts. Pre/post testing conducted by the schools suggests our program is highly effective in communicating one key idea: "Bullying hurts everyone in this school—and it takes everyone to stop it." We show children why bullying affects them personally, helping to connect them with the feelings of the bullying victims. Then we teach them how to cooperate with the bullied kids to stop the aggression in a constructive, nonviolent way.

I created the program in 2008 as the state of Florida struggled to implement its new antibullying law. Anti-bullying Through the Arts was vetted by a panel of psychologists, educators, and social activists and has become an acclaimed program in the nation's sixth largest school system, a district made up of Broward County, Florida. Program elements that can be transferred without our in-person participation have spread to school districts from California to Vermont. These include our colorful posters and our book, which was written by at-risk middle school students for their younger peers. We called the book, *I Was a Bully . . . But I Stopped.*

The title is not taken from my own experience. I was never a very good bully. I tried it out a few times as a kid but always ended up feeling bad. I can recall going home to cry hard after pushing one boy down for no reason during a baseball game, for instance. It just was not me. And I think that's part of the reason I was such a good bullying victim. Kids knew I was not aggressive by nature and possessed a distinctly sensitive side—all the makings of a good target for other children.

I also was different from most of the others. I was smart, got good grades, and had an active imagination—overactive, perhaps. I did not just go outside to kick a football around. No, I put on my football uniform to go outside and kick a football around. I wanted to feel the part, imagine myself pounding the winning field goal through the uprights. One day as I was doing this by myself, the usual neighborhood bullies could not resist stopping by to harass me.

I will never forget one boy picking up a clump of clay as he said, "Hey, Knotts! This is your head!" Then he threw it on the pavement as hard as he could, splattering the clump into small pieces of dirt. To me, this was like watching him smash my head into the ground. It wounded because I felt that someone hated me so intensely. And I wondered, "What have I done to cause this? What is wrong with me?"

My mother actually saw that incident and, for once, voiced unqualified support for me. Usually when I complained about being bullied by these same kids she offered her versions of the questions I kept asking myself: "What have you done to cause this? What is wrong with you?" I know now that she meant well. And my father always provided unconditional love and guidance for me—about bullying or anything else. That was a huge help.

But being the sensitive and reflective sort I am, of course, I have never forgotten how I felt as a bullied child. For many years, long before bullying became a front-page topic, I made the case to friends that bullying had to be viewed differently so that it would seem uncool. Like cigarette smoking, bullying had to become socially unacceptable.

I founded the Humanity Project with the goal this organization still has at its core: To help society by improving the way that individuals see themselves. I have believed for decades that many of the planet's worst problems are caused, at bottom, by a struggle for individual value. As William James wrote long ago, "The deepest principle in human nature is the craving to be appreciated." To me, this craving fuels personal, interpersonal, and intergroup problems and even international conflicts.

As I wrote in a Humanity Project booklet for our members:

> Society really is just a collection of individuals. You are humanity. So am I. The conflicts and troubles in society at large reflect the conflicts and troubles within our hearts as individuals. . . . The only genuine solution is to change the world by changing ourselves. That means we must each help improve the world from the inside out by altering the way we view ourselves and other individuals. Then we must learn to act according to this more realistic view.

Our programs include direct efforts to help accomplish that goal, especially our website for socially isolated teens and tweens. Our new website's intended audience includes many LGBT students. That site, www.thp4kids.com, is unique on the Internet to our knowledge, developed by magnet school teens from the Gay–Straight Alliance with a sophistication that appeals to smart, lonely kids of about 12 to 17 years old. Its three main sections are titled, "Bullying is SO not cool," "You're NOT alone," and "Being . . . YOU!"

But other programs, including Anti-bullying Through the Arts, use positive peer pressure to stop a problem that poses an immediate threat to emotional or physical well-being. Realizing that all kids crave the appreciation cited by William James, we designed Anti-bullying Through the Arts in a way that encourages bystanders to deny social approval to bullies. Our reasoning is that, just as with smoking, behavior can be changed fairly quickly on a broad scale by making people feel self-conscious about doing it.

Even bullies are looking for appreciation. They may want the other kids to laugh with them as they embarrass another student. Or they may seek respect as the tough girl or tough guy on campus. They may be looking for pats on the back from parents who are bullies themselves.

That's why Anti-bullying Through the Arts repeats its mantra to elementary school kids many times and in many forms: "Bullying hurts everyone in this school—and it takes everyone to stop it." Once we get bystander students as well as their teachers and administrators to show the aggressive few kids that bullying is no longer cool, most bullying will stop. Everybody wants to be seen as cool, after all, bullies included. Those bullies will find more socially acceptable outlets for their anger when bullying is denied to them as a path to appreciation— not the ultimate solution for the bullies, surely, but an immediate improvement for bullying victims, and for bystanders who must endure schools troubled by bullying.

I have wished many times during idle moments that the anti-bullying movement had been born before the middle school years when I was tormented. I know that I would felt much more supported and less isolated, even if I still had been bullied. With society in general agreement that bullying is bad, I would not have doubted myself in the same way. And I would not have asked myself those two questions so often: "What have I done to cause this? What is wrong with me?"

The scar tissue from those years still is with me, though I continue to work on letting it all go at long last. I believe that years of bullying by my schoolyard peers eventually combined with other elements of my childhood to contribute to a sense of insecurity around other people, especially those I see as peers. I can have trouble trusting them and, worse, trusting myself around them. It is a problem I work to overcome to this day.

I think that the Humanity Project's antibullying program has been helpful in this regard. Many times, the best community reforms are driven by a combination of needs that are at once very personal and very social. That is what attracted me to bullying as one of the issues on which to focus the work of the Humanity Project. I cared about it, I understood it at an intimate level—and I knew that I could find a way for this organization to help end it as a common form of violence against children.

In the future, we hope to obtain the funding that would allow us to take Anti-bullying Through the Arts to another level, creating an interactive DVD with the full program that could be used by any school anywhere. We already know how to accomplish this goal and lack only the money to carry it out just now.

But we are optimistic about our chances of making this happen in the coming years. Just as we are hopeful about the likelihood that school bullying soon will be viewed almost universally in our culture as socially unacceptable.

There's no reason any boy or girl of the future should ask themselves those terrible questions as a consequence of bullying: "What have I done to cause this? What is wrong with me?" because the answer is obvious to us now: Nothing at all is wrong with them. Once our society can convince most people to agree with this idea, placing responsibility squarely on the bullies, the era of widespread student bullying will be over.

Robert Spencer Knotts is founder and president of the Humanity Project, a South Florida nonprofit organization that seeks to build a better humanity through innovative, arts-based, and youth-led initiatives. Key programs include school-based antibullying efforts and a teen-focused safe driving effort called iCare.

COLUMBINE HIGH SCHOOL

REBEL PRIDE

A TIME TO REMEMBER

A TIME TO HOPE

4   Profiles

This chapter provides overviews of persons who have figured prominently in the history of U.S. school violence. The first half of the chapter features profiles of some of the most notorious offenders, including the Bath, Michigan, school bombing perpetrated by Andrew Kehoe in 1927; the 1999 Columbine massacre in which Eric Harris and Dylan Klebold killed 12 people and themselves; the school murders committed by Laurie Dann in 1988; Adam Lanza's December 2012 deadly rampage at Sandy Hook Elementary in Newtown, Connecticut; Kip Kinkel's family and school murders in May 1998; Barry Loukaitis's murder of two students and a teacher in 1996; Patrick Purdy's rampage at Cleveland Elementary School in 1989; Evan Ramsey's massacre of February 19, 1997; the hostage-taking and executions perpetrated by Charles Carl Roberts at an Amish school in October 2006; the Steubenville High School rape scandal of August 2012; and Jeff Weise's shootings in Red Lake, Minnesota. Additionally, the first half of the chapter includes profiles of two bullying victims who committed suicide (Phoebe Prince and Amanda Todd) and whose cases generated national and international attention.

Columbine High School conveys a message of hope after the deadly shootings that occured on April 20, 1999. (Bambi L. Dingman/Dreamstime.com)

211

The second half of the chapter includes profiles of individuals or organizations that have played important roles in helping the nation understand, respond to, and prevent school violence. Profiles include Harlem Children's Zone innovator Geoffrey Canada; historian, author, and peace activist Riane Eisler; filmmaker and author Jackson Katz; scholar and social justice educator Paul Kivel; and antihazing activist Hank Nuwer. Organizations profiled include Break the Cycle, a dating violence educational resource; the Gay, Lesbian & Straight Education Network (GLSEN), which provides information about and support for the rights of all people regardless of their sexual orientation; Students Against Violence Everywhere (SAVE), a student-driven initiative to end all forms of violence; and StopBullying.gov, a program of the U.S. Department of Health and Human Services.

Part I

Bath, Michigan, School Bombing

Unknown to many, the deadliest incidence of school violence in U.S. history did not occur at Columbine High School or at Sandy Hook Elementary. Instead, it was the small community of Bath, Michigan, that was the scene of the largest school bombing in terms of loss of life. On May 18, 1927, school board member Andrew Kehoe, 55, a resident of Bath, set bombs that blew up the north wing of Bath Consolidated School, leading to the deaths of 38 students plus five adults. Kehoe also killed his wife before the bombing and then himself afterwards, bringing the death toll to 45.

Bath Township was and is a small, largely agricultural town located 10 miles northeast of Lansing. At the time, there were no street lights in Bath and only one road, which ran through the middle of town. The town consisted of a drug store, a gas station, a small grocery store, and an auto repair and blacksmith shop. The Bath Consolidated School, located in the town's center, had recently been built, with an opening enrollment of 236 students in the first through 12th grades.

Andrew Kehoe was born in Tecumseh, Michigan, on February 1, 1872, not too far from Bath. His mother died when Kehoe was very young, and his father soon remarried. It appears that the relationship between Kehoe and his step-mother was not good, and when Kehoe was 14 years of age, his stepmother died in an accident. She was attempting to light the family's oil stove when it exploded. Kehoe was home at the time of the explosion but reportedly did little to help his step-mother, and some even believed that he was involved in the accident, although this was never substantiated.

Kehoe was known in Bath to be intelligent, meticulous, and good with machinery and electronics. He was also considered an expert in the use of dynamite and explosives, as these were common tools among local farmers, who used them for clearing land and stump removal. Kehoe was also known for having a short temper and for the cruel way he treated his farm animals. When his wife, Nellie Kehoe, contracted tuberculosis and required numerous hospitalizations, it placed a severe drain on the family finances. Additionally, Kehoe had been vocally criti-cal of the property tax rates assessed by the Bath Consolidated School District, and he eventually stopped making his mort-gage payments. Despite these criticisms, he was elected to the school board in 1924, where he served as treasurer. His rela-tionship with School Superintendent Emory Huyck was antagonistic, and Kehoe consistently accused Huyck of finan-cial mismanagement. While on the school board, Kehoe blamed the school district for his personal financial trouble and lobbied for lower taxes.

The scene of the bombing was chaotic and horrific. The school building's walls were blown outward, which caused the roof to collapse, trapping children inside of classrooms. According to witnesses, both living and dead children were vis-ible in the rubble. Monty Ellsworth, Kehoe's neighbor, and his wife had heard and even felt the explosion and raced to the school to see what had happened. Concerned about their son, who was in second grade (and was OK), the Ellsworths began pulling people from the rubble. Realizing that their rescue would require additional tools, Ellsworth and others went to their homes to retrieve the necessary items, and in the process, Ellsworth passed his neighbor Kehoe driving in the opposite direction. Kehoe smiled and waved. No one realized at that time that there had been an earlier explosion at the Kehoe farm and that a third was yet to come.

While the community pulled children from the debris, Kehoe collected any metal bits he could find, including nails, broken tools, and old farm machinery. He loaded a large quantity of dynamite behind the front seat of his car and put his loaded rifle in the passenger's seat. He drove to Bath Consolidated School, and, upon seeing Superintendent Huyck, called him over to his car. Kehoe fired the rifle into the back seat, detonating the dynamite and sending the metal bits of shrapnel everywhere. This explosion killed Huyck, Postmaster Glenn O. Smith, Smith's father-in-law, and Cleo Clayton, a second-grade student. It also killed Kehoe. Many others were injured.

Hundreds of volunteers, including Michigan governor Fred Green, came to help. They found another 500 pounds of unexploded dynamite in the school's south wing. The Michigan State Police disarmed the explosives.

Based on reports from Ellsworth, investigators went to the Kehoe farm. They found Nelly Kehoe's body, and the coroner speculated that it was not fire or explosions that killed her but instead blunt force trauma to the head. They also found all of Kehoe's animals dead in their pens and stalls. Further, investigators found a wooden sign on a fence which carried a message from Kehoe: "Criminals are made, not born." Interestingly, investigators determined that the money Kehoe had spent on explosives would have easily paid off his bills.

Columbine Massacre

The date April 20, 1999, will forever go down in history as one of the worst school shootings in history and as the first to receive extensive national and international media coverage.

That morning, Eric Harris and Dylan Klebold entered Columbine High School in Jefferson County, Colorado, dressed in trench coats and armed with multiple weapons and ammunition. Klebold and Harris had bought a rifle and two shotguns from a friend, who had bought them at a gun show. They also collected two 12-gauge shotguns and two 9 mm firearms. After researching on the Internet how to build bombs, they made 99 of them.

In a chilling rampage in which the two boys' actions were caught on video, they laughed and joked as they shot and wounded 23 of their peers and killed 12 students and a teacher. Before they could be apprehended, the boys shot themselves, counting down to ensure they would do it together. It is the most deadly shooting at a U.S. high school.

Before they entered the school, Klebold and Harris placed a fire bomb in a field near the school, set to go off at 11:14 a.m. (Mountain Daylight Time). Klebold and Harris then arrived at the school at 11:10 a.m. and parked outside the cafeteria. They had two propane bombs hidden in duffle bags that they brought into the cafeteria during the first lunch shift, which were supposed to detonate at 11:17 a.m. Klebold and Harris went to their cars to wait for the bombs to explode, but the bombs did not detonate as planned, so they took their guns and started shooting students who were outside the school eating lunch and on the staircase outside. They then shot at students in the soccer fields and threw pipe bombs, although none of the shots made their mark and the bombs did not go off. A teacher, Patti Nielson, went to see what was going on and was hit in the shoulder by shrapnel from the boys' gun shots. She ran to the library to warn students to be careful and frantically called the police from that location. At approximately 11:24 a.m. the sheriff arrived. He shot at the two school shooters. Harris shot back, and the sheriff called for backup. At that point, Harris and Klebold began running through the school, shooting at anyone who was there and throwing more pipe bombs. The two shooters then made their way to the library, which they entered at 11:29 a.m. They first threw two bombs into the cafeteria and one in the library hallway, which this time all did explode. Two teachers, two librarians, and 52 students were in the library. Harris and Klebold started yelling at everyone to quit hiding, but no one obeyed the command. They killed one student, then saw police evacuating students outside, so they shot at the police through the windows. Again, the police shot back. However, their attention quickly went back to the students inside the library, and Harris and Klebold started shooting under computer desks, where students were hiding, injuring and killing more students. They walked around, knocking down shelves and shooting more students, as well as throwing more bombs.

Witnesses have reported that Klebold and Harris starting talking to each other about how the shooting was no longer exciting to them. They thought of possibly attacking people with knives, which they thought might be more fun. Instead, they left the library at 11:42 a.m. As soon as they left, the students fled the library to get outside of the building, while others hid in the staff break room until about 3:30 p.m., when police finally found them.

Meanwhile, Klebold and Harris wandered through the school, continuing to shoot and throw bombs as they went. At 12:02 p.m., they went back into the library, which was now empty except for unconscious students on the floor. This is where, at the end of it all, Harris and Klebold killed themselves. Eric Harris, 18, shot himself in the mouth one time, and Dylan Klebold, 17, died by a single shot to his head.

At 1:09 p.m., the SWAT team entered the school. They were criticized for responding too slowly but, given that this was the first incidence of this scope, were likely not fully prepared. Further, no one knew exactly what was happening and whether there might be additional shooters in the school. At 4:30 p.m. the SWAT team declared the school to be safe, although later they found more explosives, including in Klebold's car, and it was not officially declared safe to enter again until 10:00 a.m. the next day. Officials believe the shootings lasted for 45 minutes before Klebold and Harris shot themselves, and all together, they killed 12 students and one teacher, injured 23 others, and another three were injured trying to get out of the school. The casualties of the shooting that day were Cassie Bernall, Matt Kechter, Corey DePooter, Isaiah Schoels, Daniel Rohrbough, Steve Curnow, Lauren Townsend, Kelly Fleming, Kyle Velasquez, Daniel Mauser, John Tomlin, Rachel Scott, and Coach Dave Sanders.

On April 21 police began investigating the site. Thirteen bodies remained at the school, and they were not removed to be identified until late afternoon or early evening that day. Throughout the investigation, officials held a press conference to say they believed other people had helped plan the shooting.

Many have questioned why two boys from seemingly stable families would do such an awful thing. Initial reports stated that the boys had been bullied and that they had targeted the jocks who harassed them. There is evidence that neither Klebold nor Harris fit in well and that they had endured some bullying. They were teased for being weird and accused of being gay. Before the attack, the boys made a video in which they claimed they were going to get back at all who had mistreated them. But it also is clear that they were bullies themselves. Further, they seem to have made no effort to specifically target jocks in their rampage. Other reports called attention to their apparel and connected them with a group called the Trenchcoat Mafia, a subculture of students who dressed similarly and were marginalized from the mainstream at the school. Later reports, however, showed that Harris and Klebold were not really a part of that group and that it was far from a "gang" but instead more of a loose connection of friends.

Another part of the explanation has centered on Klebold and Harris's use of violent video games. Both were avid players and had even done some programming for the ultraviolent game *Doom*. They were also fans of violent music and movies, and thus the argument is that the two had become desensitized. Yet, as many commentators have pointed out, violent music, movies, and video games are and have been popular with youth for decades, and very few who consume them act out violently.

The FBI's main investigator into the Columbine massacre as well as many psychiatrists have noted issues of mental illness. Klebold was allegedly suffering from depression, and some have speculated that Harris was a clinical psychopath and that he was essentially the leader with Klebold his follower. Both boys had previously been in trouble. On January 30, 1988, they were arrested for stealing tools from a van. They entered into a diversion program in which they had to take classes and meet with parole officers, and Harris was required to attend therapy for a year. Harris had been prescribed Zoloft because he claimed to have suicidal thoughts. Later, he switched to Luvox, which was discovered in his system when he died. These drugs have been found to increase aggression. Both were released from the program early for good behavior and then later bragged about how they had faked compliance with the program requirements.

After the attack, officials found journals and videos of the plans of Klebold and Harris. These records showed that Klebold and Harris had originally planned to bomb the school. They would then shoot any survivors and then start shooting the people who came to investigate what was happening. An investigator with the Jefferson County Sheriff's Office knew about Harris's website in which he discussed bomb-making some two years before the attack. The investigator, Michael Guerra, started looking into the website after he was informed there were threats on it against another student, Brooks Brown. Brown's parents had complained about Harris and Klebold's threats. Guerra also found blogs, written by Harris, about his hatred of society in general as well as threats against specific students at Columbine High School on the site. Harris even had a hit list on the site and a detailed description of the weapons he had. Despite these records, officials determined there was no probable cause for Guerra to obtain a search warrant to search Harris's home.

Columbine was different than some school shootings in that afterward there was no one to take to trial, since Harris and Klebold both killed themselves.

The shooting at Columbine High School opened American society's eyes to many issues with youth and safety. People were more closely scrutinizing youth violence, gun control laws, high school subcultures, bullying, and the effect of media such as video games after this shooting occurred.

Harris and Klebold also influenced many other school shootings or attempted school shootings, as other students wanted to be like them or wanted to outdo them.

Laurie Dann

On May 20, 1988, Laurie Dann attempted to poison family, friends, and acquaintances with arsenic before she entered Ravinia Elementary School in Highland Park, Illinois, where she shot and killed a boy and wounded five other children. After fleeing the scene, Dann took a family hostage, shooting one man and then killing herself.

Laurie Wasserman appeared to have a normal childhood. The daughter of an accountant and a home-maker, she grew up in Glencoe, a middle-to-upper-class suburb of Chicago. She was described as somewhat shy and withdrawn, with poor school performance. Despite her grades, Wasserman was accepted into Drake University in Des Moines, Iowa, after her high school graduation. After improving her grades, she transferred to the University of Arizona, began studying education, and started to date a premed student. Growing tired of the controlling relationship, Laurie moved back to the Chicago area and lived with her parents while she attended Northwestern University. She never completed a degree, however.

Laurie met Russell Dann, an executive with an insurance brokering firm, in the spring of 1982. They married that September. Laurie seemed troubled from the start, however. Her husband suspected she suffered from obsessive-compulsive disorder (OCD), and for a short time she saw a psychiatrist. After three years, Laurie and Russell separated. She claimed he had been violent and abusive, and indeed, the police were called to investigate fights between the two in the years after they separated. Laurie accused Russell in April 1986 of breaking into and vandalizing her parents' home, where she had been living. Shortly thereafter, Laurie purchased a gun. She continued to behave oddly and make wild accusations against Russell and other former boyfriends. In September 1986, Russell Dann accused Laurie of breaking into his home and stabbing him with an ice pick while he slept. She was not charged, as police believed Russell inflicted the wounds himself. She then accused him of raping her and of planting bombs at her home, but again no charges were ever filed.

Struggling from as yet undiagnosed mental problems, Laurie again saw a psychiatrist for her obsessive-compulsive behavior. He deemed her neither suicidal nor homicidal. She was prescribed clomipramine, a new OCD drug. When she moved to Madison, Wisconsin, in November 1987, her new psychiatrist increased the dosage and also prescribed lithium to address Laurie's many phobias.

Just one month later, Laurie purchased another gun. In March 1988, she stopped seeing her psychiatrist. She also began to plan her attacks. Laurie went to the library and stole books about poison, then stole arsenic from a lab. She was arrested for theft after she shoplifted some clothes and wigs. Concerned, her family and her former psychiatrist tried to convince her to enter a mental health facility, but she would not.

Because she made threatening phone calls that crossed state lines, Laurie became known to the FBI.

In early May 1988, Laurie mixed the arsenic she had stolen into prepared rice cereal snacks and juice boxes. She mailed some of the poisons to Russell Dann and her psychiatrist and then delivered her packages to other friends at Northwestern University. Because she had diluted the arsenic and because the smell had tipped off the recipients, no one became seriously ill. Laurie then drove to the home of a family for whom she had previously babysat, the Rushes. The kids thought she was taking them on an outing that she had promised, but instead she drove them to Ravinia Elementary School, which her former sister-in-law's children attended. Leaving the two Rush children in the car, Laurie entered the school and tried to detonate a fire bomb. No major damage was done. Laurie then drove to a local daycare facility and was prohibited from entering because she had a can of gasoline with her. Laurie then drove the Rush children to their home and gave them some poisoned milk, which they spat out. She coerced the children into the basement, then set fire to the house, trapping the two boys and their mother. Laurie then left the home and drove to Hubbard Woods Elementary. She took a boy hostage, pushing him into a restroom, and shot him with one of her three guns. She entered a classroom and demanded that all the children go to a corner. The teacher managed to get Laurie's Beretta, but she pulled a .32 from her waistband and fired several shots, wounding four and killing eight-year-old Nicholas Corwin before she fled the school.

Laurie could not escape by car due to a funeral procession, so she began running through the woods. She ran to the Andrews home and lied to Mrs. Andrews and her 20-year-old son Phillip, telling them she had been raped and was fleeing her assailant, who she had shot. Believing her, the Andrews contacted Laurie's mother. Mr. Andrews arrived home and convinced Laurie to give up her weapons. Again, they called Mrs. Wasserman, and while

Laurie spoke to her mother, Mrs. Andrews fled the house and called the police. When she saw the officers pull up, Laurie shot Phillip in the chest. He escaped and was rescued by the police and EMTs. Knowing the house was surrounded, Laurie went upstairs and shot herself.

After these tragic events, Phillip Andrew went on to become executive director of the Illinois Council Against Handgun Violence. Laurie's family was criticized for not doing more to help her and for initially refusing to allow investigators to see her medical records. Although some of Laurie Dann's victims sustained serious injuries, all recovered.

Kip Kinkel

On May 21, 1998, Kip Kinkel, a 15-year-old high school student, killed two students and wounded 25 others at Thurston High School in Springfield, Oregon. The murdered students were Ben Walker, 16, and Mikael Nickolauson, 17. The day prior, Kinkel had murdered his parents, Bill and Faith Kinkel, in their home. Their bodies were found the day after the school shooting, with a note that Kip wrote explaining that he heard voices in his head telling him to kill. The note also said that he regretted having to kill others.

On May 20, 1998, Kip bought a semi-automatic pistol from a friend. The friend had stolen it from another friend's father, although it is not clear whether Kip knew the gun had been stolen. The same day, the owner of the gun, Scott Keeney, called the school to tell them it had been taken and that he thought a student might have it. It happened that a detective was at the school for an unrelated issue, and he talked to Kip about the gun. Kip confessed that he had it. Kip Kinkel and Korey Ewert, who had stolen the gun, were both arrested and suspended from school.

Bill Kinkel was very upset and unsure of how to handle his son. He had little time to ponder it, however, as Kip shot his father in the back of the head with his rifle at about 3:00 p.m.

He put his father's body in the bathroom and put a sheet over it. At about 3:30 p.m., Kip's English teacher, Mr. Rowan, called the house. Kip spoke to him, saying he had made a mistake but not disclosing what it was. Kip also told Mr. Rowan that his father was not home. A half hour later, a friend called asking for Bill, and Kip said he was at the store. At about 4:30 p.m., students from Bill's community college class called, as Bill was late for the class he was to teach. Kip told them he was not going to make it because of family issues.

Kip then talked to his friends Tony McCown and Nick Hiaason in a conference call and said that he had not known the gun was Mr. Keeney's, that his dad was at a bar, and that he was worried what others would think about what had happened at school that day. Kip told Tony and Nick that he felt sick, that he was upset and angry, and he kept wondering when his mother would be home.

Faith Kinkel arrived home at about 6:30 p.m., and Kip joined her in the garage. After telling her he loved her, he shot her six times in the head, face, and chest. Then he covered her with a sheet, as he had his father.

Even though he was suspended, Kip went to school the following day, bringing with him three guns and a knife. He shot Ben Walker and Ryan Atteberry and then randomly shot at people in the cafeteria. After he had killed the two and injured 25, five students forced him to the ground. When police arrived, Kip told them he wanted to die. He then attacked Detective Al Warthen (the same detective who had arrested him the previous day) with a hunting knife he had strapped to his leg, shouting that he wanted them to kill him. When he calmed down, Kip confessed that he had killed his parents. Police also discovered Kip had two bullets taped to his chest. He said he intended to use those to kill himself.

These murders were not the first time Kip Kinkel had been in trouble. Even at an early age, he seemed to have difficulties controlling his anger and acted out at school. His first year in school was in Spain, and the teacher only taught in Spanish.

Kip's sister, Kristin, said this was difficult for him, and he got in trouble frequently.

In second grade Kip was tested for a learning disability, but it was not until he was retested the following year that he was diagnosed with one. In middle school, Kip and his friends started looking up how to make bombs on the Internet. His mother found out and was worried about the kind of friends he had. Kip had also started shoplifting. In eighth grade he bought a sawed-off shotgun from one of his friends. That same year he and a friend were arrested for throwing rocks of an overpass and hitting a car below. Kip was sent to Skipworth Juvenile Facility. There he saw a psychologist who felt that Kip was genuinely remorseful for these incidents and thought that Kip was improving. Kip also began seeing a therapist, Dr. Hicks, who later testified at his trial. His mother was still worried about his behavior, his depression, and his poor relationship with his father, though.

Around the same time, however, Kip was suspended for two days after he kicked another boy in the head. He said the boy pushed him. Then he was suspended again for three days after he threw a pencil at a student. Faith and Dr. Hicks felt the school had overreacted with their punishments. Dr. Hicks pre-scribed Prozac, an antidepressant, which seemed to help. That same month, Kip's father bought a 9 mm gun for Kip, with an agreement that he would not use it without his father being there and that Kip could not have full possession of it until he turned 21 years old. Kip and his parents seemed to be getting along better at this time, and his father was making more of an effort to be with him. His ninth counseling session was his last because both Dr. Hicks and his mother thought he was doing well enough to stop going.

Soon after that, Kip bought a .22 pistol from a friend without his parents' knowledge. The same year, he started high school at Thurston High. Because he seemed to be doing better, after just three months Kip went off the Prozac. His father bought him another gun, a semi-automatic rifle, with the same conditions as before.

Yet there were still signs of trouble. Kip gave a speech in class about making a bomb, including detailed pictures. Students reported that this did not seem strange, however, as other students had out-of-the-ordinary topics as well, including one on joining the Church of Satan. After this, the Pearl, Mississippi; West Paducah, Kentucky; and Jonesboro school shootings all occurred. Kip's friend commented that Kip had said the Jonesboro shooting was cool.

Kip was charged with four murders and 26 counts of attempted aggravated murder. At his trial, prosecutors argued that Kip was rational after killing his parents, pointing to the next day's newspaper read on the table, a freshly used bowl, and evidence that Kip had cleaned blood from the house and had calmly talked to his friends on the phone. They also introduced Kip's journal, in which he confessed to having thoughts of killing others and of uncontrollable rage, as well as to owning weapons including knives, chemicals, books on explosives, and "a sawed off shotgun and a handgun." Police also found a picture of the football team with one player's head circled and the word "kill" next to it. Some 50 witnesses to the shootings and their relatives gave statements, and all asked for Kip to receive the maximum sentence.

The defense tried to show that Kip was mentally ill, although they did not use an insanity defense, instead trying to obtain a plea bargain. More than one expert said Kip was mentally ill after he was in custody, diagnosing him with a learning disability, depression, low self-esteem, and early forms of schizophrenia. There was also a history of schizophrenia in Kip's family. Dr. Hicks, the only one who had helped Kip before the murders, said Kinkel was not psychotic but was definitely angry and depressed.

The trial lasted six days, and on November 9, 1999, Kip Kinkel was sentenced to 111 years in prison without parole.

He was the first juvenile in the state of Oregon to serve a life sentence.

Adam Lanza

On December 14, 2012, 20-year-old Adam Lanza shot his mother in the face, then drove to Sandy Hook Elementary in Newtown, Connecticut, and killed 26 people, including 20 elementary school students. Four teachers, the school's principal, and a school psychologist were among the victims. The victims were all hit multiple times, some as many as 11, with the semi-automatic rifle Lanza used. Lanza committed suicide after his rampage. Lanza used weapons he took from his mother, Nancy Lanza, who legally owned them. The shooting was the most deadly involving elementary school students in U.S. history and might have been worse if some of the Sandy Hook teachers had not acted quickly to usher their students to safety.

Although Lanza's precise motives cannot be discerned, many theories have been circulated. Reports months later showed that Lanza had been researching mass murders for several months before the rampage. Newspaper articles and other documents were found in Lanza's bedroom, including material about Anders Behring Breivik, the Norwegian who was convicted of killing 77 people with guns and bombs in July 2011. Connecticut state police also found evidence that Lanza was very interested in the 2006 shooting at an Amish schoolhouse in Lancaster, Pennsylvania. Based on these findings, some believe Lanza was trying to outdo other school shooters. Indeed, Lanza shot a bullet every two seconds, and the entire incident lasted less than five minutes.

Lanza was a gun enthusiast, a hobby he shared with his mother. Additionally, people close to the family say he played a lot of violent video games like *Call of Duty*, and that he was very introverted. Some have criticized Nancy Lanza for encouraging her troubled son's interest in guns. When police searched the Lanza home, they found 1,600 rounds of unspent ammunition.

They also found samurai swords and a book, published by the National Rifle Association, titled *Guide to the Basics of Pistol Shooting*. Additionally, police found a spreadsheet of mass killings.

At first, the police identified Lanza's older brother Ryan as the shooter because Lanza had some of his brother's belongings at the scene. Ryan Lanza had a solid work-related alibi, however.

Immediately after the shootings, it was revealed that Lanza had been diagnosed with Asperger's syndrome, a milder form of autism. Experts caution not to read too much into the diagnosis, as persons with Asperger's syndrome are rarely violent. Perhaps more important is the fact that Lanza suffered from tremendous anxiety, so bad that his mother had to rush him to the emergency room when he was 13. Lanza is also said to have suffered from a sensory disorder. He is also described as painfully shy, with few friends. Yet experts are quick to point out that these disorders are typically not associated with violent behavior. It is reported that his parent's divorce greatly affected Adam, as did the separation from his older brother, who moved from the home to attend college in 2006.

The tragedy prompted renewed debate about gun control in the United States. Connecticut passed one of the country's most restrictive laws as a result of the shooting. President Barack Obama stressed the need for legislation that would close the loopholes regarding who has to undergo a background check before they may purchase a firearm (current legislation only requires background checks for sales at retail establishments, so purchases made online, at gun shows, and from private sellers are exempt from this requirement). Some groups, including the NRA, suggested arming teachers and school officials, and bills to this effect were introduced into several state legislatures.

Almost a year later, the demolition of 56-year-old Sandy Hook Elementary School began. Everything was completely destroyed so that no one was able to keep any souvenirs from the infamous site.

Barry Loukaitis

Armed with a high-powered hunting rifle and two pistols, 14-year-old honor student Barry Loukaitis entered Frontier High School in Moses Lake, Washington, the school he attended, on February 2, 1996. Loukaitis immediately went to his algebra class, took the class hostage, and killed two students, Manual Vela Jr. and Arnie Fritz, as well as his algebra teacher, Leona Caires. Several others were seriously wounded before Loukaitis was overpowered by physical education teacher Jon Lane.

Barry Loukaitis had been raised in a broken and abusive home life. Before divorcing, his parents fought frequently. Reports suggest his father was an alcoholic and a womanizer, and his mother, bitter from the divorce, repeatedly confided in her son that she wished to kill his father, his father's girlfriend, and then herself. Both parents had a history of depression, and his grandmother on his mother's side seems to have suffered from depression as well, as she had attempted suicide at least once.

Although Loukaitis seemed to enjoy elementary school and had performed well academically, middle school was a different experience. Loukaitis was bullied by other students. One of his later victims, Manuel Vela Jr., was among the worst. He reportedly called Loukaitis a "faggot," spit at him, shoved him, and kicked him so many times he had bruises all over his legs. Other classmates also tormented Loukaitis, making fun of his gangly stature and the clothes he wore. Before the shooting Loukaitis had told several students that he hated everyone at the school and that he intended to go on a shooting spree.

Loukaitis was reportedly obsessed with the film *Natural Born Killers*, and the shooting prompted many to consider the role that violent media plays in desensitizing young people. Loukaitis had seen the film so many times that his classmates said he could quote it in its entirety. He also loved the song and video *Jeremy* by Pearl Jam, which featured a young man shooting his classmates after enduring their abuse. Additionally, Loukaitis was a Stephen King fan and particularly loved the horror author's book

Rage. *Rage* tells the story of a high school student who is bullied until he goes insane. He takes his class hostage and kills a teacher for revenge, much as Loukaitis did. He allegedly quoted a line from the book when he was holding the class hostage. King has expressed regret for authoring the novel.

After the shooting, the school was temporarily closed. As a result of the shooting, the district implemented a dress code, increased security, and hired security guards.

Loukaitis was waived to adult criminal court after a hearing in which it was determined that he was competent and that the severity of the incident warranted a more serious penalty than would be assigned by a juvenile court. He pleaded not guilty by reason of insanity. Defense attorneys argued that Loukaitis lived in a fantasy world. The prosecution prevailed, however, by demonstrating how Loukaitis planned the attack with great detail. He was convicted and sentenced to life without the possibility of parole. Later, questions arose about the quality of his defense, given that his primary attorney, Guillermo Romero, was being investigated by the Washington State Bar Association for providing inadequate counsel for several clients.

Patrick Purdy

On January 17, 1989, 24-year-old Patrick Purdy opened fired on students and teachers at Cleveland Elementary School in Stockton, California. Purdy shot 106 rounds of ammunition from an AK-47 rifle, killing five students and wounding 30 (29 students and one teacher) in only two minutes. The children who Purdy murdered were all Southeast Asian refugees. Three girls, Ram Chun, 8; Sokhim An, 6; and Oeun Lim, 8, were Cambodian, as was one boy, Rathanan Or, 9. The other girl who died, Thuy Tran, 6, was from Vietnam. At the time of the shooting, the neighborhood in which the school was located was 68.6 percent Asian. Although Purdy had a history of arrests, mental illness, and alcohol-related problems, his rampage was a complete surprise on a school that was unprepared for this kind of attack. Purdy had attended Cleveland Elementary School for kindergarten through third grade.

Born November 10, 1964 to Patrick Benjamin Purdy, who was stationed at Fort Lewis, Washington, and Kathleen Toscano, Purdy was raised largely by his mother, who filed for divorce when Patrick was three and moved the family to California. Kathleen alleged that her husband threatened her with a weapon. She later married Albert Gulart Sr., although the marriage lasted just six years.

Purdy's home life was less than ideal. Twice in December 1973 Child Protective Services took him and his two siblings into custody after a neighbor reported neglect. Patrick was described as a very quiet child who lacked coping skills. Neighbors remember him as weird and sometimes violent. One neighbor, Joan Capalla, recalled Purdy chasing her sons with a wooden-handled butcher knife. As a teenager he developed an alcohol problem, and his mother kicked him out of her home for hitting her when he was 13 or 14. Purdy lived with a foster parent, who told officers she feared him because he had knives and guns. Purdy also lived on the streets for a while, attending high school only sporadically.

Purdy was arrested numerous times between 1980 and 1989. The first arrest was for prostitution. He also was arrested for selling drugs, possessing illegal weapons, receiving stolen property, and being an accomplice to an armed robbery. In 1986, when his mother refused to give him money to purchase drugs, he was arrested for vandalizing her car. When he was almost 22, he told a mental health professional he had destructive thoughts. Purdy was diagnosed as having an antisocial personality, yet he never received any long-term mental health intervention. Purdy's friends described him as a nice guy, although they said he was often frustrated and angry.

When he began taking welding classes at San Joaquin Delta College in the fall of 1987, Purdy complained that there were too many Southeast Asian students there. The following year Purdy held a series of jobs, drifting among Oregon, Texas,

Connecticut, and Tennessee before returning to Stockton and renting a room at the El Rancho Motel on December 26. On August 3, during his travels, Purdy purchased the AK-47 he used in the shooting for $349.95.

Dressed in a camouflage shirt with the words "PLO," "Libya," and the misspelled "Death to the Great Satin" written on the front, Purdy lined up 100 green plastic soldiers and small tanks, weapons, and jeeps in his hotel room, placing them on shelves, on the refrigerator, and elsewhere before heading to the school. He had carved the words "Freedom," "Victory," and "Hezbollah" (a Shiite Muslim group) into his bayoneted rifle.

Purdy parked his car behind Cleveland Elementary School at approximately noon, then set it on fire with a Molotov cocktail. He entered the school and hid behind a group of portable classrooms, where he shot at the students. Purdy shot and killed himself with a pistol when he had run out of ammunition.

Investigations by the California attorney general concluded that Purdy hated minorities and blamed them for his horrible life. He particularly disliked Southeast Asians simply because he had the most contact with that group. Captain Dennis Perry of the Stockton Police Department said that Purdy was also obsessed with the military, as was evidenced by his dress and behavior at the hotel. This may have had something to do with his nonexistent relationship with his father.

The next day the school opened as workmen tried to scrub bloodstains from the floor and patch the 60 bullet holes. The school brought in psychologists and nurses, as well as interpreters, to assist the traumatized students, although only one-quarter attended.

Purdy's rampage prompted legislative efforts to restrict assault weapons, both in California and through the federal government. The California state legislature moved quickly to enact the nation's first assault weapons legislation, which banned the sale, production, and possession of certain types of assault weapons. This incident, coupled with a deadly shooting at a San Francisco high rise office building in 1993, prompted Congress to pass the Federal Assault Weapons Ban, which President Clinton signed in 1994. The ban was part of a larger crime control bill called the Federal Violent Crime Control and Law Enforcement Act of 1994. It prohibited 19 types of semi-automatic weapons, including AK-47, Uzi, Colt AR-15, and Street Sweeper, as well as copies or duplicates of these named weapons and ammunition clips that hold more than 10 rounds. Also banned were any weapons with two or more of a list of military features, including grenade launchers and flash suppressors. A 1999 study by the U.S. Department of Justice National Institute of Justice (NIJ) found that the ban helped keep assault weapons away from criminals. According to a 2004 study commissioned by the Brady Center to Prevent Gun Violence, the assault weapons ban was effective at reducing the number deaths from assault weapons by 66 percent. Despite this research showing its effectiveness, Congress and President Bush allowed the ban to expire in 2004.

Evan Ramsey

On February 19, 1997, Evan Ramsey, age 16, brought a 12-gauge shotgun to Bethel Regional High School in Bethel, Alaska. He killed 15-year-old classmate Josh Palacios and principal Ron Edwards, 50, and wounded several others. Ramsey had taken the gun from the foster home where he lived and hidden it in his loose pants when he went to school. Sources differ on the precise sequence of events; however, Ramsey himself says that both Palacios and Edwards died in a common area in the school and that he had not specifically targeted Palacios. It is unclear whether he intended to kill the principal. Police said part of the shooting was an intention to get back his CD player, which the principal had taken away. He told his friends he would take it back and then would start shooting.

It was reported that before he started shooting, Ramsey asked everyone why they would not just leave him alone.

According to reports, Palacios tried to stop Ramsey by getting up and talking to him, which instigated Ramsey to shoot him. The principal then came up behind him to see what was going on, and Ramsey turned around and shot him. His wife was nearby and cradled him as he died. Although he threatened to shoot himself, Ramsey instead surrendered to the police.

Investigations into Ramsey's motivation revealed an unstable home life. His father was in prison and his mother an alcoholic who had endured several abusive relationships. When he was in third grade, the Division of Family and Youth Services removed Evan and his two brothers from the home and placed them in different foster homes. Over the next several years, Evan lived in 11 different foster homes, enduring physical and sexual abuse in several of them.

It was also noted after Evan Ramsey's shooting that his father, Don Ramsey, had been involved in a similar incident in 1986, albeit not at school. Don Ramsey had brought an AR 180-223 semi-automatic gun to the office of the *Anchorage Times*. He too surrendered to police. Just two weeks before Evan's shooting, Don Ramsey was released from prison.

Psychiatric assessments revealed Evan to be very troubled. He had attempted suicide as a child and in high school was doing poorly in school and smoking marijuana regularly. Friends said he was often quiet and depressed and only really spoke to those he knew well. Evan described being bullied by other students, who would hang toilet paper on him, spit on his head, and call him names. At first he told teachers and the principal, but when the principal told him just to ignore it, Ramsey lashed out. Teachers and friends also said Ramsey suffered from uncontrolled anger and said they had witnessed him pushing people, punching holes in walls, and throwing garbage cans.

Another factor, as was brought up in the Columbine attack just over two years later as well as with numerous other school shootings, was Ramsey's love of violent video games. Like Eric Harris and Dylan Klebold, Ramsey was a fan of the game

Doom. He typically played with friends James Randall and Matthew Charles, both 14, who encouraged Ramsey to learn how to use a real gun. Both had warned other students about Ramsey's plans to shoot people at school, but no one took them seriously. Yet at the same time, Randall and Charles egged Ramsey on, suggesting who he should target and advising him to take pictures. Ramsey had also wanted other students to stay away, saying he was having an "evil day." According to a study by the Department of Education and the Secret Service, about 81 percent of school shooters do tell other people about their intentions, but only 4 percent of those people tell officials.

Ramsey was tried as an adult on two charges of first-degree murder. On December 2, 1998, he was sentenced to 210 years in prison. James Randall and Matthew Charles were tried as juveniles and will be out of prison at age 19.

In an interview more than 10 years later, Ramsey said he had intended to scare his tormentors and kill himself but not anyone else. He said it was his friends who convinced him to kill other people. Ramsey also stated that he thought the entire thing would be like a video game and that everyone he shot would live through it. His intent, he said, was to fix his immediate problem, and thus he did not think through the long-term consequences of his actions. Evan Ramsey now says he regrets what he did and that prison is worse than being bullied. He wishes that one of his friends would have told authorities so he could have been stopped. Many teens have written to Ramsey expressing that they feel as he did—bullied and alone.

Charles Carl Roberts IV

Charles Carl Roberts IV killed five Amish girls and himself in an Amish school in Lancaster County, Pennsylvania, on October 2, 2006. A milk-truck driver, 32-year-old Roberts lived near the Amish community in Lancaster but was not Amish. Evidently, he had planned to sexually molest the girls at the school, but when police arrived he changed his plan, killing five girls and wounding six others. Fatally shot in the head were Marian Fisher, 13; Anna Mae Stoltzfus, 12; Mary Liz Miller, 8; her sister Lena Miller, 7; and Naomi Rose Ebersole, 7.

Roberts's rampage occurred in a week of multiple school shootings. Some thought he had mimicked a 53-year-old man, Duane Morrison, who held six girls at Platte Canyon High School hostage and sexually assaulted them before killing one and then himself. Clearly the attack was planned, as Roberts was found with a checklist of supplies, all checked off, that he had purchased six days before the shooting. Roberts was found with a rifle, a shotgun, and a semi-automatic pistol as well as knives, a stun gun, and lots of ammunition. He also had a bag of tools that looked as though he had intended on staying there, with hostages, for some time. Disturbingly, Roberts also had a large board with eyebolts spaced apart that was seemingly for binding the girls to, as well as KY Jelly lubricant and other restraints.

On the day before the attack. Roberts went to work until about 3:00 a.m. He took his own children to their bus stop before proceeding to the Amish school at about 10:00 a.m., where he locked himself in by blocking the door with pieces of wood he had brought. He gathered all the students into one classroom, let the boys leave, and bound the girls' feet. A pregnant teacher as well as three other adult females who had infants with them were also allowed to leave. Two of these people called the police from a nearby farmhouse, and they arrived at 10:45 a.m. At some point, Roberts had spoken to his wife, Marie, who had found his suicide notes when she returned home from her morning prayer group. The notes stated that Roberts was seeking revenge for something but did not specify what. Roberts also called police, who by that time had surrounded the school, and told them if they did not leave he would start shooting. He did, and by the time the police entered, Roberts was dead, along with the three girls and the wounded.

Roberts had told his wife that he had a problem with sexually molesting children that started when he was 12. He also wrote a suicide note in which he described how difficult it was for him when he and Marie lost their baby Elsie just 20 minutes after she was born in 1997. Roberts said he hated God and himself. Yet Marie said she did not believe her husband was acting differently in the weeks before the shooting, although Roberts' co-workers said his mood had changed. Still, he was viewed as a peaceful man who did not have a criminal record. Marie Roberts claims he was a wonderful husband and father.

The Amish community was completely surprised by and unprepared for the attack. The Amish lifestyle is simple, and thus there was no security apparatus or real plan for what to do in a crisis situation like this. Police said that he had been watching the school after his work shifts and selected this one because it had no security. Investigators do not believe, however, that Roberts was specifically seeking an Amish school.

After the shootings, the Amish sought to forgive Charles Carl Roberts. Many have reached out to his wife and children as well. Eleven days after the attack, the community tore down the school and has built a new one.

Steubenville High School Rape Case

In the early hours of the morning of August 12, 2012, a group of boys from Steubenville High School in Steubenville, Ohio, repeatedly sexually assaulted a 16-year-old female. She was intoxicated at the time. Several of the boys took pictures and documented their attack on social media, including Facebook and Twitter. They also took video recordings of the sexual assault and sent them to friends. The pictures and videos showed the boys smiling and laughing.

During the trial, witnesses testified that, against the protests of her friends, the victim left a party at about midnight with four football players. All had been drinking. They went to a second party where the victim continued drinking and vomited.

Witnesses say she appeared "out of it." The same group left after about 20 minutes and went to the home of one of the witnesses. No adults were around. During the ride, the witnesses said that her shirt was removed and Trent Mays violated the victim with his fingers while others filmed and photographed it and her exposed breasts. Once they arrived, Mays attempted to make the girl perform oral sex on him, but she was completely unconscious. She was stripped completely naked, and Ma'lik Richmond also violated her digitally, and again photographs were taken. After the attacks, the *New York Times* reported that Mays tried to orchestrate a cover-up, telling a friend to say that the girl was at his house and pleading with the victim to drop any charges.

The victim testified that she has no memory of the rapes. She has a hazy recollection of vomiting on the street at the second party. She recalled waking up the next morning in a basement living room, naked, with Mays, Richmond, and another boy. She said she was missing her earrings, flip-flops, phone, and underwear.

On December 24, the hacker group Anonymous, dismayed at the media coverage that focused on the victim's actions, threatened to reveal the names of other alleged but unindicted assailants. The group also posted a demand that school officials and local authorities apologize for mishandling and attempting to cover up the crime in order to protect the athletes who were accused.

Other media activists took interest in the case. Blogger Alexandria Goddard and other anonymous bloggers posted messages that implicated a Steubenville boy. His parents claimed that the posts defamed their son and sought an injunction against Goddard, a public apology stating that he was not involved with the rape, and a $25,000 settlement. The case, *Saltsman v. Goddard*, was dismissed in December 2012. Goddard agreed to post that the boy was remorseful about his involvement in the rape.

To date, two of the assailants, both football players for Steubenville High School, have been convicted. Both were tried in juvenile court. On March 17, 2013, Ma'lik Richmond and Trent Mays, both 16 at the time of the sexual assault, were found guilty of rape of a minor in juvenile court. Mays was found guilty of penetrating the girl while she was unconscious and disseminating pictures of her. As she was a minor, this was considered child pornography, so Mays received a two-year sentence. Richmond received the minimum one-year sentence, to the dismay of many. Hundreds of text messages and cell-phone pictures taken by dozens of people at the parties and by the assailants were introduced as evidence. One photograph posted on Instagram by a Steubenville football player showed the unresponsive victim being carried by her wrists and ankles by two boys. Another student, former baseball player Michael Nodianos, tweeted that "Some people deserve to be peed on" and "Song of the night is definitely Rape Me by Nirvana." Several people reshared that tweet. Nodianos and others filmed a 12-minute video they later uploaded to YouTube in which Nodianos joked, "they raped her quicker than Mike Tyson raped that one girl." Mays texted someone saying she looked "like a dead body" and claimed that the semen visible on her body in other pictures was his.

The Steubenville rape case generated national attention on the issues of athletes, rape, and use of social media. As so often happens in cases of sexual assault, especially those in which drinking is involved, some people blamed the victim for the incident. Others were concerned about the negative image of the community and its football team. Even reporters from national news sources like CNN focused their coverage, to a large extent, on the fact that the convictions would ruin these boys' lives rather than on the impact on the victim. Broadcasts on CNN, Fox News, and MSNBC aired the first name of the victim on March 17, 2013, which is in violation of Associated Press guidelines for coverage.

In June 2013, a judge ruled that Trent Mays must register as a Tier II sex offender every six months for the next 20 years. Unlike adult sex offenders, however, his name will not appear on the publicly searchable database, and once he is rehabilitated, he can request that his name be removed.

In October 2013, William Rhinaman, technology director for the Steubenville City Schools, was the first adult to be indicted for crimes related to the incident. Rhinaman is charged with tampering with evidence, obstructing justice, and lying under oath. He plead not guilty and was freed on a $25,000 bond. Some have suggested that Steubenville football coach Reno Saccoccia be fired and investigated for knowing about the assault and helping to protect his players.

Jeff Weiss

Six years after the infamous Columbine High School massacre, 16-year-old Jeff Weise killed two members of his family before driving his grandfather's police car to Red Lake High School in Minnesota, where he shot and killed seven students and wounded five others before killing himself. The entire incident took less than 10 minutes. Located in northern Minnesota, Red Lake High School is located in the Red Lake Indian Reservation, home to Chippewas, with whom Weiss identified.

After murdering his sleeping grandfather and his grandfather's partner, Weise took a handgun and shotgun his grandfather owned, and upon gaining entrance to the school, he shot randomly at students and teachers. Red Lake police arrived and exchanged gun shots with Weiss, who was wounded before he escaped to a remote location within the school and shot himself.

Explanations for why Weiss committed these mass murders focused on his family history and the possibility of mental illness. Weiss's father committed suicide when he was nine, and his mother was incapacitated due to brain damage from a car accident two years later, which prompted the relocation to live with his grandparents in 1999, several hundreds of miles away. Weiss himself had been prescribed Prozac, an antidepressant, because he had twice tried to commit suicide. Additionally,

Weiss had written about zombies, identified as a goth, dressed in black, including a trench coat, and submitted numerous web posts proclaiming the brilliance of Adolf Hitler and pledging his support for neo-Nazism. Further, Weiss wrote about his enjoyment of violent video games, specifically *Grand Theft Auto*, and his interest in the film *Elephant*, which addresses the Columbine massacre. Jeff Weiss had also been in trouble at school. He was forced to repeat the eighth grade and had previously been expelled and was at the time being home-schooled. School officials and peers recall that Weiss was bullied because of his stature (he was 6 feet tall and weighed 250 pounds). Yet other students described Weiss as a good listener and friend.

Red Lake High School had installed metal detectors before the incident, which prompted national dialogue about how effective this type of intervention could be. Most research suggests that this type of technological intervention is, if anything, minimally helpful.

One of Weiss's cousins, Louis Jourdain, was arrested and charged with conspiracy after the shooting. The charge was eventually dropped, and Jourdain pled guilty to transmitting threatening messages via the Internet.

In response, the Red Lake Chippewa provided grants to Fifteen families who had been affected by the murders.

Phoebe Prince, Bullycide

A recent immigrant from Ireland, Phoebe Nora Mary Prince hung herself at her family's home on January 14, 2010. Prince had been a victim of vicious "mean girl" bullying, both in person and online. A group of girls who attended South Hadley High School in Massachusetts disliked Prince and had repeatedly harassed her verbally, in writing, and physically. On the day she committed suicide, these girls had thrown a can of Red Bull energy drink at her from a car window as Prince walked home from school.

Investigations of the incident found that the harassment had been occurring for months. These girls, as well as other students, often threw things and were referred to as "Mean Girls," so dubbed because of their resemblance to the characters in the 2004 movie. They called Prince "Irish slut" and "whore," both on social networking sites and in person. Students say the abuse started when Prince briefly dated a popular senior football player during her freshman year. It continued after Prince's suicide as the girls posted hateful comments on her Facebook page.

On March 29, 2010, authorities announced they had indicted nine teenagers, seven girls and two boys, for bullying Prince and prompting her suicide. They were charged with a variety of offenses, including statutory rape for the boys, violation of civil rights with bodily injury, criminal harassment, and stalking. Although some felt that school officials also bore some blame, given that it seemed as though they turned a blind eye even when witnessing the bullying. Investigators found that while some adults behaved in a troublesome manner, there was no criminal responsibility. Three of the girls entered not-guilty pleas on April 8, 2010. Three of the teens received probation and community service, and two others were sentenced to probation only.

Prince's case brought to the national discourse the issue of bullycide. Prior to this incident, Tyler Lee Long, 17, committed suicide after enduring years of torment at school. On October 7, 2003, Ryan Halligan killed himself after enduring similar abuse. In October 2013, 12-year-old Rebecca Sedwick of Florida committed suicide as a result of girl-on-girl harassment. After Sedwick's death, one of the bullies, a 14-year-old girl, wrote the following post on Facebook: "Yes IK I bullied REBECCA and she killed her self but IDGAF," which means "I don't give a #@@&."

Amanda Todd, Bullycide

Canadian teenager Amanda Todd committed suicide in October 2012, just one week before her 16th birthday, after enduring years of bullying in school and online. It started when Todd was in seventh grade and would go online to meet people. A stranger talked her into flashing the camera, which he then used to exploit Todd over the next several years. Despite changing schools, the bullying followed as the man continued to harass and threaten her on Facebook and all her new peers found out. They ridiculed her, calling her "porn star." She suffered from anxiety and depression, eventually turning to alcohol, drugs, and cutting to numb herself. When she transferred to yet another school she endured the harassment of a group of girls who were jealous when a boy flirted with her. The girls beat her up, and Todd attempted suicide by drinking bleach.

The hacktivist group Anonymous has allegedly tracked down Todd's blackmailer, identifying a 30-year-old man from British Columbia.

Part II

Break the Cycle

Devoted to empowering young people to enjoy safe and healthy relationships, Break the Cycle focuses on educating young people, educators, and others about the warning signs of abusive relationships and the characteristics of healthy ones. The organization also advocates for legal and policy changes and helps provide legal resources to teens, who are often ineligible for existing legal assistance. Break the Cycle was founded in Los Angeles in 1996 because advocates noticed the dearth of resources devoted to dating violence. In 2004 the organization expanded and now has a Washington, DC, office through which its programs reach a national audience. Break the Cycle's core values include (1) trusting that young people are the experts of their own lives, (2) providing services in a manner that respects culturally diverse populations, (3) collaborating and evolving as needed, and (4) constantly seeking and implementing new and creative ideas.

Break the Cycle has developed a number of curricular programs that representatives present in schools and to community groups. Safe Dates and Speak.Act.Change both teach youth about healthy and unhealthy relationships and seek to inspire them to take action in their schools and communities. The organization has also developed a School Policy Kit that helps administrators develop policies and practices to prevent and respond to dating violence in schools.

In addition to its educational programs, Break the Cycle provides information about dating violence on its website as well as legal services. Persons who need additional legal assistance are able to contact a Break the Cycle representative through the organization's website.

Three broad political priorities shape the organization's legislative initiatives. These include (1) increasing youth access to essential information and services, (2) ensuring confidentiality, and (3) providing a healthy environment for youth.

Finally, Break the Cycle provides information and ideas related to Teen Dating Violence Awareness Month, commemorated each February. To date, Break the Cycle's programs have reached more than 1 million teens.

Geoffrey Canada

Internationally known as a passionate advocate of education reform and an activist for more peaceful schools, Geoffrey Canada is founder of the Harlem Children's Zone (HCZ). Canada is president and chief executive officer of that organization, which has been called "one of the most ambitious social experiments of our time" by the *New York Times Magazine*. HCZ helps provide comprehensive services to a 100-block area of Central Harlem, serving approximately 10,000 children.

Geoffrey Canada grew up in the South Bronx. His neighborhood was generally poor and often violent. Canada was a shining star, earning a BA from Bowdoin College, then a master's degree in education from Harvard. After graduating, Canada was determined to give back to children who faced similar life circumstances to his.

Canada joined Harlem Children's Zone, Inc. (then called the Rheedlen Foundation) in 1983 as education director. Prior to that, he worked as director of the Robert White School, a private day school for troubled inner-city youth in Boston. In 1997, the agency launched the Harlem Children's Zone Project, which targets a specific geographic area in Central Harlem with a comprehensive range of services. The Zone Project today covers 100 blocks.

The *New York Times Magazine* said the Zone Project "combines educational, social and medical services. It starts at birth and follows children to college. It meshes those services into an interlocking web, and then it drops that web over an entire neighborhood. . . . The objective is to create a safety net woven so tightly that children in the neighborhood just can't slip through."

The work of Geoffrey Canada and HCZ has become a national model and has received significant media coverage. Their work has been featured on *60 Minutes, The Oprah Winfrey Show, The Today Show, Good Morning America, Nightline, CBS This Morning, The Charlie Rose Show*, and *National Public Radio's On Point*, as well in articles in the *New York Times*, the *New York Daily News, USA Today*, and *Newsday*. In October 2005, Geoffrey Canada was named one of "America's Best Leaders" by *U.S. News and World Report*. The work of Canada and HCZ was also featured in the documentary *Waiting for Superman*, which highlighted that 90 percent of public-school students who participate in HCZ programs go to college.

Drawing upon his own experiences in childhood and at HCZ, Geoffrey Canada has written two books: *Fist Stick Knife Gun: A Personal History of Violence in America*, published in 1995 by Beacon Press, and *Reaching Up for Manhood: Transforming the Lives of Boys in America*, published in 1998 by Beacon Press. *Publisher's Weekly* said of *Fist Stick Knife Gun* that a "powerful depiction of the tragic life of urban children and a more compelling plea to end 'America's war against itself' cannot be imagined."

In 2006, New York City mayor Michael Bloomberg selected Geoffrey Canada as co-chair of the Commission on Economic Opportunity, which was asked to formulate a plan to significantly reduce poverty. In 2012, he was appointed by Governor Andrew Cuomo to the New York Education Reform Commission. Canada is also the East Coast regional coordinator for the Black Community Crusade for Children. The Crusade is a nationwide effort to make saving black children the top priority in the black community. This initiative is coordinated by Marian Wright Edelman and the Children's Defense Fund.

For his years of work advocating for children and families in some of the United States' most devastated communities, Geoffrey Canada has received numerous awards. He was a recipient of the first Heinz Award in 1994 and the Harvard Graduate School of Education Medal for Educational Impact in 2012. In 2004, he was given the Harold W. McGraw Jr. Prize in Education and *Child* magazine's Children's Champion Award. In 2009, he received the Independent Sector's John W. Gardner Leadership Award. He was named to *Time* magazine's "Time 100" list of the world's most influential people in 2011.

He has also received the Heroes of the Year Award from the Robin Hood Foundation, the Jefferson Award for Public Service, the Spirit of the City Award from the Cathedral of St. John the Divine, the Brennan Legacy Award from New York University, and the Common Good Award from Bowdoin College. Canada also received the 2013 National Freedom Award from the National Civil Rights Museum.

Canada has received honorary degrees from Harvard University, Bowdoin College, the University of Pennsylvania, Williams College, John Jay College, and Bank Street College. The National Book Award–winning author Jonathan Kozol called Canada, "One of the few authentic heroes of New York and one of the best friends children have, or ever will have, in our nation."

Riane Eisler, JD

Historian, educator, women's rights advocate, and peace activist Riane Eisler is founder and president of the Center for Partnership Studies, which promotes research, education, and public policy to create more peaceful institutions. Her books include *The Chalice and the Blade*, which is now in 25 foreign editions, *The Power of Partnerships*, *Tomorrow's Children*, *Sacred Pleasure*, *Women, Men and the Global Quality of Life*, and *The Real Wealth of Nations: Creating a Caring Economics*, which Archbishop Desmond Tutu called "a template for the better world we have been so urgently seeking." Gloria Steinem referred to it as "revolutionary," and Jane Goodall described it as "a call for action." Eisler's book *Dissolution and the Equal Rights Handbook* was widely used in the campaign for the Equal Rights Amendment to the U.S. Constitution.

Born in Vienna, Austria, Riane Eisler is a refugee from Nazi Europe who grew up in the slums of Havana, Cuba. She earned degrees in sociology and law from the University of California and taught at UCLA.

Eisler has lectured worldwide, offering keynotes to the U.S. Department of State, commentary at congressional briefings, and presentations to the UN General Assembly and has given introductions to events featuring Rita Suessmuth, former president of the German parliament, and Vaclav Havel, former president of the Czech Republic. She often provides keynote addresses at major conferences as well as at universities and corporations internationally.

The Center for Partnership Studies works on issues related to gender and economic justice, the promotion of peace education in schools, and ending domestic violence. Its Caring Economy Campaign is devoted to re-envisioning what an economy can look like that invests in all its people. Eisler is also the co-founder, with Nobel Peace laureate Betty Williams, of the Spiritual Alliance to Stop Intimate Violence (SAIV). As a historian, Eisler documented that there have been two paradigms or models that have shaped human history. These she called the dominator model and the partnership model. The dominator model is one in which hierarchy, aggression, and power over others are the essential values. These are qualities more often associated with masculinity, and males are privileged in the dominator model. In contrast, the partnership model values shared power, collaboration, and nonviolent means of solving conflict. In *The Chalice and the Blade*, Eisler documented the various times and cultures in history that have been either dominator-modeled or partnership-modeled. In *Tomorrow's Children*, Eisler described how these two models have influenced schooling in the United States, emphasizing how dominator-modeled schools are unsafe and uninspiring while partnership-modeled schools are schools that teach about and for peace.

Eisler has written over 300 articles that have been published in *Behavioral Science*, *Futures*, *Political Psychology*, the *Christian Science Monitor*, *Challenge*, the *UNESCO Courier*, *Brain and Mind*, the *Human Rights Quarterly*, the *International Journal of Women's Studies*, and the *World Encyclopedia of Peace*.

Eisler has received many honors for her work, including honorary Ph.D. degrees, the Alice Paul ERA Education Award, and the Nuclear Age Peace Foundation's 2009 Distinguished Peace Leadership Award. She is included in the award-winning book *Great Peacemakers* as one of 20 leaders for world peace, along with Mahatma Gandhi, Mother Teresa, and Martin Luther King.

Gay, Lesbian & Straight Education Network (GLSEN)

In 1990, a group of Massachusetts teachers, concerned that schools frequently allow lesbian, gay, bisexual, and transgender

(LGBT) students to be bullied, be discriminated against, and fall through the cracks, came together to form GLSEN. Today, GLSEN is a national organization that advocates for the fair treatment of LGBT students in schools and outside of them. Noting that 8 out of 10 LGBT students are still harassed at school each year, GLSEN works to ensure that every student feels valued and is treated with respect regardless of her or his sexual orientation, gender identity, or gender expression. GLSEN notes that homophobia and heterosexism undermine a healthy school climate, and thus the organization works to educate teachers, students, and the general public about the damaging effects of daily harassment and an unwelcoming environment.

The organization's website lists several focus areas: (1) Conducting and disseminating research to inform evidence-based solutions for K–12 education; (2) creating age-appropriate resources for teachers to use in classroom and other settings; (3) partnering with decision-makers to make sure that safe and inclusive policies are enacted in every school; (4) working with national education organizations to share resources that will help LGBT students; and (5) empowering students to help make change in their schools and communities.

GLSEN has developed several educational guides, including a "Back to School Guide," a guide for working with LGBT youth of color, the "ThinkB4YouSpeak Guide" for educators, an "LGBT Pride Month Guide," a "Day of Silence Guide," and a "Transgender Day of Remembrance Guide," as well as a safe space kit for allies and an LGBT-inclusive curriculum. In addition, the organization's website offers a variety of lesson plans related to bullying and to acceptance of LGBT youth.

Further, GLSEN helps support youth activism by providing resources for students who want to start or enhance their gay–straight alliance (GSA). It provides ideas for students to coordinate activities for the Day of Silence on April 11, for hosting an ally week, and much more. Additionally, GLSEN's website provides references and links to crisis hotlines for youth in immediate need of assistance.

Since 1999, GLSEN has conducted research on the experiences of LGBT youth in schools. Its National School Climate Survey gauges the frequency with which LGBT youth hear discriminatory remarks and experience various forms of harassment in schools. It also assesses how teachers and school officials respond as well as what preventative programs and policies are in place. Other reports available on GLSEN's website include "Experiences of LGBT Youth Online," "LGBT Issues in Elementary Schools," "Students' and Teachers' Perceptions on School," "LGBT Students' Experiences in School Sports and PE," "LGBT Students in Rural and Small Towns," "LGBT Inclusive Curriculum," "Experiences of LGBT Students of Color," "Transgender Students in US Schools," "LGBT Issues in Middle Schools," "LGBT Parents and Their Children," "The Principal's Perspective," and "Impact of Gay–Straight Alliances."

GLSEN works with school districts as well as with Congress and the Department of Education to improve school climate and to enhance legislative protections for LGBT youth. It has helped build support for two federal laws, the Safe Schools Improvement Act and the Student Non-Discrimination Act. Another recent success involved getting the Department of Health and Human Services and the Department of Education to include sexual orientation and gender identity in national surveys they administer. It has also developed a policy kit for states, districts, and schools featuring model antibullying legislation and other policies to support transgendered and gender-nonconforming youth.

Jackson Katz

Award-winning educator, filmmaker, scholar, and activist Jackson Katz, Ph.D., specializes in the study of contemporary

U.S. masculinity. His work focuses on the social construction of gender and gender role norms that encourage male aggression and violence. Katz is an important ally in efforts against domestic violence as his work is a call to men that abuse is not a "woman's issue" but rather one that must be addressed by entire communities. Katz's work highlights the role of popular culture in reinforcing stereotypical and dangerous notions of gender. He also carefully and thoughtfully addresses other dimensions of identity, privilege, and social power such as race, social class, and sexuality.

Katz's book *The Macho Paradox: Why Men Hurt Women and How All Men Can Help* (2006) identifies violent masculine norms in the United States and provides strategies for creating safer, more equitable relations between men and women. He has also edited several scholarly collections and routinely publishes academic articles in journals and books. Katz is a regular contributor to the *Huffington Post* and, in November 2012, filmed a talk for TED (Technology, Education, Design) entitled "Violence against Women—It's a Men's Issue."

Katz is particularly well-known for the film *Tough Guise: Violence, Media, and the Crisis in Masculinity* (2000), which he worked on with Sut Jhally. An updated version of the film, which highlights how popular culture promotes dangerous gender-role norms, was released in 2013. Katz and Jhally have also collaborated for the *Dreamworlds* series (1991, 1995, 2007), in which they document the portrayal of women as sexualized objects in music and other cultural forms.

In *Wrestling with Manhood: Boys, Bullying, and Battering* (2002), Katz and Jhally focus on professional wrestling culture, which glorifies homophobia and violence. Katz discusses why professional wrestling is so popular with young men and documents the way it reinforces bullying behavior and abuse of women.

Katz coupled with cultural critic Jean Kilbourne for *Spin the Bottle: Sex, Lies, and Alcohol* (2004), which highlights U.S. media portrayals of binge drinking and other risky behaviors.

The film shows the dangerous relationship between masculinity and violence that is fueled by alcohol.

Katz is also co-founder, in 1993, of the multiracial Mentors in Violence Prevention (MVP) training program at Northeastern University's Center for the Study of Sport in Society. MVP is the most widely used gender violence prevention program in college and professional athletics. He and his staff implement training in the U.S. military, law enforcement agencies, colleges, high schools, community organizations, and small and large corporations. Katz speaks to national and international audiences. As a former all-star football player, Katz is able to draw on personal experience to address how violent masculinity hurts not just women but men as well. Research has shown MVP to be a successful means of reaching young people, in particular empowering bystanders to take action to interrupt dangerous behavior.

Paul Kivel

Known for his commitment to social justice, Paul Kivel is an educator, activist, and author. He speaks regularly at colleges, universities, and conferences about issues of race, social class, and privilege. Kivel provides workshops and training on youth violence, male violence, homophobia, and gender and class discrimination, and most notably he calls on audiences and readers to engage in their schools and neighborhoods to create stronger, safer communities.

Kivel is co-founder of the Oakland Men's Project, a community education center and prevention organization devoted to stopping male violence. In addition, Kivel has authored numerous book and curricula, including *Uprooting Racism: How White People Can Work for Racial Justice, Men's Work, Making the Peace, Young Women's Lives, Helping Teens Stop Violence, Boys Will Be Men, I Can Make My World a Safer Place,* and *You Call This a Democracy?: Who Benefits, Who Pays, and Who Really Decides.* He also authors a free newsletter called *Getting*

Together in which he shares additional thoughts and ideas. All of Kivel's curricula involve participatory, interactive methodologies for training youth and adults in a variety of settings. Kivel incorporates the concept of being allies in community struggles to end oppression and injustice to transform organizations and institutions into each of his curricula.

Kivel recently expanded his work to focus on what he has called Christian hegemony, or the everyday, pervasive, and systematic set of Christian values and beliefs, individuals, and institutions that are dominant in Western societies. Christian values and beliefs can be found in families and religious institutions but also in the social, political, and economic realms.

Hank Nuwer

Hank Nuwer is perhaps the world's leading authority on hazing. He is the author of four books and numerous articles about the topic. Nuwer's books include *Wrongs of Passage: Fraternities, Sororities, Hazing and Binge Drinking, The Hazing Reader, Broken Pledges: The Deadly Rite of Hazing,* and *High School Hazing.* Nuwer also operates a website to inform the public about hazing. The site, www.stophazing.org, features statistics, case studies, myths and facts, state laws, and resources to stop hazing. Nuwer's work has debunked myths about hazing as being a harmless prank. Instead, Nuwer has documented the dangers of hazing, including serious injury and death. Although data about the incidence of hazing is difficult to obtain, an estimated 1.5 million high school students are hazed. In 40 percent of cases in which athletes are hazed, a coach or advisor is aware of what is happening. In 1995, Nuwer began attempting to track these incidents.

Nuwer's first article focused on a study conducted with preeminent Groupthink theorist Irving Janus of Yale University. Published in 1978 in *Human Behavior Magazine,* this study propelled Nuwer's more than 30-year career studying hazing as a human rights abuse.

Nuwer teaches journalism at Franklin College in Indiana. He is frequently an invited speaker at schools and universities in the United States and Canada. Nuwer also publishes a daily blog and is an Advisory Board member of Security on Campus.

In 1999, Nuwer received a Distinguished Alumnus Award from New York's Buffalo State College and in 2006 an honorary doctorate for his work on hazing. He was inducted into the Ball State University Journalism Hall of Fame (where he once served on faculty) in 2010.

StopBullying.gov

Run by the U.S. Department of Health and Human Services, StopBullying.gov is a website that offers comprehensive information about the scope, extent, and forms of bullying, unique issues faced by at-risk groups such as youth of color and LGBT youth, tips for responding to and preventing bullying, and links to additional resources. The site is available in Spanish as well.

The site offers definitions of bullying and cyberbullying as well as a section describing the many roles kids play in bullying incidents. It highlights the importance of not labeling kids as "bullies" or "bullied" but instead referring to them as "the child who bullied" and "the child who was bullied." It also emphasizes that youth may be involved in assisting bullying by encouraging the behavior and occasionally joining in, or they may be reinforcers who provide an audience for the bullying. Outsiders are kids who are separate from the situation but who often want to help, while kids who defend are those who stand up to the bullying. These descriptions link users to additional information about those topics and especially to prevention efforts designed to help youth become defenders. Additional information provides a review of literature about bullying in elementary school and how it differs from bullying in older grades.

Cyberbullying resources include a working definition, prevention resources, and responding resources. Recommendations for prevention are targeted to both parents and educators and focus on being aware of the technology youth are using and establishing rules for its use. Model rules, policies, and procedures are provided for schools as well.

Additionally, StopBullying.gov features a tab with information outlining risk factors, warning signs, and effects of bullying. Both risk factors for students likely to be bullied and likely to do the bullying are provided. Special attention is paid to youth with disabilities and LGBT youth, as both are overrepresented in victimization statistics. While recognizing that anyone can be a victim, the site provides the following risk factors:

- Are perceived as different from their peers, such as being overweight or underweight, wearing glasses or different clothing, being new to a school, or being unable to afford what kids consider "cool"
- Are perceived as weak or unable to defend themselves
- Are depressed, anxious, or have low self-esteem
- Are less popular than others and have few friends
- Do not get along well with others, are seen as annoying or provoking, or antagonize others for attention

Similarly, anyone can be a bully, but the site provides the following factors that increase the likelihood of this behavior:

- Some are well-connected to their peers, have social power, are overly concerned about their popularity, and like to dominate or be in charge of others
- Others are more isolated from their peers and may be depressed or anxious, have low self-esteem, be less involved in school, be easily pressured by peers, or not identify with the emotions or feelings of others
- Are aggressive or easily frustrated

- Have less parental involvement or having issues at home
- Think badly of others
- Have difficulty following rules
- View violence in a positive way
- Have friends who bully others

Prevention resources focus on how to talk to children and adolescents about bullying, the role of schools in bullying prevention, and community-level efforts. School-based initiatives include assessing the scope and extent of bullying, the resources currently available, and the overall school climate; engaging parents and youth in creating programs and setting policies and rules; and educating all about the issue. The segment on community-level efforts discusses the importance of collaborations, possible partnerships, and ideas for working together. It also provides links to other community–school partnerships for bullying prevention.

The material on responding to bullying emphasizes how to spot bullying and how to empower all—from students to educators—to disrupt the act. The "Get Help Now" tab provides recommended resources for specific types of crises.

Also featured on the site are images that groups can download to use as posters or in other educational materials. Video segments are also available.

Students Against Violence Everywhere (SAVE)

SAVE is a youth-driven and youth-focused organization with chapters around the United States. Devoted to tapping into the potential youth have to make social change, SAVE seeks to spread the message of nonviolence as a means of preventing crime, solving conflict, and empowering communities. SAVE is run by a National Youth Advisory Board, a Board of Directors, three staff members, and many volunteers. SAVE's goals include (1) engaging youth in school and community violence prevention efforts;

(2) educating youth so that they have the skills, knowledge, and motivation to serve their communities and schools; (3) encouraging positive peer influence and nonviolent means of solving conflict; and (4) educating students about the effects of violence.

SAVE provides resources for its chapters, which exist all over the United States, including the *SAVE Essentials Manual*, which provides lesson plans on managing conflicts between others, active listening skills, and bullying prevention, with activities appropriate for elementary through high school ages. SAVE materials also include ideas and encouragement for students to engage in meaningful service in their schools and communities. Ideas provided on the organization's website include:

- Start a SAVE chapter in other schools.
- Sponsor a crime and violence prevention fair for your school and community.
- Decorate a bulletin board at your school, local library, or local business to spread the SAVE message.
- Have a nonviolence essay contest and send the winning essay to possibly be published on SAVE's website or in SAVE's newsletter.
- Support a local violence shelter by hosting a canned food, coat, teddy bear, clothing, or cell phone drive.
- Adopt a grandparent or assist elderly person in your community by running errands, cleaning the yard, or just providing company.
- Create a pamphlet on community or school crime prevention.
- Sponsor a photo identification booth for children at a local crime prevention fair or mall expo.
- Assist your school's safety team with coordinating a safe school site assessment.
- Clean up and revitalize a deteriorated area of your school or community.

SAVE recognizes that juveniles are twice as likely to be crime victims as any other age group. As such, the organization helps promote gun safety awareness and civic education as a means of activating youth to conform to prosocial norms. Crime prevention initiatives also focus on gangs, Internet safety, back-to-school safety, and safe driving.

In addition, SAVE operates a Speakers Bureau. Interested chapters as well as schools and community groups can request a speaker or workshop leader on virtually any facet of nonviolent conflict resolution. SAVE also hosts events and provides resources to groups who are hosting events for National Crime Victims Week and Global Youth Service Day.

Further Reading

Abad-Santos, A. (2013, April 26). What Is Steubenville Still Hiding? *The Atlantic Wire.* Retrieved October 24, 2013, from http://www.theatlanticwire.com/national/2013/04/steubenville-search-warrants-grand-jury/64627/

Armstrong, K., Davis, F., & Mayo, J. (2004, April 4). For Some, Free Counsel Comes at a High Cost. *Seattle Times.* Retrieved May 3, 2010, from http://seattletimes.nwsource.com/news/local/unequaldefense/stories/one/

Avila, J., Holding, R., Whitcraft, T., & Tribolet, B. (2008). School Shooter: 'I Didn't Realize' They Would Die." Retrieved May28, 2014, from http://abcnews.go.com/TheLaw/story?id=5040342

Bernstein, A. (2009). *Bath Massacre: America's First School Bombing.* Ann Arbor, MI: University of Michigan Press.

Bleaney, T. (2012, October 15). Amanda Todd: Suicide Girl's Mum Reveals More Harrowing Details of Cyber Bullying Campaign that Drove Her Daughter to Death. *The Mirror.* Retrieved March 28, 2014, from http://www.mirror.co.uk/news/world-news/amanda-todd-suicide-girls-mum-1379909

Brady Center to Prevent Gun Violence. (2004). On Target: The Impact of the 1994 Federal Assault Weapon Act. Retrieved May 27, 2014, from http://www.waveedfund .org/sites/waveedfund.org/files/on_target.pdf

Canada, G. (2013, May 9). Our Failing Schools. Available at http://www.ted.com/talks/geoffrey_canada_our_failing_schools _enough_is_enough.html

Clark-Flory, T. (2010, April 8). Phoebe Prince's Bullies Get Bullied. *Salon*. Retrieved May 5, 2010, from http://www .salon.com/life/broadsheet/2010/04/08/phoebe_prince_bullies _get_bullied

CNN. (2006). Police: School Killer Told Wife He Molested Family Members. Retrieved May 28, 2014, from http:// www.cbsnews.com/news/amish-forgive-pray-and-mourn/

CNN. (2006). Fifth Girl Dies after Amish School Shooting. Retrieved May 29, 2014, from http://www.cnn.com/2006/ US/10/02/amish.shooting/index.html?eref=sitesearch

CNN. (2000, May 16). Report: 12 Killed at Columbine in First 16 Minutes. Retrieved May 29, 2014, from http:// archive.today/GptXZ

Collins, D. (2006, October 4). Amish Forgive, Pray and Mourn. *CBS News*. Retrieved May 28, 2014, from http:// www.cbsnews.com/news/amish-forgive-pray-and-mourn/

Coloroso, B. (2004). *The Bully, the Bullied, and the Bystander*. New York: HarperCollins.

Columbine High School Shootings. *The Rocky Mountain News*. Retrieved December 14, 2008, from http://www.rocky mountainnews.com/news/special-reports/columbine/

Eisler, R. (1988). *The Chalice and the Blade: Our History, Our Future*. New York: HarperOne.

Eisler, R. (2000). *Tomorrow's Children*. Boulder, CO: Westview.

Eisler, R. (n.d.). Riane Eisler Biography. Retrieved October 30, 2012, from http://www.rianeeisler.com/biography.htm

Eggington, J. (1991). *Day of Fury: The Story of the Tragic Shootings that Forever Changed the Village of Winnetka.* New York: William Morrow and Co.

Fast, J. (2009). *Ceremonial Violence: A Psychological Explanation of School Shootings.* Woodstock, NY: The Overlook Press.

Fine, M., Weis, L., Pruitt, L., & and Burns, A. (2004). *Off White: Readings on Power, Privilege, and Resistance,* 2nd ed. New York: Routledge.

Finley, L. (Ed.). (2007). *Encyclopedia of Juvenile Violence.* Westport, CT: Greenwood.

Ford, B., & Siemaszko, C. (2013, October 25). Sandy Hook Elementary School Razing Begins in Newtown, Conn. *New York Daily News.* Retrieved October 28, 2013, from http://www.nydailynews.com/news/national/sandy-hook-elementary-school-destruction-begins-article-1.1496521

Gay, Lesbian & Straight Education Network (GLSEN). (n.d.). http://www.glsen.org

Grenoble, R. (2012, October 10). Amanda Todd: Bullied Canadian Teen Commits Suicide after Prolonged Battle Online and in School. *Huffington Post.* Retrieved March 28, 2014, from http://www.huffingtonpost.com/2012/10/11/amanda-todd-suicide-bullying_n_1959909.html

Gunderson, D. (2005, March 23). Who Was Jeff Weise? Minnesota Public Radio. Retrieved October 22, 2013, from http://news.minnesota.publicradio.org/features/2005/03/22_ap_redlakesuspect/

Jhally, S. (Producer). (1999). *Tough Guise: Violence, Media, and the Crisis in Masculinity* [Motion picture]. Media Education Foundation.

Jhally, S. (Producer). (2003). *Wrestling with Manhood: Boys, Bullying, and Battering* [Motion picture]. Media Education Foundation.

Jhally, S. (Producer). (2007). *Dreamworlds* [Motion picture]. Media Education Foundation.

Kaplan, J., Papajohn, G., & Zorn, E. (1991). *Murder of Innocence: The Tragic Life and Final Rampage of Laurie Dann, the Schoolhouse Killer.* New York: Warner Books.

Katz, J. (n.d.). http://www.jacksonkatz.com

Katz, J. (n.d.). Blog. *Huffington Post.* http://www.huffington post.com/jackson-katz

Kennedy, H. (2010, March 29). Phoebe Prince, South Hadley High School's "New Girl," Driven to Suicide by Teenage Cyber Bullies. *New York Daily News.* Retrieved May 29, 2014 from http://www.nydailynews.com/news/national/phoebe-prince-south-hadley-high-school-new-girl-driven-suicide-teenage-cyber-bullies-article-1.165911

Khadaroo, S. (2013, October 9). Adult Charged in Steubenville Rape Case: Will Schools Get the Message? *Christian Science Monitor.* Retrieved October 24, 2013, from http://www.csmonitor.com/USA/Justice/2013/1009/Adult-charged-in-Steubenville-rape-case.-Will-schools-get-the-message-video

The Killer at Thurston High [Documentary]. *Frontline.* Available at http://video.pbs.org/video/2318711766/

Kivel, P. (n.d.). http://www.paulkivel.com

Kivel, P. (n.d.). Challenging Christian Hegemony Project. http://www.christianhegemony.org

Kleinfeld, N., Rivera, R., & Kovaleski, S. (2013, March 28). Newtown Killer's Obsessions, in Chilling Detail. *New York Times.* Retrieved October 25, 2013, from http://www.nytimes.com/2013/03/29/nyregion/search-warrants-reveal-items-seized-at-adam-lanzas-home.html?pagewanted%253Dall&_r=0

Langman, P. (2008). *Jefferson County Sheriff's Office Columbine Documents Organized by Theme.* Retrieved May 29, 2014, from http://www.schoolshooters.info/jcso-columbine-documents.pdf

Langman, P. (2009). *Why Kids Kill: Inside the Minds of School Shooters.* New York: Palgrave Macmillan.

Leadership. (2014). *Harlem Children's Zone.* Retrieved May 28, 2014, from http://hcz.org/about-us/leadership/geoffrey-canada/

Lieberman, J., & Sachs, B. (2008). *School Shootings.* New York: Kensington Publishing Corp.

Magestro, S. (n.d.). The Warning Signs: Evan Ramsey— Bethel, Alaska. Retrieved May 29, 2014, from http://www .susanmagestro.com/susans-articles-of-interest/

McBride, R. (2007). After Shooting, Bethel Works to Prevent Bullying, Peer Abuse. Retrieved January 2, 2009, from http://www.ktuu.com.

Minnesota News Radio. (2005, March). What Happened at Red Lake? Minnesota Public Radio. Retrieved October 22, 2013, from http://news.minnesota.publicradio.org/projects/ 2005/03/redlake/

Muskal, M. (2013, June 14). Ohio Football Player, Convicted of Rape, Gets Sex-Offender Status. *Los Angeles Times.* Retrieved May 29, 2014, from http://articles.latimes.com/2013/jun/ 14/nation/la-na-nn-steubenville-football-player-sex-offender -20130614

National Public Radio. (2009, April 17). Survivors Recall 1927 Michigan School Massacre. http://www.npr.org/templates/ story/story.php?storyId=103186662

Nuwer, H. (2000). *High School Hazing.* New York: Franklin Watts.

Nuwer, H. (Ed.). (2004). *The Hazing Reader.* Bloomington: Indiana University Press.

Ollove, M. (2010, April 28). Bullying and Teen Suicide: How Do We Adjust School Climate? *Christian Science Monitor.* Retrieved May 28, 2014, from http://www.csmonitor.com/ USA/Society/2010/0428/Bullying-and-teen-suicide-How-do -we-adjust-school-climate

Parker-Pope, T. (2007, November 27). More Teens Victimized by Cyber-Bullies. *The New York Times*. Retrieved July 30. 2009, from http://well.blogs.nytimes.com/2007/11/27/more-teens-victimized-by-cyber-bullies/

Phillips, R. (2009, January 18). Purdy Recalled as Bigot and "Sick, Sick Man." Retrieved July 19, 2009, from http://www.recordnet.com/apps/pbcs.dll/article?AID=/20090118/A_NEWS/901170304/-1/A_SPECIAL0252

Raising Adam Lanza. (2013, February 19). *PBS Frontline*. Available at http://www.pbs.org/wgbh/pages/frontline/raising-adam-lanza/

Reinhold, R. (1989, January 19). After Shooting, Horror but Few Answers. *New York Times*. Retrieved July 19, 2009, from http://www.nytimes.com/1989/01/19/us/after-shooting-horror-but-few-answers.html?pagewanted=all

Reuters. (2009, January 15). Twenty Years since a Nightmare: Stockton, CA Shooting of 35 Led to Strengthening of Gun Laws. Retrieved July 19, 2009, from http://www.reuters.com/article/pressRelease/idUS226787+15-Jan-2009+PRN20090115

Ridberg, R. (Producer). (2004). *Spin the Bottle: Sex, Lies, and Alcohol* [Motion picture]. Media Education Foundation.

Segal, K., Couwels, J., & Brumfield, B. (2013, October 21). Mother of Girl Accused of Bullying Florida Teen Arrested on Unrelated Charges. *CNN*. Retrieved October 24, 2013, from http://www.cnn.com/2013/10/17/justice/rebecca-sedwick-bullying-death/index.html

Sieczkowski, C. (2012, October 16). Amanda Todd's Alleged Bully Named by Anonymous after Teen's Tragic Suicide. *Huffington Post*. Retrieved March 28, 2014, from http://www.huffingtonpost.com/2012/10/16/amanda-todd-bully-anonymous-suicide_n_1969792.html

StopBullying.gov. (n.d.). http://www.stopullying.gov

Students Against Violence Everywhere (SAVE). (n.d.). http://www.nationalsave.org

Webley, K. (2011, May 5). Teens Who Admitted to Bullying Phoebe Prince Sentenced. *Time*. Retrieved October 24, 2013, from http://newsfeed.time.com/2011/05/05/teens-who-admitted-to-bullying-phoebe-prince-sentenced/

This chapter provides charts and graphs describing various elements of school violence. The first chart shows trends in lethal school violence, as measured by the School-Associated Violent Deaths Survey. The remaining charts provide demographic data regarding the scope and impact of school violence, as measured by the Youth Risk Behavior Surveillance System (YRBSS).

Additionally, the chapter provides primary source documents relevant to proposed federal legislation. Items include the proposed Sandy Hook Elementary School Violence Reduction Act and the Safe Schools Improvement Act. Also included are the texts of President Obama's speech after the tragic massacre at Sandy Hook Elementary School in Newtown, Connecticut, and Secretary of Education Arne Duncan's 2010 speech at the Bullying Prevention Summit.

Data

Figure 5.1 shows data from the School-Associated Violent Death Study. As is clear from the chart, school-associated violent deaths peaked in 2006 and have declined significantly since.

Nicole Hockley, center, mother of Sandy Hook School shooting victim Dylan Hockley, stands with thousands of others during a rally calling for tougher gun laws at the Capitol in Hartford, Connecticut on February 14, 2013. (AP Photo/Jessica Hill)

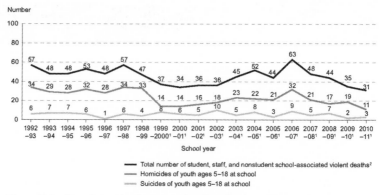

Figure 5.1   Trends in school-associated violent deaths, 1992–2010.

Source: Centers for Disease Control and Prevention. (2013, April). School-Associated Violent Death Study, http://www.cdc.gov/violenceprevention/youth violence/schoolviolence/savd.html

Figure 5.2 shows the percentage of high school students who were threatened or injured with a weapon in the last year, as measured by the YRBSS. These data show that ninth-grade students continue to be at greatest risk for threats of or actual weapon-related violence.

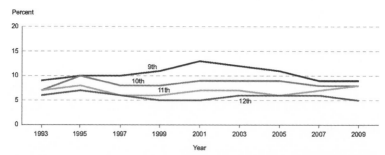

Figure 5.2   Percentage of students in grades 9–12 who reported being threatened or injured with a weapon on school property at least one time during the previous 12 months, by grade: Various years, 1993–2009.

Note: "On school property" was not defined for survey respondents.

Source: Centers for Disease Control and Prevention, National Center for Chronic Disease Prevention and Health Promotion, YRBSS, various years, 1993–2009.

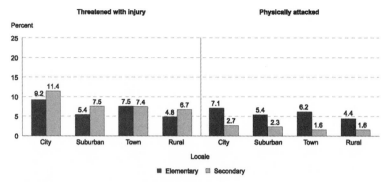

Figure 5.3 Percentage of public and private school teachers who reported that they were threatened with injury or that they were physically attacked by a student from school during the previous 12 months, by locale and instructional level: School year 2007–2008.

Note: Teachers who taught only prekindergarten students are excluded. Instructional level divides teachers into elementary or secondary based on a combination of the grades taught, main teaching assignment, and the structure of the teachers' class(es). Please see the glossary for a more detailed definition.

Source: U.S. Department of Education, National Center for Education Statistics, Schools and Staffing Survey, "Public School Teacher Data File," "Private School Teacher Data File," and "Bureau of Indian Affairs Teacher Data File," 2007–2008.

Figure 5.3, drawn from the Schools and Staffing Survey, shows teachers who work in city schools are more likely to be threatened with injury or physically attacked by students. Interestingly, the data show that elementary school teachers are more likely to endure physical assaults than are teachers at other levels.

The charts in Figure 5.4 document the percentage of 12- to 18 year-olds who were victimized in a variety of ways at school between 1995 and 2009. The charts clearly show that all types of school victimization decreased and that serious violent victimization has always been rare.

Figure 5.5 describes the degree to which 12- to 18-year-old students perceive gangs to be present at their schools. It is clear from the data that gangs are far more present in urban schools.

Figure 5.6, derived from the School Crime Supplement to the 2009 National Crime Victimization Survey, shows that

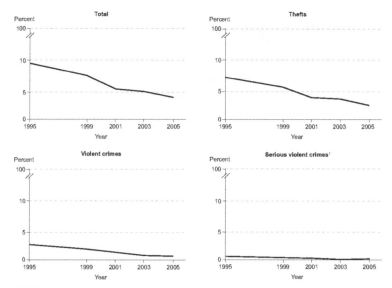

Figure 5.4   Percentage of students ages 12–18 who reported criminal victimization at school during the previous six months, by type of victimization: Various years, 1995–2009.

[1]Serious violent victimization is also included in violent victimization.

Note: "Theft" includes attempted and completed purse-snatching, completed pickpocketing, and all attempted and completed thefts, excluding motor vehicle theft. Theft does not include robbery, in which the threat or use of force is involved. "Serious violent victimization" includes rape, sexual assault, robbery, and aggravated assault. "Violent victimization" includes serious violent crimes and simple assault. "Total victimizations" includes violent crimes and theft. "At school" includes the school building, on school property, on a school bus, and, from 2001 onward, going to and from school.

Source: U.S. Department of Justice, Bureau of Justice Statistics, School Crime Supplement to the National Crime Victimization Survey, various years, 1995–2009.

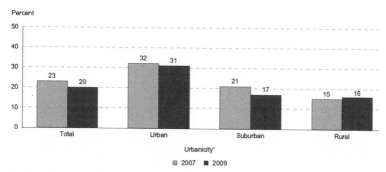

Figure 5.5 Percentage of students ages 12–18 who reported that gangs were present at school during the school year, by urbanicity: 2007 and 2009.
[1]Refers to the Standard Metropolitan Statistical Area (MSA) status of the respondent's household as defined in 2000 by the U.S. Census Bureau. Categories include "central city of an MSA (Urban)," "in MSA but not in central city (Suburban)," and "not MSA (Rural)."
Note: All gangs, whether or not they are involved in violent or illegal activity, are included. "At school" includes the school building, on school property, on a school bus, or going to and from school.
Source: U.S. Department of Justice, Bureau of Justice Statistics, School Crime Supplement to the National Crime Victimization Survey, 2007 and 2009.

hate-related graffiti is more common than other bias-related crime in both public and private schools.

Documenting what is likely the most common form of school violence, Figure 5.7 shows the percentage of students ages 12–18 who report being bullied in schools as well as the forms of bullying they endured.

Interestingly, Figure 5.8 highlights the fact that girls are more likely than boys to be victims of cyberbullying.

One of the most significant effects of school-based violence is that it deters youth from being involved in activities on school grounds, as described in Figure 5.9.

According to Figure 5.10 codes of student conduct and visitor sign-in procedures are the most common security measures in schools.

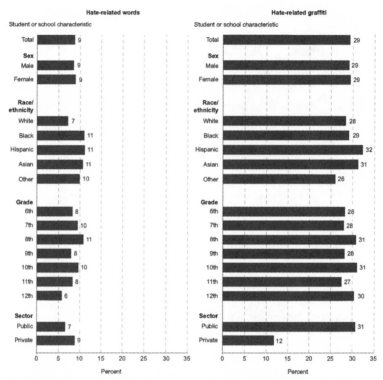

Figure 5.6 Percentage of students ages 12–18 who reported being targets of hate-related words and seeing hate-related graffiti at school during the school year, by selected student and school characteristics: 2009.

Note: Race categories exclude persons of Hispanic ethnicity. "Other" includes American Indian, Alaska Native, Pacific Islander, and two or more races. "At school" includes the school building, on school property, on a school bus, and going to and from school. "Hate-related" refers to derogatory terms used by others in reference to students' personal characteristics.

Source: U.S. Department of Justice, Bureau of Justice Statistics, School Crime Supplement to the National Crime Victimization Survey, 2009.

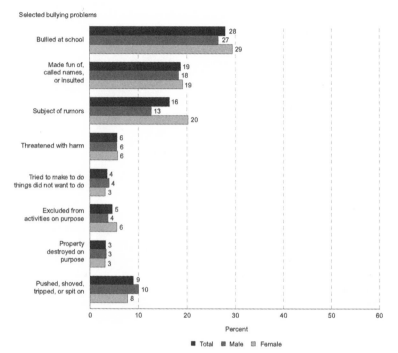

Figure 5.7 Percentage of students ages 12–18 who reported being bullied at school during the school year, by selected bullying problems and sex: 2009.

Note: "At school" includes the school building, on school property, on a school bus, or going to and from school. Bullying types do not sum to total because students could have experienced more than one type of bullying.

Source: U.S. Department of Justice, Bureau of Justice Statistics, School Crime Supplement to the National Crime Victimization Survey, 2009.

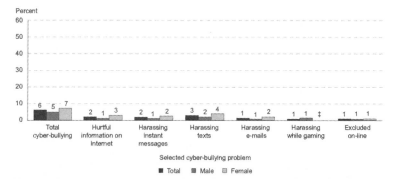

Figure 5.8   Percentage of students ages 12–18 who reported cyberbullying problems anywhere during the school year, by selected bullying problems and sex: 2009.
‡Reporting standards not met. There are too few cases.
Note: "Cyberbullying" includes students who responded that another student posted hurtful information about the respondent on the Internet; students who responded that another student harassed the respondent via instant messaging; students who responded that another student harassed the respondent via short message service (SMS) text messaging; students who responded that another student harassed the respondent via e-mail; students who responded that another student harassed the respondent while gaming; and students who responded that they were excluded online. Cyberbullying types do not sum to total because students could have experienced more than one type of cyberbullying.
Source: U.S. Department of Justice, Bureau of Justice Statistics, School Crime Supplement to the National Crime Victimization Survey, 2009.

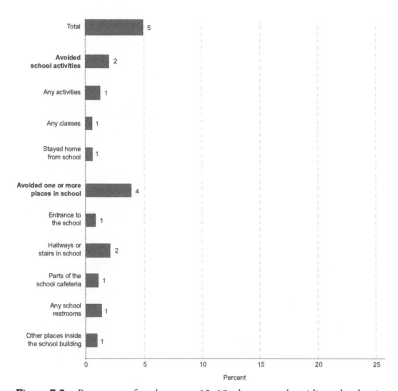

Figure 5.9   Percentage of students ages 12–18 who reported avoiding school activities or one or more places in school because of fear of attack or harm during the school year: 2009.

Note: "Avoided school activities" includes avoiding any (extracurricular) activities, skipping class, or staying home from school. Detail may not sum to totals due to rounding and because students could report avoiding more than one school activity and avoiding more than one place in school.

Source: U.S. Department of Justice, Bureau of Justice Statistics, School Crime Supplement to the National Crime Victimization Survey, 2009.

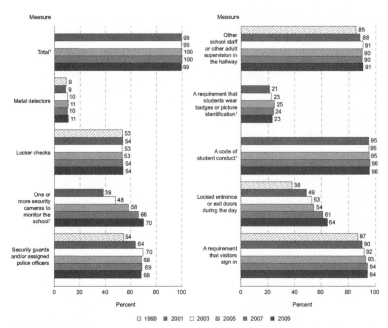

Figure 5.10 Percentage of students ages 12–18 who reported selected security measures at school: Various years, 1999–2009.

[1]Data for 1999 are not available.

Note: "At school" includes the school building, on school property, on a school bus, and, from 2001 onward, going to and from school.

Source: U.S. Department of Justice, Bureau of Justice Statistics, School Crime Supplement to the National Crime Victimization Survey, various years, 1999–2009.

Documents

Sandy Hook Elementary School Violence Reduction Act

The proposed bill detailed below was filed in direct response to the school shooting at Sandy Hook Elementary School in Newtown, Connecticut. The multifaceted proposal aims to address loopholes in gun control legislation as well as to help train educational professionals to identify early warning signs of potential threats.

A BILL

To reduce violence and protect the citizens of the United States.
1.
Short title
This Act may be cited as the Sandy Hook Elementary School Violence Reduction Act.
2.
Sense of the Senate
It is the sense of the Senate that Congress should—
(1)
support the efforts of the President of the United States to reduce violence in the United States;
(2)
promote common-sense proposals for preventing gun violence;
(3)
provide law enforcement officers with the tools necessary to combat violent crime and protect communities, and protect themselves;
(4)
ensure children can attend school free from the threat of violence;
(5)
support States and local districts to ensure schools have the safe and successful learning conditions in which all students can excel;
(6)
provide tools for identifying individuals that pose a threat to themselves or others, so they can receive appropriate assistance;

(7)

keep dangerous weapons out of the hands of criminals and individuals who are not lawfully authorized to possess them;

(8)

promote information-sharing that will facilitate the early identification of threats to public safety;

(9)

mitigate the effects of violence by promoting preparedness;

(10)

provide training for educational professionals, health providers, and others to recognize indicators of the potential for violent behavior;

(11)

examine whether there is a connection between violent media and violent behavior;

(12)

enable the collection, study, and publication of relevant research; and

(13)

expand access to mental health services, with a focus on children and young adults.

Source: S. 2: Sandy Hook Elementary School Violence Reduction Act, 113th Congress, 2013–2015. January 22, 2013.

Safe Schools Improvement Act of 2013

The Safe Schools Improvement Act is intended to provide federal guidance for states and districts in regards to keeping all youth, regardless of gender, race, sexual orientation, and other factors, safe in schools.

A BILL

To amend the Elementary and Secondary Education Act of 1965 to address and take action to prevent bullying and harassment of students.

1.

Short title

This Act may be cited as the Safe Schools Improvement Act of 2013.

2.

Findings

Congress finds the following:

(1)

Bullying and harassment foster a climate of fear and disrespect that can seriously impair the physical and psychological health of its victims and create conditions that negatively affect learning, thereby undermining the ability of students to achieve their full potential.

(2)

Bullying and harassment contribute to high dropout rates, increased absenteeism, and academic underachievement.

(3)

Bullying and harassment include a range of behaviors that negatively impact a student's ability to learn and participate in educational opportunities and activities that schools offer. Such behaviors can include hitting or punching, name-calling, intimidation through gestures or social exclusion, and sending insulting or offensive messages through electronic communications, such as internet sites, e-mail, instant messaging, mobile phones and messaging, telephone, or any other means.

(4)

Schools with enumerated anti-bullying and harassment policies have an increased level of reporting and teacher intervention in incidents of bullying and harassment, thereby reducing the overall frequency and number of such incidents.

(5)

Students have been particularly singled out for bullying and harassment on the basis of their actual or perceived race, color, national origin, sex, disability status, sexual orientation, gender identity, or religion, among other categories.

(6)

Some young people experience a form of bullying called relational aggression or psychological bullying, which harms individuals by damaging, threatening, or manipulating their relationships with their peers, or by injuring their feelings of social acceptance.

(7)

Interventions to address bullying and harassment conduct to create a positive and safe school climate, combined with evidence-based discipline policies and practices, such as Positive Behavior Interventions and Supports (PBIS) and restorative practices, can minimize suspensions, expulsions, and other exclusionary discipline policies to ensure that students are not pushed-out or diverted to the juvenile justice system.

(8)

According to one poll, 85 percent of Americans strongly support or somewhat support a Federal law to require schools to enforce specific rules to prevent bullying.

(9)

Students, parents, educators, and policymakers have come together to call for leadership and action to address the national crisis of bullying and harassment.

3.

Safe Schools improvement

(a)

In general

Title IV of the Elementary and Secondary Education Act of 1965 (20 U.S.C. 7101 et seq.) is amended by adding at the end the following:

D

Safe Schools improvement

4401.

Purpose

The purpose of this part is to address the problem of bullying and harassment conduct of students in public elementary schools and secondary schools.

4402.

Anti-bullying policies

(a)

Bullying

In this part, the term *bullying* includes cyber-bullying through electronic communications.

(b)

Policies

A State that receives a grant under this title shall require all local educational agencies in the State to carry out the following:

(1)

Establish policies that prevent and prohibit conduct, including bullying and harassment, that is sufficiently severe, persistent, or pervasive—

(A)

to limit a student's ability to participate in, or benefit from, a program or activity of a public school or local educational agency; or

(B)

to create a hostile or abusive educational environment, adversely affecting a student's education, at a program or activity of a public school or local educational agency, including acts of verbal, non-verbal, or physical aggression or intimidation.

(2)

The policies required under paragraph (1) shall include a prohibition of bullying or harassment conduct based on—

(A)

a student's actual or perceived race, color, national origin, sex, disability, sexual orientation, gender identity, or religion;

(B)

the actual or perceived race, color, national origin, sex, disability, sexual orientation, gender identity, or religion of a person with whom a student associates or has associated; or

(C)

any other distinguishing characteristics that may be defined by the State or local educational agency, including being homeless or the child or ward of a member of the Armed Forces.

(3)

Provide—

(A)

annual notice to students, parents, and educational professionals describing the full range of prohibited conduct contained in such local educational agency's discipline policies; and

(B)

grievance procedures for students or parents to register complaints regarding the prohibited conduct contained in such local educational agency's discipline policies, including—

(i)

the name of the local educational agency officials who are designated as responsible for receiving such complaints; and

(ii)

timelines that the local educational agency will establish in the resolution of such complaints.

(4)

Collect annual incidence and frequency of incidents data about the conduct prohibited by the policies described in paragraph (1) at the school building level that are accurate and complete and publicly report such data at the school level and local educational agency level. The local educational agency shall ensure that victims or persons responsible for such conduct are not identifiable.

(5)

Encourage positive and preventative approaches to school discipline that minimize students' removal from instruction and ensure that students, including students described in paragraph (2), are not subject to disproportionate punishment.

4403.

State reports

The chief executive officer of a State that receives a grant under this title, in cooperation with the State educational agency, shall submit a biennial report to the Secretary—

(1)

on the information reported by local educational agencies in the State pursuant to section 4402(b)(5); and

(2)

describing the State's plans for supporting local educational agency efforts to address the conduct prohibited by the policies described in section 4402(b)(1).

. . .

(b)

Free speech and expression laws

Nothing in this part shall be construed to alter legal standards regarding, or affect the rights (including remedies and procedures) available to individuals under, other Federal laws that establish protections for freedom of speech or expression.

Source: H.R. 1199: Safe Schools Improvement Act of 2013, 113th Congress, 2013–2015.

Barack Obama's Statement on the School Shooting in Newtown, Connecticut

President Obama has been a vocal advocate of tightened gun control legislation, as exemplified in his emotional speech after the Sandy Hook shooting.

THE PRESIDENT: This afternoon, I spoke with Governor Malloy and FBI Director Mueller. I offered Governor Malloy my condolences on behalf of the nation, and made it clear he will have every single resource that he needs to investigate this heinous crime, care for the victims, counsel their families.

We've endured too many of these tragedies in the past few years. And each time I learn the news I react not as a President, but as anybody else would—as a parent. And that was especially true today. I know there's not a parent in America who doesn't feel the same overwhelming grief that I do.

The majority of those who died today were children— beautiful little kids between the ages of 5 and 10 years old. They had their entire lives ahead of them—birthdays, graduations, weddings, kids of their own. Among the fallen were also teachers—men and women who devoted their lives to helping our children fulfill their dreams.

So our hearts are broken today—for the parents and grandparents, sisters and brothers of these little children, and for the families of the adults who were lost. Our hearts are broken for the parents of the survivors as well, for as blessed as they are to have their children home tonight, they know that their children's innocence has been torn away from them too early, and there are no words that will ease their pain.

As a country, we have been through this too many times. Whether it's an elementary school in Newtown, or a shopping mall in Oregon, or a temple in Wisconsin, or a movie theater in Aurora, or a street corner in Chicago—these neighborhoods are our neighborhoods, and these children are our children. And we're going to have to come together and take meaningful action to prevent more tragedies like this, regardless of the politics.

This evening, Michelle and I will do what I know every parent in America will do, which is hug our children a little tighter and we'll tell them that we love them, and we'll remind each other how deeply we love one another. But there are families in Connecticut who cannot do that tonight. And they need all of us right now. In the hard days to come, that community needs us to be at our best as Americans. And I will do everything in my power as President to help.

Because while nothing can fill the space of a lost child or loved one, all of us can extend a hand to those in need—to remind them that we are there for them, that we are praying for them, that the love they felt for those they lost endures not just in their memories but also in ours.

May God bless the memory of the victims and, in the words of Scripture, heal the brokenhearted and bind up their wounds.

Source: The White House. Available at http://www.white house.gov/the-press-office/2012/12/14/statement-president -school-shooting-newtown-ct

The Myths about Bullying: Secretary Arne Duncan's Remarks at the Bullying Prevention Summit

The following is a speech presented by Secretary of Education Arne Duncan at the 2010 Bullying Prevention Summit. In it, Duncan aims to inspire educators, policy-makers, and service providers that they play important roles in ending bullying. Duncan notes the importance of school safety on students' moral development as well as on their academic success.

Thank you, Kevin, for that generous introduction.

This is an important day in so many respects. It is the very first federal summit on bullying. We have an extraordinary range of NGOs, corporate leaders, state and local officials on hand, as well as the members of the Federal Partners in Bullying Prevention Working Group.

This summit culminates months of unprecedented collaboration and hard work across federal agencies.

We have not only joined forces but, more important, we are committed to using this summit to launch a sustained commitment to address and reduce bullying.

For all the promise of this summit, it is incumbent on everyone in this room and every educator and school leader to ask: What can we do to sustain that commitment to reduce bullying? To answer that question, we should start with another leading question that this summit itself raises. And that is: Why have these agencies not come together for a federal summit on bullying before today?

The answers to that basic question are many. But they start, and end, with the fact that the problem of bullying has been shrouded in myth and misunderstanding for far too many years. As educators, as state and local officials—and yes, absolutely at the federal level—we simply have not taken the problem of bullying seriously enough. Too often, bullying gets shrugged off.

You have heard all the excuses. You have heard the lineup of reasons to minimize the gravity of bullying and to dismiss the potential of effective programs to reduce it. "What can you do," people say, "bullying has been going on forever. Kids are mean." Or "she just made a bad joke." "He didn't mean to hurt anyone." "It was just a one-time thing." "Bullying may be wrong. But it really isn't an educational issue." At the heart of this minimization of bullying, is a core belief that bullying is an elusive concept that can't really be defined.

Every one of those myths and excuses I've just cited is flat-out wrong. Bullying is definable. It has a common definition, and a legal definition in many states. Good prevention programs work to reduce bullying. And bullying is very much an education priority that goes to the heart of school performance and school culture.

The truth is that bullying is ultimately an issue of school safety. Kevin Jennings often talks about the fact that school safety is a much broader issue than the shootings and gang violence that make the evening news.

Bullying is part of that continuum of school safety. It is troubling in and of itself. But bullying is doubly dangerous because if left unattended it can rapidly escalate into even more serious violence and abuse. Just as you have gateway drugs, bullying is gateway behavior. Too often it is the first step down the road to one of the tragic incidents of school violence we all have watched in horror on the evening news.

As the CEO of the Chicago Public Schools for seven years, I dealt every day with the issue of school safety—and it's a subject that I am passionate about. We are simply not doing nearly enough as a nation, or as school leaders, to keep children safe. Keeping my students safe, not just in school, but in their communities, was by far my toughest challenge. Our inability as adults to secure the safety of innocent children was a failure that haunts me every day.

For the record, let me state my basic, operating premise, both in Chicago and Washington DC: No student should feel unsafe in school. Take that as your starting point, and then it becomes inescapable that school safety is both a moral issue, and a practical one.

The moral issue is plain. Every child is entitled to feel safe in the classroom, in the hallways of school, and on the playground. Children go to school to learn, and educational opportunity must be the great equalizer in America. No matter what your race, sex, or zip code, every child is entitled to a quality education and no child can get a quality education if they don't first feel safe at school.

It is an absolute travesty of our educational system when students fear for their safety at school, worry about being bullied, or suffer discrimination and taunts because of their ethnicity, religion, sexual orientation, disability, or a host of other reasons.

The job of teachers and principals is to help students learn and grow—and they can't do that job in schools where safety is not assured.

The practical import of school safety is just as plain as the moral side of the equation. A school where children don't feel safe is a school where children struggle to learn. It is a school where kids drop out, tune out, and get depressed. Not just violence but bullying, verbal harassment, substance abuse, cyber-bullying, and disruptive classrooms all interfere with a student's ability to learn.

I have to tell you—I have very little patience for the arguments that "kids will be kids" and there is not much that schools can do to make schools much safer. I hate the excuses, and I hate the passivity.

I know that effective prevention programs have the power to dramatically improve school environment and school safety. The default position of schools, parents, and communities should be that school violence, bullying, and harassment are completely unacceptable.

The fact is that no school can be a great school until it is a safe school first. A positive school climate is foundational to start academic achievement. That is one reason why in Chicago we established school safety as a metric on our report cards for every school, just as we did with academic metrics like measuring the number of students who exceeded state standards in reading and math.

What does a safe school look like? As all of you know, it is obvious from the minute you walk in the door. A safe school is one where students feel like they belong. The students feel secure, valued, and are surrounded by adults that they trust.

Safe schools also cultivate a culture of respect and caring—and have little tolerance for disruptiveness. At a safe school, students don't curse or threaten teachers. They don't spend most of their class time texting other students or tune out on their iPods. Students don't roam the hallways.

At safe schools, teachers are primarily engaged in helping students learn and grow—and students, empowered by feeling safe, are more likely to feel free to explore, and even fail as they learn. At safe schools, all the building's staff pitches in to create a culture of respect—from the teachers and principals to the receptionists, lunch room attendants and custodial staff.

Now, I've just talked about what a safe school feels like. But I have to tell you that I have been in many schools that don't feel safe. And this is a tragedy we can avoid.

This isn't just a big-city problem. Bullying is epidemic in urban, suburban, and rural schools. The statistics are frankly staggering. In 2007, nearly one out of three students in middle school and high school reported that they had been bullied at school during the school year. That means that 8.2 million students a year are suffering at the hands of bullies in school.

The most common form of bullying is being made fun of or being the subject of mean-spirited rumors. But more violent forms of bullying are common, too.

One out of nine secondary school students, or 2.8 million students, said they have been pushed, shoved, tripped, or spit on during the last school year.

Another one-and-a-half million students said they were threatened with harm, and one million students reported they had their property destroyed during the school year.

Cyber-bullying, as you know, is a new and especially insidious form of bullying. In 2007, more than 900,000 secondary students reported being cyber-bullied. Cyber-bullying allows bullies to do their work at a distance, outside of schools, in front of a broad audience and sometimes under the protection of anonymity. New technologies provide bullies with new tools to hurt students in old ways.

We have all been told that bullying has been going on in schools forever.

But the truth is that it doesn't have to keep going on forever. Bullying is not something that school leaders, teachers, or parents can shrug off. Children are never born as bullies—it is a learned behavior. And if they are learning to bully from their peers, or parents, they can learn to behave differently, too.

Bullying is not the occasional bad joke or the child who gets a bit too aggressive.

Bullying is deliberate. The bully wants to hurt someone. Bullying is usually repeated, with the bully targeting the same victim again and again—and the bully takes advantage of an imbalance of power by picking victims that he or she perceives are vulnerable.

Bullying can occur through physical, verbal, or relational means where bullies try to destroy their victims' relationships through vicious rumors and social exclusion.

Bullying, in other words, is not just a "boy" behavior or a "mean girl" behavior. It is a problem that often has an impact on children who are neither bully nor victims.

It often occurs in groups. It shapes the way that everyone—bullies, victims, and bystanders alike—view a school's environment.

Ultimately, bullying is really a form of physical and mental abuse. If you don't stop it when it starts, it usually spreads.

A powerful testament to the fact that bullying is not part of the natural order of things is that most people can remember, even decades later, the feeling of being bullied or bullying another individual. Or they may feel haunted by the memory of standing by while a friend or classmate was bullied.

The fact that those memories are seared into our brains suggests that bullying leaves long-lasting scars on children.

Why does bullying have such long-lasting effects? Why are the victims of bullying more likely to drop out of school and get depressed? Because bullying is insidious—it tends to get enveloped in a code of silence and shame. It is underreported because children are embarrassed or don't recognize behavior as bullying. Maybe they fear retaliation, don't have an adult they trust to talk to about what is going on, or they think nothing can be done to stop the bullying.

The situation is much the same with cyber-bullying and "sexting." Adolescents suffer from what you might call the Las Vegas syndrome—they feel that what happens online stays online.

Now, one of the antidotes to this culture of silence is sunshine—teachers, parents, and the peers of students should be encouraged to expose and confront bullying behavior. We want children to learn to be assertive and stand up for themselves. But we do not want to encourage them to respond to bullying with violence and force themselves.

Instead, schools should be cultivating a culture of trust and accountability. A culture of trust empowers students to tell teachers and other adults when bullying is occurring. It teaches students that should have a sense of responsibility for the well-being of other students. In schools that just say no to bullying, students who report other students are not tattle-tales, but acting responsibly, keeping students safe, and holding bullies accountable for their mistreatment.

When 11-year old Ziainey Stokes got tired of being bullied, she wrote President Obama a letter. And the president wrote her back that her letter "demonstrates a desire to change the culture of your classroom as well as your community." I believe Ziainey is here today. And I'd ask you all to give her a round of applause.

Schools, in short, can have an enormous impact in reducing bullying. Ideally, all schools should have a code of conduct that sends a message to the students, staff, and community that it has high expectations for them and little tolerance for cruelty and disrespect.

But a code of conduct can't just be punitive. Schools must teach and reward positive behavior as well.

Part of setting clear expectations is being consistent. Principals, teachers, and parents send messages to children about how they should behave all the time, even when they are unaware of it. All the hallmarks of great schools—student support, a sense of connection to caring adults, clarity of mission, inclusiveness, parental involvement—are also the hallmarks of safe schools.

Now I want to switch gears for a moment, to talk about a related school safety concern, the problem of disruptive and disorderly classrooms. For many parents and teachers, disruptive and disorderly schools are a serious problem because so little learning can take place in classrooms that are in a state of perpetual chaos.

The department's latest survey data indicate one in three teachers nationwide think that student misbehavior interferes with their teaching—and roughly the same proportion of teachers think tardiness and class cutting is impeding learning in their classrooms.

Interestingly, students themselves think disruptive classrooms are an even bigger problem. In one recent national survey of 10,000 tenth graders in more than 650 high schools, three fourths of tenth graders said that other students often disrupted their classes.

In urban schools, the problem is ever worse. Twelve percent of secondary school teachers—nearly one of every eight instructors—reports that they were threatened with physical injury the previous year by a school student. Five percent of urban teachers say they were actually attacked by a student the previous year.

It is absolutely inexcusable that so many teachers are attacked, threatened, or face persistently chaotic classrooms. And just as you can usually tell a safe school when you walk in the door, you can tell an unsafe one, too. Just as good practice echoes through a school, so does bad practice.

The famous broken windows theory suggests that the root problem in schools is not so much shootings on the playground but the message that disorder and disruption sends to the students—it's the broken window that goes unfixed that signals to students no one is really in control here and taking care of things.

That's just one more reason schools and districts need to do a better job of setting clear expectations, minimizing classroom disruption, and disciplining students who prevent other students from learning.

School leadership matters tremendously in school safety. That encouraging fact—that what we do in schools matters—is still true even when violence occurs away from school. Does anyone here know the most dangerous hour of the day for adolescents in the United States, the time when violent teen crime peaks? It is 3:00 p.m., not midnight.

That is one reason why I so strongly support an extended school day. Keeping kids off the street and having them do something productive, either at school or with community-based organizations, is critical to adolescent safety. It doesn't have to be expensive. Community organizations have an important role to play—to work with schools to provide students with more opportunities. You don't have to have teachers staying to all hours at the school.

What we did in Chicago was open schools to great providers to run after-school programs. We brought in the Boys Club and the Girls Club, after-school tutoring programs, the YMCA, college-readiness programs, counseling initiatives, adult education providers, and other non-profits and community-based organizations.

We made the schools centers of the community where adolescents could continue to participate after the school day was over. To steal a phrase from Robert DeNiro, it's all about creating a circle of trust. And if you build it they will come. Teens are looking for structure and positive activities to engage in.

I encourage you to take away three messages when you leave here today.

First, our department has a renewed commitment to enforcing the law, including civil rights law that applies to racial, sexual, or disability harassment.

Second, we are committed to collecting better data to document the contours of bullying more fully, and to formulate solutions.

And finally, we will be providing more dollars to places with the biggest problems.

Outside of this room, I am not sure that many educators and parents realize that bullying can constitute racial, sexual, or disability harassment prohibited by the civil rights laws enforced by our department's Office for Civil Rights.

OCR will be issuing policy guidance to schools explaining the relationship between bullying and discriminatory harassment, and it will be outlining schools' civil rights responsibilities to protect students from discriminatory harassment. As part of the enhanced civil rights data collection that OCR has instituted, we will also be gathering new and better data on harassment.

We understand that stopping the plague of bullying will take time. It takes sustained commitment. It takes resources. And, I promise you, we are in this fight for the long haul.

The department has stepped up its support for HHS's Stop Bullying Now campaign, managed by Captain Stephanie Bryn, helping fund the expansion of the campaign to include a focus on elementary school children.

Bullying starts young—and we need to reach students when they are young with the message that bullying is not OK. Within our department, we're backing that stepped-up commitment with increased resources.

Both our budget and our blueprint for reforming the Elementary and Secondary Education Act calls for a 12 percent increase in funding for programs that ensure students feel safe, healthy, and supported in school.

The Successful, Safe, and Healthy Students program in our Blueprint will enable states and districts to measure school safety, including bullying, at the building level. It will provide federal funds for interventions in those schools with the greatest needs.

And just as important, we will be getting information about school safety not just from incident data but also from surveying the real experts on school climate—our students themselves. For the first time, students will be given a formal role in shaping our efforts to make schools safer. Even before reauthorization, we're piloting this program through our new Safe and Supportive School program. Historically, why have we been so reluctant to ask students how they felt about their schools.

As important as all of these steps are, the department cannot do this alone. We have gathered so many partners here today because it will take sustained commitment and resources from all of us to meet this challenge.

The Department of Education stands ready to assume a role of leadership. But we need your help. This challenge requires all the assets of the federal government. I am so pleased to have so many partner agencies here today, and to have great leaders such as Surgeon General Benjamin and Associate Attorney General Perrelli speaking later in the program.

Preventing bullying will take leadership from state and local authorities, like the officials you will hear tomorrow from the state of Iowa and the district of Sullivan County, Tennessee. The Sullivan County school system is a beautiful illustration of how a district used a school climate survey to empower students by giving them a voice, formulate solutions, and help develop buy-in from all members of the community for reform. Not surprisingly, academic achievement is up in Sullivan County and disciplinary issues are down.

To keep making progress in the battle to reduce bullying, we need the support and involvement of corporate, civic, and nonprofit leadership. And this will take action by individual students, teachers, school staff, parents, and concerned citizens. We all have to play a part.

Let me close by saying that as part of your leadership, we need your ideas. This summit seeks to collect the most knowledgeable experts on the issue of bullying in America in one place, at one time, to get the best thinking about what needs to be done to bring this plague to an end.

We will never have all the answers in the U.S. Department of Education. But I believe that, with the collective knowledge and wisdom of those assembled here today, we can identify, and highlight, the most effective solutions.

I ask you to be daring, to think imaginatively, to challenge us and yourselves, and to listen carefully over the next day and a half. To break the cycle of bullying, we must be bold. The status quo cannot stand. With your courage, with your imagination, with your leadership, let this summit be a turning point where America finally tackles the problem of bullying with tenacity—and leaves the myths of bullying behind, once and for all.

Thank you.

Source: U.S. Department of Education. Available at http://www.ed.gov/news/speeches/myths-about-bullying-secretary-arne-duncans-remarks-bullying-prevention-summit

The resources in this chapter are recommended for educators, policy-makers, and parents seeking to learn more about school violence. The list of books has been categorized for easy searching. Also included is a list of scholarly journals that often feature articles about various facets of school violence as well as specific citations for recent (2010 to 2014) peer-reviewed articles. Further, the chapter includes a description of recommended websites as well as films and documentaries about school violence.

Books

School Violence

Balfour, S. (Ed.) (2005). *How Can School Violence Be Prevented?* Farmington Hills, MI: Greenhaven.

Bellini, J. (2001). *Child's Prey.* New York: Pinnacle.

Benbenishty, R., & Astor, R. (2005). *School Violence in Context: Culture, Neighborhood, Family, School, and Gender.* New York: Oxford University Press.

Derek Brown, right, a former Vice Lords gang chief, speaks to a student who had a problem during the school day at William Penn Elementary School in Chicago. Brown donates his time for an after-school boxing program that gives young kids an option to being on the streets and getting in trouble. (AP Photo/Hadi Mizban)

Blanchard, K. (2003). *How to Talk to Your Kids about School Violence.* New York: Onomatopoeia.

Brezina, C. (2000). *Deadly School and Campus Violence.* New York: Rosen Publishing.

Carr, P., & Porfilio, B. (Eds.). (2012). *Educating for Peace in a Time of "Permanent War."* New York: Routledge.

Casella, R. (2001). *At Zero Tolerance: Punishment, Prevention, and School Violence.* New York: Peter Lang.

Casella, R. (2001). *"Being Down": Challenging Violence in Urban Schools.* New York: Teachers College.

Chalmers, P. (2009). *Inside the Mind of a Teen Killer.* Nashville, TX: Thomas Nelson.

Cornell, D. (2006). *School Violence: Fears versus Facts.* Lawrence Erlbaum & Associates.

DiGuilio, R. (2001). *Educate, Medicate, or Litigate? What Teachers, Parents, and Administrators Must Do about Student Behavior.* New York: Corwin Books.

Fearnley, F. (2004). *I Wrote on All Four Walls: Teens Speak Out on Violence.* Toronto, Canada: Annick.

Finley, L. (2012). *Building a Better World: Creative Peace Education for the 21st Century.* Charlotte, NC: Information Age.

Finley, L. (Ed.). (2011). *Encyclopedia of School Crime and Violence.* Santa Barbara, CA: ABC-CLIO.

Fisher, B., & Sloan, J. (2007). *Campus Crime: Legal, Social, and Policy Perspectives.* Charles C. Thomas.

Gerler, E. (2004). *Handbook of School Violence.* Binghamton, NY: Haworth.

Hunnicutt, S. (Ed.). (2006). *School Shootings.* Farmington Hills, MI: Greenhaven.

King, M. (2014). *School Violence: Crisis and Opportunity.* CreateSpace Independent Publishing Platform.

Kohn, A. (2005). *Shooters: Myths and Realities of America's Gun Cultures.* New York: Oxford University Press.

Langman, P. (2009). *Why Kids Kill: Inside the Minds of School Shooters.* Palgrave MacMillan.

Lawrence, R. (2006). *School Crime and Juvenile Justice,* 2nd ed. New York: Oxford.

Lieberman, J. (2006). *The Shooting Game: The Making of School Shooters.* Santa Ana, CA: Seven Locks Press.

Moore, M., Petrie, C., Braga, A., & McLaughlin, B. (Eds.). (2003). *Deadly Lessons: Understanding Lethal School Violence.* Atlanta, GA: National Academies Press.

Newman, K., Fox, C., Roth, W., & Mehta, J. (2005). *Rampage: The Social Roots of School Shootings.* New York: Basic

Orr, T. (2001). *Violence in Our Schools: Halls of Hope, Halls of Fear.* New York: Franklin Watts.

Paludi, M. (2008). *Understanding and Preventing Campus Violence.* Westport, CT: Praeger.

Sexton-Radek, K. (2005). *Violence in Schools: Issues, Consequences, and Expressions.* Westport, CT: Praeger.

Stevenson, L. (2003). *From the Inside Out: A look into Teen Violence and Rebellion.* Authorhouse.

Thomas, R. (2006). *Violence in America's Schools: Understanding, Prevention, and Responses.* Lanham, MD: Rowman & Littlefield.

Turk, W. (Ed.). (2004). *School Crime and Policing.* Upper Saddle River, NJ: Prentice Hall.

Webber, J. (2003). *Failure to Hold: The Politics of School Violence.* Lanham, MD: Rowman & Littlefield.

Weill, S. (2002). *We're Not Monsters: Teens Speak Out about Teens in Trouble.* New York: HarperTempest.

Winslade, J., & Williams, M. (2011). *Safe and Peaceful Schools: Addressing Conflict and Eliminating Violence.* New York: Corwin.

Bullying

Bazelon, E. (2013). *Sticks and Stones: Defeating the Culture of Bullying and Rediscovering the Power of Empathy.* New York: Random House.

Cianciotti, J., & Cahill, S. (2012). *LGBT Youth in America's Schools.* Ann Arbor, MI: University of Michigan Press.

Coloroso, B. (2003). *The Bully, the Bullied, and the Bystander: From Preschool to High School—How Parents and Teachers Can Help Break the Cycle of Violence.* New York: HarperCollins.

DeWitt, P. (2012). *Dignity for All: Safeguarding LGBT Students.* New York: Corwin.

Englander, E. (2013). *Bullying and CyberBullying: What Every Educator Needs to Know.* Cambridge, MA: Harvard University Press.

Fried, S. (2003). *Bullies, Targets, and Witnesses: Helping Children Break the Pain Chain.* New York: M. Evans.

Goodstein, A. (2007). *Totally Wired: What Teens Are Really Doing Online.* New York: St. Martin's Press.

Hinduja, S. (2008). *Bullying beyond the Schoolyard: Preventing and Responding to CyberBullying.* New York: Corwin.

Katz, A. (2012). *Cyberbullying and E-Safety: What Educators and Other Professionals Need to Know.* Philadelphia, PA: Jessica Kingsley Publications.

Kelsey, C. (2007). *MySpace: Helping Your Teen Survive Online Adolescence.* New York: Marlowe.

Klein, J. (2013). *Bully Society: School Shootings and the Crisis of Bullying in America's Schools.* Albany, NY: New York University Press.

Kowalski, R., Limber, S., & Agatston, P. (2007). *Cyber Bullying: Bullying in the Digital Age.* Malden, MA: Wiley-Blackwell.

Olweus, D. (2004). *Bullying at School: What We Know and What We Can Do.* Cambridge, MA: Blackwell.

Patchin, J., & Hinduja. S. (2013). *Words that Wound: Delete Cyberbullying and Make Kindness Go Viral.* Minneapolis, MS: Free Spirit Publishing.

Phillips, R., Linney, J., & Pack, C. (2008). *Safe School Ambassadors: Harnessing Student Power to Stop Bullying and Violence.* San Francisco, CA: Jossey-Bass.

Porter, S. (2013). *Bully Nation: Why America's Approach to Childhood Aggression Is Bad for Everyone.* St. Paul, MN: Paragon House.

Savage, D,, & Miller, T. (2012). *It Gets Better: Coming Out, Overcoming Bullying, and Creating a Life Worth Living.* New York: Plume Press.

Simmons, R. (2002). *Odd Girl Out: The Hidden Culture of Aggression in Girls.* New York: Harcourt.

Twemlow, S., & Sacco, C. (2011). *Preventing Bullying and School Violence.* Arlington, VA: American Psychiatric Publications.

Weisman, R. (2002). *Queen Bees and Wannabees: Helping Your Daughter Survive Cliques, Gossip, Boyfriends, and Other Realities of Adolescence.* New York: Three Rivers Press.

Willard, N. (2007). *Cyberbullying and Cyberthreats: Responding to the Challenge of Online Social Aggression.* Champaign, IL: Research Press.

Specific Cases

Bellini, J. (2001). *Child's Prey.* New York: Pinnacle.

Bernstein, A. (2009). *Bath Massacre: America's First School Bombing.* Ann Arbor, MI: University of Michigan Press.

Berry, H. (2013). *Massacre in Newtown: Adam Lanza's Dark Passage to Madness.* CreateSpace Independent Publishing Platform.

Cullen, D. (2009). *Columbine.* New York: Twelve.

Eggington, J. (1991). *Day of Fury: The Story of the Tragic Shootings that Forever Changed the Village of Winnetka.* New York: William Morrow and Co.

Gibson, G. (1999). *Gone Boy: A Walkabout.* New York: Anchor.

Greenhill, J. (2006). *Someone Has to Die Tonight.* New York: Pinnacle.

Kaplan, J., G. Papajohn, & E. Zorn. (1991). *Murder of Innocence: The Tragic Life and Final Rampage of Laurie Dann, the Schoolhouse Killer.* New York: Warner Books.

Merritt, R., & Brown, B. (2002). *No Easy Answers: The Truth behind Death at Columbine.* Lantern.

Hazing

Guynn, K. L., & Aquila, F. D. (2005). *Hazing in High Schools: Causes and Consequences.* Bloomington, IN: Phi Delta Kappa Educational Foundation.

Holmes, R. (2013). *How to Eradicate Hazing.* Authorhouse Self-Publishing.

Johnson, J., & Holman, M. (Eds.). (2004). *Making the Team: The Inside World of Sport Initiations and Hazing.* Toronto: Canadian Scholar's Press.

Lipkins, S. (2006). *Preventing Hazing: How Parents, Teachers, and Coaches Can Stop the Violence, Harassment, and Humiliation.* San Francisco, CA: Jossey-Bass.

Nuwer, H. (2000). *High School Hazing: When Rites Become Wrongs.* London: Franklin Watts.

Nuwer, H. (Ed.). (2004). *The Hazing Reader.* Bloomington: Indiana University Press.

Civil Liberties

Dupre, A. (2009). *Speaking Up: The Unintended Costs of Free Speech in Schools.* Cambridge, MA: Harvard University Press.

Finley, L., & Finley, P. (2005). *Piss Off! How Drug Testing and Other Privacy Violations Are Alienating America's Youth.* Monroe, ME: Common Courage.

Gender

Brown, L. M. (2003). *Girlfighting: Betrayal and Rejection among Girls.* New York: New York University Press.

Chesney-Lind, M. (2007). *Beyond Bad Girls: Gender, Violence, and Hype.* London: Routledge.

Duncan, N. (1999). *Sexual Bullying: Gender Conflict and Pupil Culture in Secondary Schools.* London: Routledge.

Ferguson, A. (2001). *Bad Boys: Public Schools in the Making of Black Masculinity.* Ann Arbor, MI: University of Michigan Press.

Garbarino, J. (2007). *See Jane Hit: Why Girls Are Growing More Violent and What We Can Do about It.* New York: Penguin.

Hinshaw, S. (2009). *The Triple Bind: Saving Our Teenage Girls from Today's Pressures.* New York; Random House.

Jones, N. (2009). *Between Good and Ghetto: African American Girls and Inner City Violence.* New Brunswick, NJ: Rutgers University Press.

Katz, J. (2006). *The Macho Paradox: Why Some Men Hurt Women and How All Men Can Help.* Naperville, IL: Sourcebooks.

Kellner, D. (2008). *Guys and Guns Amok: Domestic Terrorism and School Shootings from the Oklahoma City Bombing to the Virginia Tech Massacre.* New York: Paradigm.

Kimmel, M. (2009). *Guyland: The Perilous World Where Boys Become Men.* New York: Parker.

Kindlon, D. (2007). *Alpha Girls: Understanding the New American Girl and How She Is Changing the World.* New York: Rodale.

Meyer, E. (2009). *Gender, Bullying, and Harassment: Strategies to End Sexism and Homophobia in Schools.* New York: Teachers College Press.

Prothrow-Stith, D., & Spivak, H. (2007). *Sugar and Spice and No Longer Nice: How We Can Stop Girls' Violence.* San Francisco, CA: Jossey-Bass.

Dating and Sexual Violence

Finley, L. (Ed.). (2013). *Encyclopedia of Domestic Violence and Abuse.* Santa Barbara, CA: ABC-CLIO.

Mignon, S., Larson, C., & Holmes, W. (2002). *Family Abuse: Consequences, Theories, and Responses.* Boston, MA: Allyn & Bacon.

Miles, A. (2005). *Ending Violence in Teen Dating Relationships.* Minneapolis, MN: Augsburg Books.

Murray, J. (2007). *But He Never Hit me.* Lincoln, NE: iUniverse.

Suicide, Eating Disorders, and Self-Harm

Bornstein, K., & Quin, S. (2006). *Hello Cruel World: 1010 Alternatives to Suicide for Teens, Freaks and Other Outlaws.* New York: Seven Stories Press.

Martin, C. (2007). *Perfect Girls, Starving Daughters: The Frightening New Normalcy of Hating Your Body.* Glencoe, IL: Free Press.

Mendelsohn, S. (2007). *It's Not about the Weight: Attacking Eating Disorders from the Inside Out.* Lincoln, NE: iUniverse.

Turner, V. (2002). *Secret Scars: Uncovering and Understanding the Addiction of Self-Injury.* Center City, MN: Hazelden.

Theories and Explanations

Fast, J. (2008). *Ceremonial Violence: A Psychological Explanation of School Shootings.* New York: Overlook Press.

Garbarino, J. (2000). *Lost Boys: Why Our Sons Turn Violent and How We Can Save Them.* New York: Anchor.

Katch, J. (2001). *Under Dead Man's Skin: Discovering the Meaning of Children's Violent Play.* Boston: Beacon.

Kohn, A. (2005). *Shooters: Myths and Realities of America's Gun Culture.* New York: Oxford University Press.

Langman, P. (2009). *Why Kids Kill: Inside the Minds of School Shooters.* New York: Palgrave MacMillan.

Schier, H. (2008). *The Causes of School Violence.* Minneapolis, MN: Abdo Publishing.

Responses

Aronson, E. (2000). *Nobody Left to Hate: Teaching Compassion after Columbine.* New York: W. H. Freeman & Co.

Bodine, R., Crawford, D., & Schrumpf, F. (2003). *Creating the Peaceable School: A Comprehensive Program for Teaching Conflict Resolution.* Champaign, IL: Research Press Publishers.

Cohen, R. (2005). *Students Resolving Conflict.* New York: Good Year Books.

Cornell, D., & Sheras, P. (2006). *Guidelines for Responding to Student Threats of Violence.* New York: Sopris West.

Cremin, H. (2007). *Peer Mediation: Citizenship and Social Inclusion in Action.* Maidenhead, UK: Open University Press.

DiGuilio, R. (2000). *Educate, Medicate, or Litigate? What Teachers, Parents, and Administrators Must Do about Student Behavior.* New York: Corwin.

Eisler, R., & Miller, R. (Eds.). (2004). *Educating for a Culture of Peace.* Portsmouth, NH: Heinemann.

Fox, J., & Burstein, H. (2010). *Violence and Security on Campus: From Preschool to College.* Westport, CT: Praeger.

Galtung, J., & Udayakumar, S. (Eds.). (2011). *More Than a Curriculum: Education for Peace and Development.* Charlotte, NC: Information Age.

...

Harber, C. (2004). *Schooling as Violence: How Schools Harm Pupils and Societies.* New York: RoutledgeFarmer.

Harris, I., & Morrison, M. (2003). *Peace Education,* 2nd ed. Jefferson, NC: McFarland.

Hemphill, B., & LeBanc, B. (Eds.). (2010). *Enough Is Enough: A Student Affairs Perspective on Preparedness and Response to a Campus Shooting.* Sterling, VA: Stylus.

Hiber, M. (2008). *Should Juveniles Be Tried as Adults?* New York: Greenhaven.

Hinduja, S., & Patchin, J. (2012). *School Climate 2.0: Preventing Cyberbullying and Sexting One Classroom at a Time.* New York: Corwin.

Holtham, J. (2009). *Taking Restorative Justice to Schools: A Doorway to Discipline.* Tulsa, OK: Homestead Press.

Lin, J., Brantmeier, E., & Bruhn, C. (2008). *Transforming Education for Peace.* Charlotte, NC: Information Age Publishing.

Monaghan, T., & Torres, R. (Eds.). (2009). *Schools under Surveillance: Cultures of Control in Public Education.* Rutgers, NJ: Rutgers University Press.

Muschert, G., Henry, S., Bracy, N., & Pequero, A. (2013). *Responding to School Violence: Confronting the Columbine Effect.* Boulder, CO: Lynne Rienner.

Reardon, B. (1988). *Comprehensive Peace Education: Educating for Global Responsibility.* New York: Teachers College Press.

Saltman, K., & Gabbard, D. (Eds.). (2011). *Education as Enforcement: The Militarization and Corporatization of Schools.* New York: Routledge.

Shapiro, S. (2010). *Educating Youth for a World beyond Violence: A Pedagogy for Peace.* New York: Palgrave.

Smith, M., Monteverde, M., & Lily, H. (2012). *School Violence and Conflict Resolution.* New York: Rosen Publishing Group.

Thornton, T., Craft, C., Dahlberg, L., Lynch, B., & Baer, K. (2002). *Best Practices of Youth Violence Prevention: A Sourcebook for Community Action.* Atlanta, GA: Centers for Disease Control and Prevention, National Center for Injury Prevention and Control.

Trump, K. (2000). *Classroom Killers? Hallway Hostages? How Schools Can Prevent and Manage School Crises.* New York: Corwin.

Winslade, J., & Williams, M. (2011). *Safe and Peaceful Schools: Addressing Conflict and Eliminating Violence.* New York, NY: Corwin.

Media

Coleman, L. (2004). *The Copycat Effect: How the Media and Popular Culture Trigger the Mayhem in Tomorrow's Headlines.* New York: Simon & Schuster.

Jones, G. (2003). *Killing Monsters: Why Children Need Fantasy, Super Heroes, and Make-Believe Violence.* New York: Basic.

Potter, W. (2002). *The 11 Myths of Media Violence.* Thousand Oaks, CA: Sage.

Rafter, N. (2000). *Shots in the Mirror.* New York: Oxford University Press.

Ravitch, D., & Vilerette, J. (2003). *Kid Stuff: Marketing Sex and Violence to America's Children.* Baltimore, MD: Johns Hopkins University Press.

Strasburger, V. (2002). *Children, Adolescents and the Media.* Thousand Oaks, CA: Sage.

Recommended Journals

Contemporary Issues in Criminology & Criminal Justice

Contemporary Justice Review

Crime, Law, and Social Change

Criminal Justice Policy Review

Criminal Justice Studies: A Critical Journal of Crime, Law and Society

Criminology & Public Policy

Critical Criminology

Critical Issues in Justice and Politics

Educational Researcher

International Journal of Violence in Schools

Journal of Contemporary Criminal Justice

Journal for Crime, Conflict and the Media

Journal of Educational Administration and Policy Studies

Journal of Gang Research

Journal of Interpersonal Violence

Journal of Knowledge and Best Practices in Juvenile Justice and Psychology

Journal of Law and Conflict Resolution

Journal of Peace Education

Journal of Research in Crime and Delinquency

Journal of School Safety

Journal of School Violence

Journal of Youth and Adolescence

Juvenile Justice Journal

Social Problems

Victims and Offenders

Violence and Victims

Youth & Society

Youth Violence & Juvenile Justice

Journal Articles, 2010–Present

Ackers, M. (2012). Cyberbullying: Through the Eyes of Children and Young People. *Educational Psychology in Practice, 28*(2), 141–57.

Agnich, L., & Miyazaki, Y. (2013). A Multi-level Cross-National Analysis of Direct and Indirect Forms of School Violence. *Journal of School Violence, 12*(4), 319–339.

Avor, R., Guerra, N., and Van Acker, R. (2010). How Can We Improve School Safety Research? *Educational Researcher, 39* (1), 69–78.

Biag, M. (2014). Perceived School Safety: Visual Narratives from the Middle Schools. *Journal of School Violence, 13*(2), 165–87.

Borum, R., Cornell, D., Modzeleski, W., & Jimerson, S. (2010). What Can Be Done about School Shootings? A Review of the Evidence. *Educational Researcher, 39*(1), 27–37.

Brady, N. (2011). Student Perceptions of High-Security School Environments. *Youth & Society, 43*(1), 365–95.

Chin, J., Dowdy, E., Jimerson, S., & Rime, J. (2012). Alternatives to Suspensions: Rationale and Recommendations. *Journal of School Violence, 11*(2), 156–73.

Daniels, J., Volungis, A., Pshenshny, E., Gandhi, P., Winkler, A., Cramer, D., & Bradley, M. (2010). A Qualitative Investigation of Averted School Shooting Rampages. *The Counseling Psychologist, 38*(1), 69–95.

De Venanzi, A. (2012). School Shootings in the USA: Popular Culture as Risk, Teen Marginality, and Violence against Peers. *Crime, Media, Culture, 8*(3), 261–78.

Dishman, A., Lewis, J., & Pepper, M. (2011). "A Student [Came] Down and Said 'There's a … Guy in the … English Classroom with a Gun' ": Recovering from Violent

Invasion. *Journal of Cases in Educational Leadership, 14*(1), 48–58.

Dittirch, C., Beran, T., Mishna, F., Hetherington, R., & Sharif, S. (2013). Do Children Who Bully Their Peers Also Play Violent Video Games? A Canadian National Study. *Journal of School Violence, 12*(4), 297–318.

Estrada, J., Gilreath, T., Astor, R., & Benbenishty, R. (2014). Gang Membership, School Violence, and the Mediating Effects of Risk and Protective Behaviors in California Schools. *Journal of School Violence, 13*(2), 228–51.

Lund, E., Blake, J., Ewing, H., & Banks, C. (2012). School Counselors' and School Psychologists' Bullying Prevention and Intervention Strategies: A Look into Real-World Practices. *Journal of School Violence, 11*(3), 246–65.

Mark, L., & Ratliffe, K. (2011). Cyber Worlds: New Playgrounds for Bullying. *Computers in the Schools: Interdisciplinary Journal of Practice, Theory, and Applied Research, 28*(2), 92–116.

Maume, M., Kim-Godwin, Y., & Clements, C. (2010). Racial Tensions and School Crime. *Journal of Contemporary Criminal Justice, 26*(3), 339–58.

Menard, S., & Grotpeter, J. (2014). Evaluation of Bully-Proofing Your School Antibullying Prevention. *Journal of School Violence, 13*(2), 188–209.

Nurmi, J. (2013). Expressions and Projections of Evil in Mass Violence. *Deviant Behavior, 34*(11), 859–874.

Obermann, M. (2011). Moral Disengagement among Bystanders to School Bullying. *Journal of School Violence, 10*(3), 239–57.

Raby, R. (2010). "Tank tops Are OK but I Don't Want to See Her Thong": Girls' Engagements with Secondary School Dress Codes. *Youth and Society, 41*, 333–56.

Rose, C., Monda-Amaya, L., & Espelage, D. (2011). Bullying Perpetration and Victimization in Special Education: A Review of the Literature. *Remedial and Special Education*, *32*(2), 114–30.

Sanchez, J., Yoxsimer, A., & Hill, G. (2012). Uniforms in the Middle School: Student Opinions, Discipline Data, and School Police Data. *Journal of School Violence, 11*(4), 343–56.

Waasdorp, T., Pas, E., O'Brennan, L., & Bradshaw, C. (2011). A Multilevel Perspective on the Climate of Bullying: Discrepancies among Students, School Staff, and Parents. *Journal of School Violence, 10*(2), 115–32.

Welch, K., & Payne, A. (2010). Racial Threat and Punitive School Discipline. *Social Problems, 57*(1), 25–48.

Wilken, I., & Van Aardt, A. (2012). School Uniforms: Tradition, Benefit or Predicament? *Education as Change, 16* (9), 159–84.

Wylie, L., Gibson, C., Brank, E., Findacaro, M., Smith, S., Brown, V., & Miller, S. (2010). Assessing School and Student Predictors of Weapons Reporting. *Youth Violence and Juvenile Justice, 8*(4), 351–72.

Zaykoswki, H., & Gunter. W. (2012). Youth Victimization: School Climate or Deviant Lifestyles? *Journal of Interpersonal Violence, 27*(3), 431–52.

Websites and Organizations

Advocates for Youth (www.advocatesforyouth.org):
    Helps youth make good choice regarding reproductive and sexual health.

American Academy of Pediatrics (www.aap.org):
    Recommendations for safe and healthy children and youth.

American Civil Liberties Union (www.aclu.org):
    Civil rights watchdog, often involved in cases related to
    students' rights.

Amnesty International (www.amnesty.org):
    Human rights watchdog with information relevant to
    school violence, youth activism, and teaching human rights.

Brady Campaign to Prevent Gun Violence (www.bradycenter
.org):
    Devoted to informing the public and lobbying for greater
    control of handguns.

Break the Cycle (www.breakthecycle.org):
    National organization devoted to providing information
    and resources related to dating violence and healthy
    relationships.

Bully Free (www.bullyfree.com):
    Resources for ending bullying.

Bully Police USA (www.bullypolice.org/):
    Provides details about school violence and a detailed
    description of state laws to address bullying.

Center for Effective Discipline (www.stophitting.com):
    Advocates for an end of corporal punishment. Provides
    statistics and reports.

Center for Media Literacy (www.medialit.org):
    Research and information related to critical analysis of
    media.

Center for Partnership Studies (www.partnershipway.org):
    Sociological and historical information about creating
    partnership-based schools.

Center for the Prevention of School Violence (http://test
.ncdjjdp.org/cpsv/resource_room.html):
  Provides information, statistics, and links related to school
  violence.

Center for the Study and Prevention of Violence (www
.colorado.edu/cspv):
  Disseminates research and reports on school violence.

Centers for Disease Control and Prevention School Violence
Resources (www.cdc.gov/violenceprevention/youthviolence/school
violence/index.html):
  Resources for preventing and responding to school
  violence.

Coalition for Safe and Effective Schools (http://safeand
effectiveschools.com/welcome.asp):
  Nonprofit organization devoted to promoting safe,
  supportive, and exemplary learning climates in schools.

Conflict Resolution Education Center (http://creducation.org):
  Offers extensive resources related to teaching conflict
  resolution skills, including lesson plans, videos, articles,
  role plays, and more.

The Cool Spot (www.thecoolspot.gov/):
  The Young Teen's Place for Info on Alcohol and Resisting
  Peer Pressure.

Defending Childhood (www.justice.gov/defendingchildhood/):
  Initiative started by Attorney General Eric Holder to provide supports for early education and families in need as a
  means of preventing violence.

Do Something (www.dosomething.org):
  Information, project ideas, and grant money for young
  people seeking to make their world better.

Free Child (www.freechild.org):
> Provides tools and training to young people and adults so that youth can help make social change.

Gay, Lesbian, & Straight Education Network (GLSEN) (www.glsen.org):
> Advocacy group for LGBT students with a particular focus on bullying.

Hamilton Fish Institute (www.hamfish.org/):
> Rigorous academic work devoted to safe and healthy children.

The Humanity Project (www.thehumanityproject.com):
> This nonprofit "passionately believes society can improve —if individuals understand why they benefit from moving beyond a purely self-centered life. We offer practical, psychology based ways for both kids and grownups to act not for 'me' alone but rather for 'us.'"

Ignitus Worldwide (http://www.ignitusworldwide.org/) Student-led groups help prevent crime and bullying.

Inside Hazing (www.insidehazing.com/):
> Statistics, stories, and resources about hazing at all levels.

iSafe (www.isafe.org):
> Provider of Internet safety education.

It Gets Better Project (www.itgetsbetter.org):
> Emphasizes how to support LGBT youth.

Mentors in Violence Prevention (www.mvpstrategies.net/):
> Programs designed to help athletes and others as bystanders to crime and violence.

National Center for Victims of Crime Dating Violence Resource Center (www.victimsofcrime.org/help-for-crime-victims/get-help-bulletins-for-crime-victims/bulletins-for-teens/dating-violence):
    Statistics, warning signs, and additional resources related to dating violence.

National Crime Prevention Council (www.ncpc.org):
    Addresses the prevention of all forms of crime

National Peace Academy Peace, Peacebuilding and Peace-Learning Guides (http://nationalpeaceacademy.us):
    Peace education curricula for use with children and youth.

National School Safety Center (www.schoolsafety.us):
    Provides resources to schools on how to stay safe and how to respond to crises.

National Youth Violence Prevention Resource Center (http://vetoviolence.cdc.gov/basics-overview.html):
    Information on a variety of types of school and campus violence.

Ophelia Project (www.opheliaproject.org/):
    Resources and ideas for addressing girl-on-girl bullying and other issues relevant to girls.

The Oregon Social Learning Center (www.oslc.org):
    Multidisciplinary center that promotes the scientific understanding of children's health and well-being.

Pacer Center Kids Against Bullying (www.pacerkidsagainstbullying.org/#/home):
    Features videos, games, and kid-friendly information about bullying.

PBS Frontline: "The Killer at Thurston High" (www.pbs.org/
wgbh/pages/frontline/shows/kinkel/):
> Informative video and resources on Kip Kinkel.

Peace and Justice Studies Association (www.peacejusticestudies
.org):
> Provides resources, training, and consultation on peace-
> making, peacebuilding, and peace education.

Prevention Institute (www.preventioninstitute.org):
> Provides online workshops related to a number of topics.

Rethinking Schools (www.rethinkingschools.org):
> Critically examines how and what is taught and offers lesson
> ideas for teaching peace, social justice, and human rights.

Safe and Drug-Free Schools Program, U.S. Department of
Education (www.ed.gov/offices/OESE/SDFS):
> This government organization provides resources, statistics,
> support, and funding to many of the other publicly run
> organizations that are focusing on ending school violence.

Stomp Out Bullying (www.stompoutbullying.org):
> Antibullying and anticyberbullying organization for kids
> and teens.

Stop Bullying (www.stopbullying.gov):
> Managed by the U.S. Department of Health and Human
> Services, this website provides definitions and information
> about risk and protective factors, as well as ideas and best
> practices for responding to and preventing bullying.

Stop Bullying Now! (www.stopbullyingnow.com):
> Information, resources, and links related to preventing
> and responding to bullying.

Stop Cyberbullying (www.stopcyberbullying.org):
   Devoted to providing information about cyberbullying
   and its effects.

Stop Hazing (www.stophazing.org):
   Statistics, stories, and resources about hazing at all levels.

Street Law (www.streetlaw.org):
   Resource for materials on crime and violence, especially
   for classroom educators.

Students Against Violence Everywhere (www.nationalsave
.org):
   The emphasis is on students as key to preventing school
   violence. Their goals are crime prevention, conflict management, and service projects.

Teachers Without Borders Peace Education (www.teachers
withoutborders.org):
   Detailed peace education curriculum and professional
   development resources for educators.

Teaching Tolerance (www.tolerance.org):
   Articles and lesson plans on a variety of topics related to
   civil liberties, human rights, and social justice.

TED Talks (www.ted.com and http://ed.ted.com):
   Amazing compilation of short videos by experts in all
   fields. TED Ed shows educators how to use these tools
   and offers ways to contribute lessons.

Teens Against Bullying (www.pacerteensagainstbullying.org/#/
home):
   Information and personal stories directed at inspiring
   teens to get involved to stop bullying.

United States Institute of Peace (www.buildingpeace.org):
    Toolkits and training manuals for peace educators at all
    levels.

Violence Policy Center (www.vpc.org):
    Performs research, investigation, analysis, and advocacy
    related to making the United States safer.

Working Against Violence Everywhere (www.waveamerica.com):
    Implements awareness campaigns based on the principles
    of leadership, resolve, respect, and responsibility.

Yes Magazine (www.yesmagazine.org):
    Teacher materials include lesson plans, ideas, student
    competitions, visual aids and more.

Zinn Education Project (www.zinnedproject.org):
    In honor of historian and educator Howard Zinn, site
    features a compilation of lesson plans and teaching ideas
    related to civil rights and equality.

Films

American Yearbook (2004):
    Should bullying victims take revenge? This film grapples
    with the choices faced by victims of school bullying.

April Showers (2009):
    Writer/director Andrew Robinson, a Columbine sur-
    vivor, shows how students coped with the aftermath of
    Columbine and the loss of their friends.

Bang Bang, You're Dead (2002):
    Students bully Trevor, that is, until he calls in a phony
    bomb threat with a working bomb. After that, everyone
    but a group of outcasts is afraid of him, and Trevor takes

the blame for anything that goes wrong at the school. One caring drama teacher is Trevor's only salvation.

Basketball Diaries (1995):

The film adaptation of Jim Carroll's descent into drug addiction. Jim is a great basketball player, but little else in his life is great. It is only through drugs that he manages to escape the harsh reality of his life. Depicts a dream sequence in which Jim (played by Leonardo DiCaprio) goes on a shooting rampage in his school.

Blackboard Jungle (1955):

Classic film starring Sidney Poitier that shows an urban school rife with verbal and physical violence. Spawned numerous remakes.

Bowling for Columbine (2002):

Award-winning documentary by filmmaker Michael Moore addresses the culture of violence in the United States. Attempts to more deeply understand what motivated the Columbine shooters by looking at gun control, media, governmental violence, welfare policy, and many other factors. Includes interviews with the creators of *South Park*, Charlton Heston, and Marilyn Manson.

Bully (2001):

Not overtly about schools, *Bully* depicts what happens when a victim tires of being bullied and seeks revenge. He and a group of friends suffer the repercussions of their naive actions.

Cry for Help (2009):

PBS documentary examining teenage mental illness, suicide, and how to help. Can be viewed online at http://www.pbs.org/wnet/cryforhelp/

CyberBully (2011):
ABC Family dramatic portrayal of cyberbullying and its consequences.

Dangerous Minds (1995):
Award-winning film documenting the lives of urban youth and how one teacher, an ex-marine, can help. Starring Michellle Pfeiffer.

Dead Poets Society (1989):
Set in an elite boarding school, the film depicts the tension students face to succeed and how one dedicated and creative teacher can help them explore their true passions.

Detention: The Siege at Johnson High (1997):
Starring Rick Schroeder, Freddy Prince Jr., Rodney Dangerfield, and Henry Winkler; largely depicts the school hostage situation perpetrated by Eric Houston at Lindhurst High School in 1992.

Duck! The Carbine High Massacre (2000):
First film released after Columbine massacre, a black comedy showing the problems with moral panics and conspiracy theories.

Elephant (2003):
Award-winning film from writer/director Gus Van Sant based on the Columbine shootings. Documents the lead-up to a school massacre by seemingly "normal" students.

Freedom Writers (2007):
Starring Hilary Swank; tells the true story of a Long Beach, California, high school teacher who helps her at-risk students develop skills and empathy.

Hidden Rage (2008):

Documents the traumatic effects of school bullying. The website www.hiddenrage.com provides resources for discussing school violence.

High School High (1996):

A satire that mixes parts of *Dangerous Minds* and parts of *Stand and Deliver*. Shows how a caring teacher can change a student's life.

The Interruptors (2011):

PBS Frontline documentary focusing on community and youth-led efforts to stop gang activity.

The Killer at Thurston High:

PBS Frontline episode that tells the story of school shooter Kip Kinkel. The website http://www.pbs.org/wgbh/pages/frontline/shows/kinkel/ provides more information about the case and other school shooters.

Lean on Me (1989):

Morgan Freeman stars as Joe Clark, the principal of a dangerous urban school in which test scores are so bad it is close to being shut down. Shows the power of expectations.

Light It Up (1999):

Starring musician Usher and actress Rosario Dawson, *Light it Up* tells the story of a group of urban students who stand up for their right to be educated and treated fairly. After a school police officer mistreats one of them, the students take over the school and demand a quality education.

Mean Creek (2004):

A bullied teen and his friends lure the bully into a boat trip and seek revenge. Shows what can happen when students believe revenge is the answer.

O (2001):

A modern-day retelling of Shakespeare's *Othello*, the film is set in a high school. "O," played by Mekhi Phifer, is the star of the team and the only African American student. He is love with Desi (Julia Stiles), the dean's daughter. Jealous teammate Hugo (Josh Hartnett) is addicted to steroids. He initiates the problems that explode into major atrocities.

One Eight Seven (1997):

Starring Samuel L. Jackson, the film shows how high school teachers deal with gang violence.

The Path to Violence (2013):

Tells the story of schools that thwarted attacks and highlights how schools can prevent violence.

School Ties (1992):

A cast of stars (Brendan Fraser, Matt Damon, Chris O'Donnell) shows the problems with elite schools, including elitism, privilege, cheating, and anti-Semitism. When working-class newcomer David Greene takes over the quarterback position at an exclusive prep school, the animosity hits a boiling point.

Stand and Deliver (1988):

True story of tough and demanding teacher Jaime Escalante, who shows urban high school students in a violence and gang-infested school that it is OK to succeed.

Teachers (1984):

A so-called "day-in-the-life" film, *Teachers* depicts troubled students and how their teachers deal with them, both good and bad.

Tomorrow's Children (2001):

Documentary featuring the work of historian Riane Eisler. Shows how schools have been modeled on domination and hierarchy and the promise of a different model.

Tough Guise (1999):

Documentary by Media Education Foundation that discusses how gender roles contribute to many forms of violent behavior today.

Tough Guise, II (2013):

Updated documentary about the problems with stereotypical gender roles.

Varsity Blues (1999):

Shows how football in small-town Texas is king. The team is everything and can get away with anything. Athletes drink illegally, use performance-enhancing drugs, and cheat.

Wrestling with Manhood (2003):

Media Education Foundation documentary showing how big-time wrestling reinforces bullying behavior.

Zero Day (2003):

A fictional depiction of the Columbine massacre. Shows the planning stages, including how the student acquired the weapons. Acclaimed by journalist and author Dave Cullen as a realistic depiction.

Starting with the first widely discussed incident of school violence in 1927, this timeline includes high-profile school shootings and bullycides as well as the dates for important speeches, legislation, and court decisions.

- May 18, 1927: School board member Andrew Kehoe, 55, kills his wife and sets fire to his farm buildings. Bombs he had planted over the course of months explode at Bath Consolidated School, killing 45 and injuring 58.
- August 1, 1966: Charles Whitman, 25, shoots and kills 14 and wounds 32 others, mostly from an observation tower at the University of Texas at Austin.
- February 8, 1968: Policemen kill three and wound 27 unarmed South Carolina State University students who were protesting the segregation of a local bowling alley.
- May 4, 1970: Ohio National Guard fires 67 rounds in just 13 seconds, killing four unarmed Kent State University students who were protesting the expansion of the Vietnam War into Cambodia.

Children from the Boys and Girls Club raise their hands to show their commitment to the Team Up to Stop Bullying campaign run by Sears stores in 2013. (John Konstantaras/AP Images for Sears)

- May 14/15, 1970: Police shoot and kill two Jackson State College students who were protesting the Vietnam War. Twelve others were wounded.

- May 15, 1974: Three members of the Democratic Front for the Liberation of Palestine shoot and kill 22 Israeli high school students in Ma'alot, Israel.

- December 30, 1974: Anthony Barbaro, 18, sets off home-made bombs and firearms at school in Olean, New York. He fires at janitors and responding firefighters, then commits suicide while awaiting trial.

- January 22, 1975: Supreme Court determines in *Goss v. Lopez* that students have due process rights in school disciplinary hearings.

- May 28, 1975: Michael Slobodian, 16, kills a classmate and an English teacher and wounds 13 at Brampton Centennial Secondary School in Ontario, Canada. Slobodian commits suicide in a school bathroom.

- October 21, 1975: Robert Poulin, 18, shoots and kills one and wounds five others, then commits suicide at St. Pius X High School in Ottawa, Canada.

- July 12, 1976: Custodian Edward Charles Allaway, 37, kills two and wounds seven in the library basement at California State University–Fullerton. He is committed to the California state mental hospital system.

- May 19, 1978: Honors student John Christian, 13, shoots and kills his teacher in Austin, Texas.

- October 15, 1978: Robin Robinson, 13, was paddled by school administrators after a disagreement with another student. He returns to the school and shoots the principal in Lanett, Alabama.

- January 29, 1979: Brenda Spencer, 16, shoots and kills one principal and one janitor and wounds nine students and adults in San Carlos, California. She uses a sniper rifle she had received for Christmas.

- March 19, 1982: Patrick Lazotte kills one and wounds two at Valley High School in Las Vegas, Nevada. Lazotte had been bullied for 12 years.

- January 20, 1983: David F. Lawler, a freshman, kills one student when he opens fire in a study hall classroom at Parkway South Junior High School in St. Louis. Lawler committed suicide.

- January 15, 1985: Supreme Court determines in *New Jersey v. T.L.O* that school officials can search students based on reasonable suspicion.

- January 21, 1985: James Alan Kearby, 14, kills his principal and three other students who were bullying him at his junior high in Goddard, Kansas.

- March 2, 1987: Twelve-year-old Nathan Ferris kills the boy who had picked on him and then kills himself at a Missouri school.

- February 11, 1988: Jason Harless and Jason McCoy use stolen guns to kill Principal Richard Allen and wound two others at Pinellas Park High School in Pinellas Park, Florida.

- May 20, 1988: Laurie Dann, 30, attempts to poison family and friends and then kills one boy and wounds five other students at an elementary school in Winnetka, Illinois. She then takes a family hostage and shoots another man before killing herself.

- September 30, 1988: James William Wilson Jr., 19, shoots and kills one student and wounds 14 elementary school students and a teacher with a .22 caliber pistol in Greenwood, South Carolina.

- December 16, 1988: Nicholas Elliott, 16, kills one teacher and wounds another in Virginia Beach, Virginia.

- December 6, 1989: Marc Lepine, 25, orders all the men to leave a classroom at the University of Montreal School of Engineering, then kills nine women. Lepine kills five more outside the classroom, then himself.

- September 27, 1990: Curtis Collins shoots one student at El Dorado High School in Las Vegas, Nevada.
- November 1, 1991: Gang Lu, 28, shoots and kills four faculty members and one student at the University of Iowa. Another student is wounded before Lu commits suicide.
- May 1, 1992: Eric Houston, 20, shoots and kills four students and wounds 10 at his former high school in Olivehurst, California.
- August 24, 1992: Dr. Valery I. Frabricant kills four colleagues and wounds a staff member at Concordia University in Montreal, Quebec.
- November 20, 1992: Joseph White, 15, shoots another student at Tilden High School in Chicago, Illinois. The shooting is gang-related.
- December 14, 1992: Wayne Lo, 18, kills one student and one professor and wounds four others at Simon's Rock College of Bard in Massachusetts before surrendering to the police.
- January 18, 1993: Gary Scott Pennington, 19, holds a teacher and a custodian hostage at his high school in Grayson, Kentucky.
- February 22, 1993: Robert Heard, 15, shoots a student who had transferred to Reseda High School in California to flee gang violence.
- March 18, 1993: Edward Gillom, 15, kills one and wounds another student at Harlem High School in Harlem, Georgia. He claims to have been bullied.
- March 25, 1993: Lawanda Jackson, 19, shoots and kills her ex-boyfriend at Sumner High School in St. Louis, Missouri.
- March 26, 1993: Five students get into a fight over the previous night's track meet at Lamar High School in Bryan, Texas. One student is stabbed to death.

- April 12, 1993: Karter Reed, 16, stabs and kills one student who he thought was someone else at Dartmouth High School in Dartmouth, Massachusetts.

- April 14, 1993: Max Martinez, 17, kills one student who had insulted his girlfriend at Nimitz High School in Irving, Texas.

- May 15, 1993: Eric Schmitt, 42, takes 21 students and their teacher hostage at Commandant Charcto Nursery School in Neuilly-sur-Seine, France.

- December 1, 1993: Leonard McDowell, 21, shoots and kills an associate principal who had suspended him from school at Wauwatosa West High School in Milwaukee, Wisconsin. McDowell had entered the building in violation of a restraining order sought by a teacher with whom he was obsessed.

- April 4, 1994: Flemming Nielsen, 35, shoots and kills two and wounds two others at Aarhus University in Denmark.

- April 12, 1994: James Osmanson, 10, shoots and kills a classmate on the playground at Margaret Leary Elementary School in Butte, Montana. Osmanson was aiming at another boy who had been bullying him for years.

- May 26, 1994: Clay Shrout, 17, kills his parents and two younger sisters, then takes a class hostage at his high school. Assistant Principal Steve Sorrell convinces Shrout to give up his gun before anyone else is hurt.

- November 7, 1994: Keith Ledeger, 37, a former student, kills a custodian and wounds three others at Wickliffe Middle School in Wickliffe, Ohio.

- January 26, 1995: Supreme Court rules in *Vernonia School District v. Acton* that drug testing students who seek to participate in extracurricular sports is constitutional.

- October 12, 1995: Suspended student Toby Sincino, 16, kills three people with a .32 caliber revolver in Blackville, South Carolina.

- November 15, 1995: Jamie Rouse, 17, kills a teacher and student and wounds another teacher at Richland High School in Lynnville, Tennessee.

- February 2, 1996: Barry Loukaitis, 14, opens fire on a junior high school algebra class, killing two students and one teacher and wounding another student in Moses Lake, Washington.

- March 13, 1996: Thomas Hamilton kills 16 children and one teacher and wounds 10 others at Dunblane Primary School in Scotland.

- March 25, 1996: Anthony Gene Rutherford, 18; Jonathon Dean Moore, 15; and Joseph Stanley Burris, 15, kill a student they believe planned to tell about their plot to attack the school in Patterson, Missouri.

- August 15, 1996: Frederick Martin Davidson, a 36-year-old graduate student, shoots and kills three professors at San Diego State University.

- September 17, 1996: Jillian Robbins, 19, kills one student and wounds another at Pennsylvania State University.

- February 19, 1997: Evan Ramsey, 16, kills one student and the school principal and wounds two others with a shotgun he uses in the high school commons room in Bethel, Alaska.

- March 30, 1997: Mohammad Ahman al-Nazari, 48, shoots and kills six and wounds 12 with an illegally obtained assault rifle at Tala'I Private School in Sanaa, Yemen.

- October 1, 1997: Luke Woodham, 16, kills his own mother, then shoots two students and wounds seven at his high school in Pearl, Mississippi.

- December 1, 1997: Michael Carneal, 14, kills three students and wounds five who were involved in a prayer circle at his high school in West Paducah, Kentucky.

- December 15, 1997: Joseph "Colt" Todd, 14, shoots two students he said humiliated him in Stamps, Arkansas.

- March 9, 1998: Jeffrey Lance Pennick II, 18, kills one student and wounds two at Central Avenue Elementary School in Summit, Washington.
- March 24, 1998: Mitchell Johnson, 13, and Andrew Golden, 11, kill one teacher and four students and wound 10 others when they shoot at their school from the nearby woods in Jonesboro, Arkansas.
- April 24, 1998: Andrew Wurst, 14, kills one teacher and wounds one teacher and two students at a school dance for Parker Middle School in Edinboro, Pennsylvania.
- May 21, 1998: Kip Kinkel, 15, kills both his parents, then two students, and wounds 23 when he opens fire on his high school cafeteria in Springfield, Oregon.
- June 15, 1998: Quinshawn Booker, 14, shoots one teacher and wounds a guidance counselor in the hallway of his high school in Richmond, Virginia.
- April 20, 1999: Eric Harris, 18, and Dylan Klebold, 17, shoot and kill 14 students, one teacher, and themselves at Columbine High School in Littleton, Colorado. Twenty-three students and teachers are wounded in the attack.
- April 28, 1999: Todd Cameron Smith, 14, shoots and kills one student and wounds another in what is believed to be a Columbine "copycat" at W.R. Myers High School in Taber, Alberta, Canada.
- May 20, 1999: Thomas "T.J." Solomon, 15, wounds six students with a .22 caliber rifles at his high school in Conyers, Georgia.
- November 19, 1999: Victor Cordova, 12, kills one student with a .22 caliber handgun in the lobby of his school in Deming, New Mexico.
- December 6, 1999: Seth Trickey, 13, wounds four students when he shoots them with a 9 mm semi-automatic gun at his middle school in Fort Gibson, Oklahoma.

- February 29, 2000: Dedrick Owens, 6, finds a loaded gun at his uncle's house and brings it to school, shooting 6-year-old Kayla Rolland at Buell Elementary School in Flint, Michigan.
- March 16, 2000: Nathaniel Brazill, 13, kills his teacher with a .25 caliber semi-automatic pistol on the last day of classes in Lake Worth, Florida.
- March 5, 2001: Charles Andrew "Andy" Williams, 15, kills two students in the high school bathroom in Santee, California.
- March 7, 2001: Elizabeth Catherine Bush, 14, shoots and wounds a female student in the high school cafeteria in Williamsport, Pennsylvania.
- March 22, 2001: Jason Hoffman, 18, kills four students and two teachers at his high school in El Cajon, California.
- May 7, 2001: Jason Pritchard, 33, cuts and stabs four elementary school students on their playground in Anchorage, Alaska.
- June 8, 2001: Mamoru Takuma fatally stabs 8 and injures 13 at Ikeda Elementary School in Osaka, Japan.
- Chris Buschbacher, 17, takes two students and one teacher from his high school hostage in Caro, Michigan. He releases all of them, then commits suicide.
- December 5, 2001: Corey Ramos, 17, stabs and kills his principal in Springfield, Massachusetts.
- January 16, 2002: Peter Odighizuwa, 43, a former student, shoots and kills three and wounds three others at Appalachian School of Law in Grundy, Virginia.
- April 29, 2002: Dragoslav Petkovic, 17, shoots and kills one teacher and wounds another before committing suicide at his high school in Vlasenica, Bosnia-Herzegovina.
- March 2, 2002: Mike Placencia, 14, stabs a student who made a racist remark in Cashmere, Washington.

- April 26, 2002: Robert Steinhauser, 19, kills 13 teachers, two students, and one police officer at Johann Gutenberg Secondary School in Erfurt, Germany. Steinhauser commits suicide.

- April 29, 2002: Dragoslav Petkovic, 17, shoots and kills a teacher and wounds another before he commits suicide in Vlasenica, Bosnia-Herzegovina.

- October 28, 2002: Robert Flores Jr., 41, kills three female nursing professors and then himself at the University of Arizona.

- June 27, 2002: Supreme Court rules in *Board of Ed. of Pottawatomie Schools v. Earls* that drug testing students seeking to participate in any extracurricular activity is constitutional.

- April 14, 2003: Steven Williams and James Tate kill one student at John McDonogh High School in New Orleans, Louisiana.

- April 24, 2003: James Sheets, 14, shoots and kills his middle school principal and then himself in Red Lion, Pennsylvania.

- May 9, 2003: Biswanath Halder, a former student, kills one student and wounds a professor and a student at Case Western Reserve University in Cleveland, Ohio.

- September 24, 2003: Jason McLaughlin, 15, shoots and kills two students at Rocori High School in Cold Spring, Minnesota.

- September 1, 2004: A group of Muslim pro-Chechen rebels take more than 1,200 schoolchildren and adults hostage in Beslan, North Ossetia-Alania. After a three-day standoff, Russian security forces storm the building. A series of explosions followed by a fire and gunfire exchanges result in the death of at least 334 hostages, including 186 children.

- March 21, 2005: Jeff Weise, 16, kills his grandfather and grandfather's girlfriend before shooting and killing five students, a teacher, a security guard, and then himself at his high school on Red Lake Indian Reservation in Minnesota.

- November 8, 2005: Kenny Bartley, 15, kills Assistant Principal Ken Bruce and wounds two other administrators at his high school in Jacksboro, Tennessee.
- August 24, 2006: Christopher Williams, 27, shoots and kills his ex-girlfriend's mother. He then attempts to find his ex-girlfriend at the school where she taught. When he cannot, Williams kills another teacher and wounds another. He attempts suicide but is instead captured.
- September 13, 2006: Kimveer Gill, 25, shoots 20 at Dawson College in Montreal, Canada. One victim dies on the spot. Gill commits suicide after being shot in the arm by a police officer.
- September 27, 2006: Duane Morrison, 53, takes six girls hostage for hours, molesting them before shooting and killing one girl and then himself at Platte Canyon High School in Bailey, Colorado.
- September 29, 2006: Eric Hainstock, 15, shoots and kills his principal in Cazenovia, Wisconsin.
- October 2, 2006: Charles Roberts, 32, ties up and then kills five girls at an Amish school in Nickel Mines, Pennsylvania. Five others are injured before Roberts kills himself.
- November 20, 2006: Sebastian Bosse, 18, shoots five people at his former high school in Emsdetten, Germany. Police commandos find Bosse dead.
- April 16, 2007: Seung-Hui Cho, a senior, shoots and kills 32 and wounds many others at Virginia Tech College in Blacksburg, Virginia.
- September 21, 2007: Loyer Braden, 18, shoots and kills two fellow Delaware State University students.
- October 10, 2007: Asa Coon, 14, shoots and kills two students and two teachers, then commits suicide at SuccessTech alternative high school in Cleveland, Ohio.

- November 7, 2007: Pekka-Eric Auvinen, 18, shoots and kills eight people and then himself at a high school in Tuusula, Finland.

- February 8, 2008: Latina Williams, 23, shoots and kills two students, then commits suicide at Louisiana Tech College in Baton Rouge, Louisiana.

- February 12, 2008: Brandon McInerney, 14, shoots and kills Lawrence King because he was gay at E.O. Green School in Oxnard, California.

- February 14, 2008: Steven Kazmierczak, 27, a former student, shoots and kills 6 people and wounds 18 on the campus of Northern Illinois University.

- August 21, 2008: Jamar Siler, 15, shoots and kills a fellow student at Central High School in Knoxville, Tennessee.

- September 23, 2008: Matti Juhani Saari, 22, shoots and kills 10 people at the vocational college he attended in Kauhajoki, Finland.

- October 26, 2008: Four men (Kawin Brockton, 19; Kelsey Perry, 19; Mario Tony, 20; and Brandon Wade, 20) shoot and kill two University of Central Arkansas students and wound a visitor.

- November 13, 2008: Teah Wemberly, 15, shoots and kills friend Amanda Collette at Dillard High School in Ft. Lauderdale, Florida.

- March 6, 2008: Alaa Abu Dhein, 26, shoots and kills 8 students and wounds 11 at Mercaz HeRav Yeshiva, a religious school in Jerusalem, Israel.

- March 11, 2009: Tim Kretschmer, 17, a former student, shoots and kills 15 at Albertville Secondary School in Winnenden, Germany.

- April 30, 2009: Farda Gadyrov, 29, kills 12 and wounds 13 before killing himself at Azerbaijan State Oil Academy in Azerbaijan.

- June 25, 2009: Supreme Court rules in *Safford v. Redding* that strip-searching a student for allegedly having ibuprofen is unconstitutional.
- September 15, 2009: Andy Rodriquez, 17, stabs classmate to death in Coral Gables, Florida.
- September 23, 2009: A 16-year-old student stabs a special education teacher in Tyler, Texas. The teacher later dies from the attack.
- October 16, 2009: Trevor Varinecz, 16, is shot and killed by a school resource officer after allegedly stabbing the officer in an altercation in Conway, South Carolina.
- January 14, 2010: Phoebe Prince commits suicide after being bullied at South Hadley High School in Massachusetts.
- February 12, 2010: Biology professor Amy Bishop kills three faculty members and wounds three employees at the University of Alabama at Huntsville.
- February 23, 2010: Bruco Strongeagle Eastwood, 32, allegedly shoots at middle school students as school lets out in Littleton, Colorado. Two eighth-grade students are injured.
- March 9, 2010: Nathaniel Brown, 51, a custodian who had been told he was being fired, kills a co-worker and wounds another at Ohio State University.
- March 17, 2010: Wayne Treacy, 15, brutally beats and stomps Jose Lou Ratley in Deerfield Beach, Florida. Ratley survives the attack.
- April 2010: Xu Yuyuan, 47, stabs 28 children and two adults in an elementary school in China. This is China's fifth attack on schoolchildren in just over a month.
- September 2010: A spate of gay teens commit suicide after being bullied by peers.
- October 2010: President Obama, Education Secretary Arne Duncan, and Secretary of State Hilary Clinton speak out against bullying.

- October 24, 2011: Cape Fear High School, Fayetteville, North Carolina. Ta'Von McLoren, 18, and another 15-year-old student shoot 15-year-old Caitlyn Abercrombie.
- January 10, 2012: North Forest High School, Houston, Texas. Eighteen-year-old Warren Lewis shoots at three students who had bullied him A 16-year-old bystander is wounded.
- February 27, 2012: Chardon High School, Chardon, Ohio. Seventeen-year-old Thomas "T.J" Lane opens fire in the school cafeteria, killing three and wounding three others. Lane is sentenced to three life sentences.
- March 6, 2012: Episcopal School of Jacksonville, Jacksonville, Florida. Twenty-eight-year-old former Spanish teacher Shane Scheumerth shoots and kills headmistress Dale Regan after being fired.
- April 7, 2012: Oikos University, Oakland, California. Seven students are killed and three others wounded in a classroom by One L. Goh, 43.
- August 24, 2012: Banks County High School, Homer, Georgia. A 16-year-old student commits suicide in a school restroom.
- August 27, 2012: Perry Hall High School, Perry Hall, Maryland. Fifteen-year-old Robert Wayne Gladden fires two shots in the cafeteria; a 17-year-old student is injured. The shooter is sentenced to 35 years for attempted murder.
- September 26, 2012: Stillwater Junior High School, Fairmount, North Dakota. Thirteen-year-old Cade Poulos commits suicide in front of classmates while wearing a villain costume from the Batman series.
- October 10, 2012: Canadian teenager Amanda Todd commits suicide after enduring in-person and online bullying.
- December 14, 2012: Sandy Hook Elementary School, Newtown, Connecticut. Twenty-year-old Adam Lanza kills 20 first-grade students, six adults, and his mother, wounding two more before committing suicide.

- December 22, 2012: The New York *Journal News* publishes the names and addresses of gun owners in Westchester and Rockland Counties. Public outrage prompts New York and six other states to exempt gun permit data from public records requests.

- January 3, 2012: Governor Daniel Malloy creates Sandy Hook Commission to make legislative recommendations on school safety, mental health, and gun violence following the mass shooting at Sandy Hook Elementary School.

- January 7, 2014: Secretary of Education Arne Duncan and Attorney General Eric Holder author a document critiquing zero tolerance laws.

- January 10, 2013: Taft Union High School, Taft, California. Sixteen-year-old Bryan Oliver targets classmates who bullied him. One student is wounded. Oliver is charged with two counts of attempted murder.

- January 10, 2013: Colorado Governor John Hickenlooper says he would consider universal background checks if it would have prevented the mass shooting in an Aurora, Colorado, movie theater in July 2012.

- January 12, 2013: Osborn High School, Detroit, Michigan. A 16-year-old student is shot after a basketball game and hospitalized.

- January 15, 2013: Stevens Institute of Business and Arts, St. Louis, Missouri. A former student shoots and wounds an administrator and then wounds himself in a stairwell.

- January 15, 2013: Governor Andrew Cuomo signs the SAFE Act to tighten the state's assault weapons ban, limit gun magazine capacity, require background checks for gun and ammunition sales, toughen penalties for illegal gun use, and exempt gun permit data from public records requests.

- January 16, 2013: Chicago State University, Chicago, Illinois. A 17-year-old student is shot and killed after a high school basketball game. Michael McNabb, 32, and Stephen Gilbert, 29, are charged.

- January 16, 2013: President Barack Obama signs 23 executive orders designed to reduce gun violence. He also calls on Congress to pass universal background checks and address assault weapons.

- January 31, 2013: Price Middle School, Atlanta, Georgia. A 14-year-old student is shot in the neck by another student, 15. The shooter is charged with aggravated assault.

- March 8, 2013: Governor Dennis Daugaard signs the "school sentinels" bill to allow teachers, staff, and volunteers to carry guns in classrooms.

- March 14, 2013: Republican Governor Bill Haslaim signs a bill permitting handgun owners to store guns in their cars in virtually any parking lot, including at schools.

- March 18, 2013: University of Central Florida, Orlando, Florida. Former student James Oliver Seevakumaran, 30, attempts to execute a mass killing outside a dormitory. The plan is foiled and the perpetrator commits suicide.

- March 20, 2013: Colorado governor signs into law three new gun-related laws mandating limits on magazine size, authorizing fees for background checks, and requiring background checks for all gun transfers.

- April 4, 2013: Connecticut governor Dan Molloy signs into law a requirement limiting magazine size, mandating background checks, and expanding the definition of assault weapons.

- June 7, 2013: Santa Monica College, Santa Monica, California. John Zawahri kills three people in a library after killing his father and brother. Zawahri is killed by police.

- August 19, 2013: Ronald E. McNair Discovery Learning Academy, Decatur, Georgia. Twenty-year-old Michael Brandon Hill fires shots in an elementary school, but nobody is injured. Front office employee Antoinette Tuff talks him down, and Hill is arrested.

- August 30, 2013: Carver High School, Winston-Salem, North Carolina. Eighteen-year-old Christopher Lamont Richardson shoots a 15-year-old student in the neck. The victim survives.
- October 21, 2013: Sparks Middle Schools, Sparks, Nevada. A 12-year-old student shoots and kills a teacher and two other students before committing suicide.

Adolescence: A stage in the life course between childhood and adulthood, typically characterized by marginal social status and identity, uncertain roles, and minimal power or meaningful participation in U.S. social life.

Anger Management Programs: Courses, often but not always court-mandated, that help attendees understand what triggers their anger and work on managing anger in healthy, constructive ways.

Anomie: Concept developed by French sociologist Emile Durkheim to explain conditions of normlessness that are a result of rapid social change.

Antisocial Behaviors: Behaviors that involve violating social norms and suggest a disregard for the feelings of others.

Antisocial Personality Disorder: A personality disorder that is characterized by impulsivity, inability to follow societal customs and laws, and a lack of anxiety and guilt.

Arts-Based Programs: Prevention or therapeutic efforts that involve music, theater, dance, or other forms of art.

Assessment: The evaluation of an individual's development, behavior, intellect, interests, personality, cognitive processes, emotional functioning, or social functioning for the purpose of identifying needs. Assessment methods include interviewing, systematic observation, and psychometric testing.

Atavism: Concept developed by Cesare Lombroso, an early criminologist, suggesting that there are "born criminals" who are less evolved and who share certain body structures and features.

Attention-Deficit Disorder (ADD) and Attention-Deficit/ Hyperactivity Disorder (AD/HD): Syndrome typically identified in childhood that involves a short attention span, impulsivity, and sometimes hyperactivity.

Biological Theories: A category of theories explaining abuse as the result of heredity, childhood trauma, or head injuries.

Birth Order: Order of birth relative to one's siblings, found in some studies to impact propensity for delinquency.

Borderline Personality Disorder: A personality disorder that features various manifestations, including impulsivity, mood instability, and perhaps even functional psychosis. Patients typically experience periods of normalcy as well.

Bullying: Physical, sexual, verbal, emotional, and other forms of harmful or violent behavior perpetrated by one person over another. Typically associated with youth but shares the same power–control dynamic as in dating and domestic violence.

Bystander Intervention Programs: Educational programs focused on informing participants about a phenomenon and providing them with skills to intervene safely to disrupt harmful behavior like bullying and abuse.

Case Management: The arrangement, coordination, and monitoring of services to assist victims and their families.

Child Protective Services (CPS): In most states, the designated social services agency to receive reports of, investigate, and provide intervention and treatment services to children and families in which child maltreatment has allegedly occurred.

Child Victim: A child for whom an incident of abuse or neglect has been substantiated or indicated by an investigation or assessment by authorities.

Child Witness: Refers to a child who is present when abuse occurs, regardless whether she or he sees the abuse.

Chivalry Hypothesis: A concept that suggests that females are treated more leniently by police and other formal systems of social control.

Choice Theories: Criminological theories which emphasize offenders' free will and ability to make rational choices about their behavior.

Cognitive Behavioral Therapy: A treatment approach that focuses both on observable behavior and on the thinking or beliefs that accompany the behavior. The goal of cognitive behavioral therapy is to replace maladaptive behaviors, thoughts, and beliefs with more adaptive ones.

Community Violence: Community violence refers to both predatory violence (e.g., robbery) and violence arising from nonfamily interpersonal conflicts and may include brutal acts such as shootings, rapes, stabbings, and beatings.

Compassion Fatigue: Occurs when advocates experience a state of exhaustion, often accompanied by depression and hopelessness, due to the challenging nature of working with traumatized populations.

Comprehensive Crime Control Act: Enacted in 1984 and considered to be one of the most dramatic changes in U.S. crime control policy, it generally broadened the courts' powers to assign lengthy sentences for specific offenses.

Conduct Disorder: Term used by the American Psychiatric Association to describe adolescents whose behavior routinely violates the rights of others and major conduct norms.

Conflict Resolution: Strategies that help people identify the causes of conflict and weigh possible resolutions. Programs may or may not include mediators who help both parties negotiate an agreeable resolution.

Conflict Theories: Criminological theories derived from the work of Karl Marx which focus on class conflict and power differentials as the basic reasons for crime and violence.

Containment Theory: Theory developed by Walter Reckless to explain both internal and external pushes and pulls toward delinquency.

Corporal Punishment: Physical punishments dispensed by schools and other authority figures with the goal of modifying misbehaviors.

Correlates of Delinquency: The statistical association between certain social and demographic characteristics and the propensity to engage in delinquent or violent behavior.

Court-Appointed Representative: A person appointed by a judge or court official to represent a person in neglect or abuse proceedings.

Cultural Competence   Help that is sensitive and responsive to cultural differences. Mental health professionals are aware of the impact of their own culture and possess skills that help them provide services that are culturally appropriate in responding to people's unique cultural differences, such as race and ethnicity, national origin, religion, age, gender, sexual orientation, or physical disability.

Cyberbullying: An aggressive behavior directed at another person using various communication technologies such as e-mails, instant messaging, texting, or sending images via cell phones, blogs, Web pages, and chat rooms. Aggressors often torment, threaten, harass, humiliate, or embarrass the victim repeatedly. Cyberbullying is also referred to as online social cruelty or electronic bullying.

Dating Violence: Controlling behavior perpetrated by one partner in a dating relationship against the other partner. May include emotional, verbal, social, physical, and sexual forms.

Deterrence Theory: A part of classical criminological theory, the notion that stern and prompt punishment will prevent offenders from reoffending and will stop others who might be inclined to do so as well.

Developmental Perspective: An approach that takes into account the growth and change of human beings as they age, including cognitive development, social development, language development, moral reasoning, and self and gender identity formation.

Differential Association Theory: Theoretical perspective developed by Edwin Sutherland focusing on crime as learned behavior.

Differential Identification Theory: Authored by Daniel Glaser, a theoretical perspective maintaining that crime is learned from those with whom one identifies.

DSM-IV: The *Diagnostic and Statistical Manual of Mental Disorders*, Fourth Edition, is the official manual of mental health problems developed by the American Psychiatric Association. This reference book is used by psychiatrists, psychologists, social workers, and other health and mental health care providers to understand and diagnose a mental health problem. Insurance companies and health care providers also use the terms and definitions in this manual when they discuss mental health problems.

Evidence-Based Practices: Evidence-based practices, sometimes referred to as empirically validated treatments or empirically supported therapy, are practices that have been clearly specified and found to be supported by scientific evidence.

Feminist Theories: Theories that emphasize the study, analysis, and explanation of crime as it relates to gender.

Gun-Free Schools Act: Passed in 1994, an act that requires states receiving federal funds to enact legislation mandating specific punishments for guns, drugs, and other forms of violence on school grounds.

Hazing: Any activity expected of someone joining a group (or to maintain full status in a group) that humiliates, degrades, or risks emotional or physical harm, regardless of the person's willingness to participate.

Interpersonal Violence: Violence between two individuals.

Intervention: Services, activities, or treatments developed and implemented to change or improve knowledge, attitudes, behavior, or awareness. Interventions are purposeful responses, which can be acute and provided either in the immediate aftermath of a traumatic event or after an event has already occurred.

Keeping Children and Families Safe Act: Enacted in 2003 (P.L. 108-36), this legislation included the reauthorization of the Child Abuse Prevention and Treatment Act (CAPTA). CAPTA provides minimum standards for defining child physical abuse and neglect and sexual abuse that states must incorporate into their statutory definitions in order to receive federal funds.

Labeling Theories: Sociological explanations for crime and violence that focus on the impact societal labeling and stigmas may have on producing criminal or deviant behavior.

Learning Theories: Criminological theories that emphasize that crime is a learned behavior.

Medical Trauma: Trauma associated with an injury or accident, chronic or life-threatening illness, or painful or invasive medical procedures.

Mentoring: Efforts to involve successful older people as role models for youth.

Neglect: Child neglect involves the failure to provide needed, age-appropriate care although financially able to do so or offered financial or other means to do so. This includes physical neglect (e.g., deprivation of food, clothing, or shelter), medical neglect (e.g., failure to provide the child with access to needed medical or mental health treatments or to consistently administer prescribed medications), and educational neglect (e.g., withholding child from school, failure to attend to special education needs).

No Child Left Behind Act: Legislation enacted in 2001 that mandates drug prevention and response programs, new initiatives to increase graduation rates, and efforts to ensure safe school climates, among other foci.

Peace Education: Education that includes content about peace, justice, and nonviolence, typically delivered via egalitarian and participatory teaching methods.

Physical Abuse: Actual or attempted infliction of bodily pain or injury, including the use of severe corporal punishment. Physical abuse is characterized by physical injury (for example, bruises and fractures) resulting from punching, beating, kicking, burning, or otherwise harming a child. In some cases, the injury may result from overdiscipline or physical punishment that is inappropriate to the child's age or condition.

Posttraumatic Stress Disorder: An anxiety disorder defined in the *DSM-IV* that can develop after exposure to a terrifying event or experience in which grave physical harm occurred or was threatened. Diagnostic criteria for PTSD include exposure to a traumatic event, re-experiencing of the event (e.g., nightmares, flashbacks), persistent avoidance of things associated with the trauma (e.g., avoiding certain activities, avoiding talking about the event), and increased physiological arousal. To meet diagnostic criteria for PTSD, an individual must exhibit a certain number of symptoms for a duration of more than one month and experience clinically significant distress or impairment.

Primary Prevention: Efforts to prevent domestic violence from occurring. Typically these include efforts to reduce gender inequalities and address gender role stereotypes, decrease violent media, educate young people about healthy relationships, and more.

Profiling: Efforts to identify potential perpetrators through use of statistical data.

Protective Factor: A variable that decreases the chance that a phenomenon will occur.

Psychological Maltreatment: Sometimes called emotional abuse, psychological maltreatment includes acts or omissions by parents or caregivers that have caused, or could cause, serious behavioral, cognitive, emotional, or mental disorders. Examples include verbal abuse (e.g., insults, belittling, threats of violence), bullying and the use of coercive control, emotional neglect (e.g., shunning, withdrawal of love), and intentional social deprivation (e.g., isolation, confinement).

Psychopathology: Mental disorders. Some theorists maintain that batterers suffer from various psychopathologies.

Public Health Perspective: An approach that focuses on health promotion and disease prevention for the population at large. A public health perspective considers behavioral and environmental risk factors and targets primary, secondary, and tertiary prevention and intervention strategies to populations depending on their levels of risk.

Refugee Trauma: Exposure to war, political violence, or torture. Refugee trauma can be the result of living in a region affected by bombing, shooting, or looting as well as forced displacement to a new home due to political reasons.

Resiliency: Qualities that allow individuals to adapt and remain strong despite risk and adversity.

Restorative Justice: Method of justice that involves victims, offenders, and community members in identifying an appropriate strategy for repairing the harm done.

Risk Factor: A variable that increases the chance that a phenomenon will occur.

School Climate: The quality and character of school life, including student and staff morale, belief in a common vision, and inclusivity, among other factors.

School Resource Officer: A sworn officer assigned to a particular school or district with the goal of reducing crime and violence and increasing youth support for police.

Secondary Prevention: Targeting at-risk populations for services in order to decease risk factors, thereby decreasing domestic violence.

Secondary Trauma: A risk incurred when engaging compassionately or empathically with a traumatized adult or child.

Self-Defense: Legal right to defend oneself when facing an imminent threat.

Self-Directed Violence: Violence perpetrated against one's self, like cutting, eating disorders, and suicide.

Sexual Abuse: Child sexual abuse includes a wide range of sexual behaviors that take place between a child and an older person. Behaviors that are sexually abusive often involve bodily contact, such as in the case of sexual kissing, touching, fondling of genitals, and intercourse. However, behaviors may be sexually abusive even if they do not involve contact, such as in the case of genital exposure ("flashing"), verbal pressure for sex, and sexual exploitation for purposes of prostitution or pornography.

Sexual Harassment: May include offers to exchange sexual favors of some sort, called quid pro quo, or persistent and derogatory remarks, jokes, exposure to images, or other factors that result in a hostile environment.

Social Control Theories: A category of criminological theories that emphasize the importance of social capital and social bonds in constraining people from offending.

Sociopath: A person who cannot differentiate right from wrong and who is incapable of feeling guilt or remorse for his or her actions.

Stalking: Unwanted and repeated visual or physical proximity or nonconsensual communication resulting in fear for the targeted person.

Standard of Care: Current procedure and practice; generally agreed upon principles of practice.

Strain Theories: Criminological theories that place the origin of crime and violence in the disjuncture between the idea of what it means to be a success and the realistic ability to achieve it.

Systemic Violence: Violence that is built into how an institution or society operates. Might include harsh and discriminatory teaching and disciplinary techniques as well as overall school climates.

Teacher-Perpetrated Violence: Violence committed by teachers against students.

Techniques of Neutralization: Criminological theory developed by Gresham Sykes and David Matza to explain how juveniles can rationalize or neutralize the negative impacts of their behavior, including denying the victim, denying responsibility, denying harm, condemning the condemners, and appealing to higher loyalties.

Terrorism: The U.S. Department of Defense defines terrorism as "the calculated use of violence or the threat of violence to inculcate fear, intended to coerce or to intimidate governments or societies in the pursuit of goals that are generally political, religious, or ideological." Terrorism includes attacks by individuals acting in isolation (e.g., sniper attacks).

Tertiary Prevention: Attempts to minimize the effects of domestic violence by identifying and holding abusers accountable and providing resources to victims.

Tracking: Educational strategy that involves grouping students according to ability level, as identified by standardized test scores and academic performance.

Trauma Reminders: People, places, activities, internal sensations, or other things that trigger memories of a trauma experience. Trauma reminders can cause feelings of fear or distress or put people "on alert." Trauma reminders can "restart" posttraumatic stress reactions or behavior even years after a traumatic event has occurred.

Traumatic Grief: Childhood traumatic grief occurs following the death of a loved one when the child objectively or subjectively perceives the experience as traumatic. The cause of death can be due to what is usually described as traumatic, such as an act of violence, accident, disaster, or war, or it can be due to natural causes. The hallmark of childhood traumatic grief is that trauma symptoms interfere with the child's ability to navigate the typical bereavement process.

Treatment Manual: A written guide with step-by-step instructions for conducting individual, family, or group treatment. Treatment manuals typically cover multiple sessions and describe the techniques used by the clinician, key elements of various phases of treatment, and activities to be done by the client or patient.

Zero Tolerance Laws: Controversial laws mandating suspension or expulsion for specific offenses, typically drugs, weapons, and alcohol.

Abuse, 10, 22, 23, 64–65, 96–97, 232–34
Action Markers, 161
Adler, Freda, 86
Agnew, Robert, 77
Alcohol, 91
American Association of University Women (AAUW), 9
American Bar Association, 116
American Psychological Association (APA), 11, 70
Anonymous tip lines, 105–106
Asperger's Syndrome, 37, 69, 227
Atavists, 66
Attention Deficit Disorder (ADD), 5–6, 88–89
Attention Deficit Hyperactivity Disorder (ADHD), 5–6, 88–89
Auvinen, Pekka-Eric, 32–33

The Basketball Diaries, 24
Bath Consolidated School bombing, 18–19, 211, 212–14

Beslan School Massacre, 29–30
Biochemical theories, 68
Birth order, 94–95
Board of Education of Independent School District No. 92 of Pottawatomie County v. Earls, 44–45
Bosse, Sebastian, 32
Brain dysfunction, 68–69
Brazill, Nathaniel, 28–29
Break the Cycle, 212, 242–43
Breivik, Anders Behring, 36
Brewer, Michael, 34–35
Bullycide, 33–34, 149, 211
Bullying, xv, 4, 283–93
  against teachers, 11, 65, 99, 266–67
  bullycide, 33–34, 64, 240–41, 241–42
  cyberbullying, 7–8, 33–34, 102–103, 240–41, 241–42, 253–54
  disability, 5–6, 69–70
  effects, 63–66
  gender, 12, 13, 33–34, 86–87, 136–38, 239–40, 265–67

legislation, 21, 28, 28, 37–40, 116–120

LGBTQ youth, 6–7, 34, 102, 145–64

personal stories, 133–136, 136–138, 204–208

physical, 4

prevention programs, 103, 253–54, 255–57

protective factors, 100–105, 150–151, 253–54

race, 13–14, 265–67

risk factors, 87–100, 150–51, 253–54

school shootings, 11–12, 21, 22, 24, 26–27, 64

social, 4

statistics, 5, 13, 14–15, 253–54, 266–74

verbal, 4

Bully Police, 117–18

Bystander interventions, 93, 103, 180–98

Canada, Geoffrey, 212, 243–46

Canine searches, 47, 114–15

Carneal, Michael, 22

Center for the Study and Prevention of Violence, 106–107

Centers for Disease Control and Prevention (CDC), 10, 12, 13, 87–88, 95, 100, 103, 180–98

Chambliss, William, 83

Chivalry hypothesis, 86–87

Circle Model, 190–92

Cloward Richard, 76–77

Cohen, Albert, 76

Columbine High School, 26–27, 32, 67, 74, 90, 105–106, 211, 215–19

Coming Out, 152–55

Comprehensive Crime Control Act, 37–38

Conflict resolution, 100, 110–11

Coon, Asa, 96

Corporal punishment, 41–42, 98–99

Curricula, 102–104, 162

Cyberbullying, 7–8, 102–103, 283–93

Dann, Laurie, 20, 90, 211, 219–22

Dating violence, 10, 64–65, 103

education, 103, 120, 199–203, 212

Davis v. Monroe County Board of Education, 9, 42–43

Democratic Front for the Liberation of Palestine (DFLP), 19

Differential Association theory, 79–80

Differential Identification theory, 79–80

Do Something, 5

Doom, 22, 27
Dress codes, 107–108
Drug testing, 43–45
Due process, 41
Dugdale, Richard, 66
Duncan, Arne, 34, 158–59, 265, 283–93
Durkheim, Emile, 74–75

Eisler, Riane, 212, 246–47
Estabrook, Arthur, 66
Eugenics, 66–67

Family size, 94–95
Female perpetrators, 12, 19–20
Focal concerns, 77–78
Fourteenth Amendment, 156
Franklin v. Gwinnett County Public School, 9
Free speech, 40–41, 107–108
Freud, Sigmund, 70

Gangs, 76–77, 99–100, 105, 266–67
Gang Resistance Education and Training (G.R.E.A.T), 105
Gay, Lesbian and Straight Education Network (GLSEN), 6–7, 34, 147, 162, 212, 247–49
Gay-Straight Alliances, 102, 148, 162–63, 248
General Theory of Crime, 85
Golden, Andrew, 25
Goss v. Lopez, 41

Goring, Charles, 66
Gottfredson, Michal, 85
Greenberg, David, 84
Gun control laws, 21, 28, 29, 37, 37–40, 227, 231–32
Gun-Free Schools Act, 38, 115
Gun-Free School Zones Act, 38, 115

Halligan, Ryan, 33, 241
Hamilton, Thomas, 21
Harlem Children's Zone, 212, 243–46
Harris, Eric, 26–27, 32, 67, 74, 90, 211, 215–19
Hazing, 7–8, 252–53
  harassment hazing, 8
  laws, 120
  subtle hazing, 8
  violent hazing, 8
Hirschi, Travis, 81–82, 85
Humanity Project, The, 204–208

In loco parentis, 43–44
Ingraham v. Wright, 11, 41–42
Insanity pleas, 21–22
IQ, 87–88, 100

Jeremy, 21, 228
Johnson, Mitchell, 25
Johnston, Jeffrey, 33

Katz, Jackson, 93, 212, 249–50

Kehoe, Andrew, 18–19, 211, 212–14
Kindness Clubs, 189
King, Lawrence, 34
Kinkel, Kip, 26, 69, 211, 222–26
Kivel, Paul, 212, 251–52
Klebold, Dylan, 26–27, 32, 67, 74, 90, 211, 215–19
Kretschmer, Tim, 33

Lanza, Adam, 36–37, 69, 211, 226–29
Laub, John, 85
Lead exposure, 68
Learning disabilities, 5–6, 69–70, 87–88, 222–26
Legislation, 21, 28, 28, 37–40, 116–20, 158–59, 265, 275–81
Lemert, Edwin, 82–83
Liberation hypothesis, 86
Life-course theory, 85
Lombroso, Cesar, 66
Long, Tyler, 241
Loukaitis, Barry, 21–22, 211, 228–29

Measuring school violence, 12–18, 265–74
    limitations, 17–18
Media literacy, 101
Meier, Megan, 33
Mental illness, 90–91, 219–22, 222–26, 226–29
Merton, Robert, 75–76

Metal detectors, 97–98, 108–109
Microaggressions, 138–42, 145–64
Militarism, 176–99
Miller, Walter, 77–78
Moffitt, Terrie, 85
Monitoring the Future, 16–17
Moral panic, 65, 164–66
Morrison, Duane, 31
Movies, 21, 24, 92, 93, 228, 250
Music, 21, 94, 228

National School Climate Survey, 6–7, 147
Natural Born Killers, 21, 228
Neblett, Rachel, 33
No Child Left Behind Act, 39
Nuwer, Hank, 212, 252–53

Obama, Barack, 34, 265, 281–82
Ohlin, Lloyd, 76–77
Olweus Bullying Prevention Program, 103
Owens, Dedrick, 27–28

Parenting, 94–96, 100–101
PeaceJam, 166–76
PeacePals, 110
Peaceable schools, 111–12
Peace education, 103–104, 180, 192–99, 246–47
Peer mediation, 110–11

People's Court, 142–45
Prescription drugs, 26,
    88–90, 215, 217–18,
    219–22, 239–40
Prince, Phoebe, 33–34, 211,
    241–42
Profiling, 106–107
Prothrow-Stith, Deborah, 86
Prozac, 26, 89–90, 239–40
Psychological disorders,
    70–71
Purdy, Patrick, 20–21, 211,
    229–32

Quinney, Richard, 83–84

Rachel's Challenge, 189
Rage, 21, 228
Ramsey, Evan, 22, 96, 211,
    232–34
Rational Choice theory,
    72–73
Restorative Justice, 112
Restoring Conflict Creatively
    Program, 111–12
Ritalin, 89
Roberts, Charles, 31–32, 211,
    234–36
Rollins, Kayla, 27–28
Routine Activities theory,
    73–74

Safe and Drug-Free Schools
    Act, 38–39
Safe Schools Improvement
    Act, 120, 265

*Safford United School District
    #1 v. Redding*, 45–46
Sampson, Robert, 85
Sandy Hook Elementary
    School, 36–37, 226–29,
    281–82
Sandy Hook Elementary
    Violence Reduction Act,
    265, 275–81
School-Associated Violent
    Death Study, 14,
    265, 266
School climate, 97–98,
    101–104, 145–64,
    166–76
School police officers, 112–14
School shootings, xv, 11–12,
    14, 19–33, 34–37
    abuse, 22, 23, 229–32
    adults, 18–19, 19–20,
    20–21, 29–30, 31–32,
    212–14, 234–26
    gender, 12, 19–20, 219–22
    international, 19, 21,
    29–30, 32–33
    racial hatred, 20–21,
    229–32
    suburban, 21–25
    violent media, 21–22
Search and seizure, 43–45,
    45–46, 47, 98–99, 113
Seductions of crime
    theory, 74
Sedwick, Rebecca, 241
Sexual harassment, 8–10, 42–43
    gender, 9–10

hostile environment, 8–9
Quid pro quo, 8
school liability, 9
teachers, 10
Sexting, 241–42
Sheldon, William, 67
Social bond theory,
   81–82, 85
Social disorganization theory, 78
Somatotyping, 67
Status frustration, 76
Spencer, Brenda, 19–20
Steinhauser, Robert, 29
Steubenville Rape Scandal,
   211, 236–39
Stopbullying.gov, 5, 212,
   253–55
Strip searches, 45–46
Students Against Violence
   Everywhere (SAVE), 212,
   255–57
Supreme Court Cases, 40–47
Sutherland, Edwin, 79–80
Systemic violence, 10–11
   corporal punishment,
      10–11, 41–42
   drug testing, 43–45
   strip searches, 45–46, 98–99

Teaching Students to Be
   Peacemakers, 110
Techniques of Neutralization
   theory, 80–81
Terrorism, 29–30
Theories to explain school
   violence, 66–87

biological theories, 66–70
choice theories, 72–74
conflict theories, 83–85
feminist theories, 86–87
integrated theories, 85–87
labeling theories, 82–83
psychological theories, 70–72
social control theories, 81–82
social learning theories,
   79–81
social strain theories, 74–78
Tinker v. Des Moines
   Independent Community
   School District, 40–41,
   108, 155
Title IV of the 1964 Civil
   Rights Act, 9
Title IX of the Education Amen-
   dment Acts of 1972, 158
Todd, Amanda, 241–42
Tough Guise, 92, 250
Tracking, 98
Treacy, Wayne, 34–36
Trenchcoat mafia, 27
Turning points theory, 85
Twins, 68

United States v. Place, 114
United States Department of
   Health and Human
   Services, 5, 118–120,
   212, 253–55

Vernonia School District 47 J v.
   Acton, 43–44
Video cameras, 110

Video games, 22, 27, 92, 232–34

Violent media, 21–22, 24, 25, 29, 32–33, 37, 79–80, 92–94, 138–42, 217–18, 249–50

Visibility Markers, 160–61

Weise, Jeff, 30–31, 211, 239–40

Wimberley, Teah, 34–35, 199–203

Woodham, Luke, 22–23

Wrestling with Manhood: Boys, Bullying and Battering, 93, 250

Wurst, Andrew, 25–26

Youth Risk Behavior Surveillance System (YBRSS), 12–13, 266

Zero tolerance laws, 97–98, 115–16

About the Author

Laura L. Finley earned her Ph.D. from Western Michigan University in 2002. Prior to earning her doctoral degree in sociology, Dr. Finley was a high school social studies teacher. Since then she has taught at a variety of colleges and universities in Michigan, Colorado, and Florida. She is currently associate professor of sociology and criminology at Barry University in Miami Shores, Florida, where she teaches courses on crime, justice, and human rights. Dr. Finley is the author, co-author, or editor of 13 books as well as numerous book chapters and peer-reviewed journal articles. Additionally, Dr. Finley is actively involved with a number of local, state, and national initiatives. She serves on the boards of No More Tears, which helps victims of domestic violence; the Humanity Project, an antibullying organization; Floridians for Alternatives to the Death Penalty; and the Peace and Justice Studies Association. Dr. Finley is also a mentor for at-risk girls, co-chair of the South Florida Diversity Alliance, and an organizer of the College Brides Walk.